THIRTEEN PERFECT FUGITIVES

THIRTEEN PERFECT FUGITIVES

The True Story of the Mob, Murder, and the World's Largest Art Heist

GEOFFREY KELLY

Post Hill Press

A POST HILL PRESS BOOK

Thirteen Perfect Fugitives:
The True Story of the Mob, Murder, and the World's Largest Art Heist

ISBN: 979-8-89565-317-3
ISBN (eBook): 979-8-89565-318-0

Cover design by Conroy Accord
Interior design and composition by Greg Johnson, Textbook Perfect

All people, locations, events, and situations are portrayed to the best of the author's memory. While all of the events described are true, many names and identifying details have been changed to protect the privacy of the people involved.

Post Hill Press
New York, NY
www.republicbookpublishers.com

Published in the United States of America
3 4 5 6 7 8 9 10

For Sonia, Jack, and Will
(in no particular order)

Contents

Prologue

Olly olly oxen free!

—TRADITIONAL SAYING

On June 22, 2011, James "Whitey" Bulger was captured in Southern California. At the time of his arrest, he was number two on the FBI's list of Ten Most Wanted Fugitives, second only to Osama bin Laden. Bulger's apprehension came as the direct result of a nationwide publicity campaign launched by the FBI that targeted his girlfriend, Catherine Greig, who had joined Bulger shortly after he fled Boston. Aware that Bulger's girlfriend had a penchant for plastic surgery and teeth cleanings, the FBI took out advertisements in relevant trade magazines, which paid huge dividends when a plastic surgeon came forward with updated photographs of Greig. The FBI aired public service announcements featuring these newly obtained images, all the while touting the $2 million reward being offered for her squirrely boyfriend.

After years of exhaustive investigation by an FBI task force, in the end it was a former Icelandic beauty pageant winner who finally ended Bulger's flight from justice. She recognized those images of Bulger's longtime moll and contacted the FBI, and within days, the high-profile fugitive was arrested inside a Santa Monica parking garage. Bulger had successfully evaded capture for nearly seventeen years.

There were a couple of reasons why I took note of Bulger's apprehension. At the time, I was a special agent assigned to the FBI's Boston division, an office that had deservedly taken its share of criticism for harboring the corrupt agent who tipped off Bulger to the pending indictment, thus facilitating his flight from justice. We were all relieved to finally have some closure to this dark chapter in the FBI's history. But for me, the most important aspect of Bulger's arrest stemmed from the fact that it represented yet another example of publicity leading directly to the capture of a wanted fugitive.

For twenty-two years, I was the FBI's lead investigator on the Gardner Museum heist, searching (spoiler alert) in vain for the thirteen works of art that had been stolen back in March 1990 by two ersatz police officers. And the strategy that ultimately resulted in Bulger's apprehension was similar to the one I'd implemented in the Gardner case. When the investigation was first assigned to me in December 2002, the statute of limitations—that is, the time period in which a case must be charged—had been expired for more than seven years. So I chose to take a more unorthodox approach to recovering the lost artwork, and instead of working it as a traditional stolen property case, I worked it as a fugitive investigation.

Essentially, I was searching for thirteen fugitives. Unlike their human counterparts, however, these fugitives never got cavities or experienced the heartbreak of psoriasis. They had no need for driver's licenses, and they never went food shopping. They had no landlord, and they never took the bus. And of course, they had no need for plastic surgery or teeth cleanings.

All of this made them perfect fugitives.

Thirteen perfect fugitives, to be precise.

Unencumbered by those everyday tasks, the mundane appointments and the pedestrian chores that eventually lead to any fugitive's undoing, they have the luxury of time. And so they hide, in casual insouciance, perhaps under a bed or up in the attic, behind a furnace or tucked inside a book, biding their time, cautiously awaiting their eventual and inevitable discovery.

And the key to any fugitive investigation is publicity; the more the better. I hoped that if we saturated the media with images of my fugitives, then perhaps one of these might resonate with somebody, somewhere.

This book contains my reflections and observations of the case, gleaned from more than two decades of investigation into the world's largest art heist. During that time, I changed squad assignments a number of times, yet the case always remained with me. For an agent to be assigned the same case for such a lengthy period of time is not a testament to my investigative prowess; rather, it is a testament to the FBI. During my tenure on the Gardner case, I went 0 for 13, yet the Bureau continued to entrust me with the investigation, to wear either as a badge of honor on my chest or as an albatross around my neck, depending on your perspective.

There is little doubt that being the case agent on the Gardner Museum investigation was a dubious distinction. I was often introduced to other agents as the *he's-got-the-Gardner-case* guy, and the response was usually a furrowed brow and a sympathetic head tilt—gestures typically reserved for next of kin or those afflicted with psoriasis and its heartbreaking consequences.

Through the years, I was profoundly impressed with the FBI's forbearance on the Gardner case, since it followed none of the conventions and protocols of a typical investigation. It remains, of course, a pending matter, and typically when the FBI is pressed for details regarding an ongoing case, the official response is a laconic "no comment." This case was different, however, and the overwhelming majority of agents in executive management, both in Boston and at FBI Headquarters, rightly understood that an investigation this unique required an equally unique approach. I argued that publicity was key to solving this case and apprehending the fugitives, all thirteen of them, and they listened.

Through the years, the Bureau implemented media campaigns that highlighted the lost treasures. We posted frequently on social media, rented billboard space, and even produced some pretty slick videos. And while I would not be so disingenuous as to bloviate that I wrote this book as some type of public service announcement, I do believe that the story which underpins the Gardner Museum robbery is a fascinating one, a damned good yarn that lies at the intersection of true crime and art theft. And more to the point, not only does my mom want to read about the Gardner case, but so do a lot of my mom's friends. So, there you go.

There are instances in this book where I provide opinions. These are my own, and not necessarily those of the FBI. And while I've attempted to present the information as accurately as possible, I readily acknowledge that the very nature of the case—that is, a pending fugitive investigation in which the fugitives are still very much pending—may necessitate a bit of conjecture and supposition. Those instances are noted.

So check the attic; look under your bed and behind the furnace.

They're out there, somewhere.

These thirteen perfect fugitives.

CHAPTER 1

81 minutes

No plan survives first contact with the enemy.

—HELMUTH VON MOLTKE

March 18, 1990, is a cold night in Boston. Although the temperature hovers in the mid-forties, the city's proximity to the ocean always makes it feel a bit chillier. A damp breeze sweeps across the city, a shallow breath that slinks through narrow, haphazard streets and alleys and finally exhales at the Fenway, a swirling tendril of green that negotiates those tight spaces as it inexorably wends its way toward Boston before finally emptying into the Common. Frederick Law Olmsted designed the Emerald Necklace more than a century earlier and created a series of serpentine parks—the Fens being one of them—that link downtown Boston with the nether regions of its western suburbs. And dangling from that necklace like a homely bauble is Fenway Court, home to the Isabella Stewart Gardner Museum and the erstwhile residence of its iconoclastic namesake.

The museum isn't much to look at from the outside, just an austere rectangle of buff-colored brick whose main architectural feature is a pair of chimneys on its front façade that join together on the second floor like some racy décolletage; a lone bay window serves as its cleavage. The building sits like a giant Amazon delivery box, plunked down as it were on the corner of Palace Road and Park Drive. But it's more accurate and fairer still to think of Fenway Court as a giant geode—austere and unimpressive on the outside but filled with a sparkling cluster of gems once cracked open.

And tonight it will be cracked open. Tonight will be historic. Not because it's St. Patrick's Day in Boston; that happens every year, when college students almost grudgingly partake in a green-tinted beer bacchanal to celebrate the holy Irishman's allegorical expulsion of all the snakes of Ireland. And not because a serendipitous confluence of circumstance this year has caused the holiday to fall on a Saturday night, thus allowing for maximum effort and recovery time before Monday classes and a fresh workweek. No, tonight will be historic because it will be the night when the world's largest art heist will occur. Tomorrow morning, seismic shudders will radiate out from the Fenway and register around the world within the art community, museum officials, and law enforcement writ large. It will be monumental.

But tonight, it's only quiet.

It's just after midnight, and inside the museum, security guard Richard Abath doesn't have much to do. Rick is a self-styled musician, a drop-out of nearby Berklee College of Music, and a denizen of Boston's late-night music scene. Just three days earlier, Rick gave his two-week notice at the museum, and now he's just killing time and checking off his last few night shifts like a prisoner awaiting parole. His partner that night, Randy,* is manning the watch desk, a fancy name for the console where the guards monitor the alarms or use the phone. In a few minute's time, they'll switch off assignments.

The image of Rick does little to imbue anyone with a sense of security. A frizzy explosion of dark locks tumbles out from beneath

* Last name redacted.

a comically large cowboy hat that seems so utterly out of place in Boston. His pale blue security guard shirt is worn almost with contempt, untucked and unbuttoned over a multicolored T-shirt, a jarring juxtaposition of polyester and tie-dye. Contrary to popular belief, the primary role of a night guard isn't to thwart art theft; it's only in the movies where you'll find museums with a retinue of armed tactical guards on the midnight shift, ready to respond to an intrusion with deadly force. In reality, the main job of the humble museum night watchman is to detect the biggest threat to the museum: fire. Keep flames to a minimum (preferably none) and listen for the sound of a burst water pipe and you'll be all right. You can do your homework. You can read a book. Just don't let the place burn down.

Desultory rounds do little to eliminate the boredom, and Rick's remaining hours in the employ of the Gardner Museum are marked with obligatory sweeps of his Detex wand on the sensors discreetly placed throughout the various galleries. The predecessor of this circa-1990 engineering marvel was the mechanical watchman's clock, a leather-clad, five-pound timepiece lugged around by square badges on their midnight shifts as they performed their nightly scavenger hunt, seeking out keys tethered to various points along their rounds. Guards would insert the key into their clock, imprinting a strip of paper with the unique signature of that particular key, thus proving that they were completing their appointed rounds and not off somewhere "cooping." But this is 1990, and the World Wide Web is only a few years away, and by now an electronic wand has replaced the chronographic man-purse once carried by all those poor schmoes unfortunate enough to find themselves working the graveyard shift in crepe-soled shoes and a clip-on tie.

In addition to the Detex, the Gardner Museum is equipped with an array of motion sensors sprinkled throughout the galleries. They bear silent witness to anyone and everyone who passes, with each trespass duly recorded on a dot matrix printer perched atop the watch desk, where an eternal sheet of perforated paper unfurls with its distinctive mosquito buzz. Computers will soon be a big deal, and many people will come to own one, but back in 1990 they are a novelty, and computer memory is an esoteric construct. Years later, every layman will understand the shared concepts of hard drives and RAM storage, but tonight it's quite logical to think of that printer like a typewriter. And you would forgive any museum thief (and perhaps even a soon-to-be-unemployed museum security guard) who believes that by pilfering those paper printouts they will erase any record of which galleries were visited that night.

Or more to the point, the exact time when *one* particular gallery was visited.

Back to Rick. It's now 12:27 a.m., and he's still doing his rounds. He's just swiped the magnetic Detex strip hidden inside the Blue Room, a first-floor gallery that's filled with objects reflecting Mrs. Gardner's personal relationships and close friends. The gallery contains an impressive array of pieces by John Singer Sargent, who was Mrs. Gardner's first artist in residence; in fact, the museum boasts 256 Sargents in its collection.[1] The Blue Room is sandwiched between two hallways, and each one has its own doorway into the gallery. In 1990, the east hallway was the main entrance into the museum and the west hallway was the public's exit, and motion sensors were positioned in each hallway, effectively bracketing the gallery.

Rick's presence in the Blue Room, as well as his subsequent exit, has been dutifully registered by those motion sensors. Simply put, tonight there is no way Rick—or anyone else for that matter—can enter or exit the Blue Room without triggering those motion sensors.

At 12:34 a.m., Rick takes over the watch desk from Randy. We know this because *Operator: Abath, R.* has edited the computer's database, a few rapid sweeps of the dot matrix printer head memorializing the action on perforated paper. As he mans the desk, Rick sporadically taps the computer keyboard, silencing the notifications from the incessant motion-sensor activations that are tripped by Randy as he makes his rounds upstairs. Other than monotonously pecking computer keys to silence those alarms, Rick has little else to do.

So why is Rick back in the Blue Room at 12:53 a.m.? We know he's in there because he triggered the motion sensors upon his arrival. Back at the unmanned watch desk, the gathering spool of paper advises no one that "*Someone is in the Blue Room. Investigate immediately!!!*," a surfeit of exclamation points imparting a sense of urgency. Rick is supposed to be watching that paper spool, since the responsibility of visiting the galleries has already been passed along to Randy; instead, Rick *is* that Someone in the Blue Room.

Four minutes later and Rick has just opened the exterior door to the rear courtyard, a door that's just a few steps away from the Security Office, an impressive-sounding name for what amounts to a glorified broom closet. The cramped space contains the VCR used to record video from a paltry array of security cameras, a file cabinet, an upholstered swivel chair, and a week's worth of VHS tapes, with the last few days partially obscured by an empty can of Budweiser (tactical ninjas they are not). One minute later and Rick is now in the rear courtyard, an outdoor space whose boundaries are defined by the rear of the museum, the carriage house, and a high brick wall bisected by a tall metal gate.

About the same time as Rick is inexplicably perambulating the rear courtyard, a group of teenagers is winding their way down Palace Road, trading off piggyback rides and struggling to maintain their balance. They're coming from a college dorm party, despite the fact that they're still in high school; it is, after all, St. Patrick's Day. As the teens draw near the museum, they observe a car parked along the curb, adjacent to the rear courtyard gate. At roughly the same time, Rick is on the other side of the gate, making the rounds he's not supposed to be making, separated from the car by that courtyard gate and the breadth of a Boston sidewalk.

The car that has drawn the teens' attention is not just any car; they will later describe it as a Dodge Daytona, model year 1985 through

1988. And while two of the teens share—with an exacting degree of specificity—the make and model of the vehicle, they differ wildly on the color; one claims it's gray, while the other is certain it's red. And while they may have different recollections about the color, they agree on one very sobering fact: There are two men sitting inside that Dodge, and the driver is a Boston cop. Under the sickly yellow glow of a sodium-arc streetlamp they can clearly see his profile silhouetted in the dark; they see the police uniform, as well as the keystone-shaped Boston Police patch on his left shoulder. The driver stares at them impassively, challenging them to make the next move. Underage and probably under the influence, the teens wisely decide to continue their revelry elsewhere, and—to use the local vernacular—screw.

At 1:03 a.m., Rick opens and closes the Palace Road service door, a stone's throw from the Dodge. He later claims that he was simply following security protocol by testing the alarms on the door; however, that is most definitely *not* protocol. In fact, it had been drilled into the museum's security guard contingent that those doors were never to be opened at night.

Two minutes later, those teenagers are driving to the train station; one of them has to catch the last trolley home, and it leaves at 1:20 a.m. He checks his watch and confirms the time with a quick glance at the clock on the dashboard: *1:05*.

At precisely 1:24 a.m., the night bell buzzes at the museum's service door. From his position back at the watch desk, Rick glances up at an overhead monitor, which displays a quadrant of black-and-white surveillance images, and sees two uniformed police officers standing outside. Rick keys the intercom and the officers announce themselves:

"Boston Police. We got a call of a disturbance."

Rick buzzes them inside.

And not since a Trojan night watchman signed for that big wooden horse has a greater lapse in security led to such dire consequences.

The exterior door leads into a mantrap; basically, a small anteroom with a window into the watch desk area. As he stands before that window, the taller cop gives Rick a quick wave, at which time Rick notices that he's wearing a pair of dark gloves. Rick buzzes the two officers through, and once they've cleared the mantrap, they plant themselves in the lobby and the taller one speaks to Rick. His tone is imperious and self-assured, the bearing of a seasoned city cop working the midnight shift. From years of hard-worn experience, this guy knows that on St. Paddy's Day it's better to be handling false alarms at museums than breaking up bar fights on Lansdowne Street. His partner, the shorter cop, skulks in the shadows, fidgeting uncomfortably, letting his partner do all the talking. His face is tight and narrow, with a pair of ordinary eyeglasses perched atop an ordinary nose.

When the taller cop asks if Rick is alone, Rick reveals that his partner is upstairs, doing his rounds. He is instructed to call him down, so he calls Randy over the walkie-talkie and summons him to the watch desk. As they wait for Randy to arrive, there is absolutely no conversation; add in a ticking clock and it would be the very definition of an awkward silence.

When Randy joins the group at the watch desk about a minute later, the taller cop studies Rick for a moment and then tells him that there might be a warrant out for his arrest. He asks Rick for a name and demands identification as he orders him out from behind the watch desk—away from the panic button that, if pressed, would immediately summon the real police. With minimal conversation, Rick produces his driver's license and museum identification card. After a perfunctory look at the documents, the officer informs Rick that there is, in fact, a warrant for his arrest, and he orders him to "assume the position." Rick, having seen his share of 1980s cop shows, stands spread-eagled, facing the wall. As Rick is handcuffed, the shorter officer does the same with Randy. After Rick and Randy are both restrained, the taller cop reveals the true motive of this late-night visit:

"Gentlemen, this is a robbery."

The most remarkable aspect of our subjects is how truly unremarkable they are: white males, one a bit shorter than the other, both in their twenties or thirties and sporting shiny mustaches, possibly fake. With such ambiguous descriptions, Boston's pool of potential suspects has dropped nary a bit.

* * * *

Rick and Randy are brought downstairs to the museum's basement, a labyrinth of hallways and crawl spaces that stretch for nearly a city block. Obscured headroom is further impeded by low-hanging steam pipes and ventilation ductwork. Its darkness is absolute; with four stories of Gothic museum perched above this subterranean cavern, no light can penetrate. The basement is an area of the museum that few employees have ever seen, and far fewer would venture down to visit unless out of necessity, and yet our subjects move through here with impunity, demonstrating a comfort level that's almost startling.

Randy is escorted to a small washroom under the staircase, handcuffed to a slop sink, and then partially mummified with a few loops of duct tape around his face. He is asked if he's comfortable, since he'll be there all night. Meanwhile, Rick is marched down corridor after corridor, past recesses and alcoves and dead ends, to the farthest reaches of the basement, where he's restrained to an electrical box located next to the boiler. Rick is already handcuffed, but his captor adds insult to injury by wrapping his head—and with it that impressive mane of metal hair—with overwrought laps of duct tape. The image of Rick Abath, handcuffed in the farthest reaches of the museum's dank cellar, cowboy hat by his side and hair circumnavigated many times over with liberal amounts of duct tape, could almost be comical. Except it's not.

The subjects take the guards' licenses as a veiled threat, since they contain their home addresses, and in a parting salvo fired off as they head back upstairs, yell down to their charges:

"If everything goes all right, then you'll get a nice reward in about a year's time."

* * * *

Using the same motion sensors that tracked Rick on his nocturnal wanderings an hour earlier, we can trace the exact route taken by our subjects that night. They first enter the museum proper at 1:47 a.m., ascending the main staircase to the second floor; they are both in the Dutch Room one minute later. With an utter disregard for time—something unheard of in the world of art theft—they methodically set to work. At 1:50 a.m., one subject passes through the Early Italian and Raphael rooms and enters the Short Gallery while his partner stays behind.

At 1:56 a.m., both subjects are back together in the Dutch Room and, aside from one subject's brief visit to the Short Gallery twelve minutes later, remain there for the duration. And with good reason, since there is much work to be done in this gallery. They remove two large Rembrandts from the wall, *A Lady and Gentleman in Black* and the iconic *Christ in the Storm on the Sea of Galilee*. The latter piece is Rembrandt's only known seascape, and it discreetly depicts the artist in the stern, clinging to a shroud and literally holding on to his hat—a kind of Old Masters version of *Where's Waldo*. Both pieces are large oils on canvas, about four feet by five, and both were neatly sliced out of their frames, most likely with a box cutter or similar instrument. The cuts are clean and straight, using the frames as straight edges, and the paucity of paint chips recovered from the gallery's tile floor the next morning points to relatively little damage suffered by the pieces from their ordeal.

The subjects take the time to unscrew a tiny framed Rembrandt self-portrait etching from the Flemish cabinet to which it is mounted. They take even more time to meticulously remove the etching from its frame and backing, leaving both items on a nearby table where they will be recovered the next morning.

Landscape with an Obelisk, an oil on panel by Govaert Flinck, is removed from its stand atop a small table. Up until a few years before the heist, the piece had been attributed to Rembrandt; it had only recently been determined to have been painted by one of his students. Also taken is *The Concert* by Johannes Vermeer, an oil on canvas that butted up against the Flinck. Its frame and a fresh jigsaw puzzle of shattered glass lie on the floor. One of only thirty-six pieces ever painted by the artist, it will come to hold the dubious distinction of being the world's most valuable piece of stolen art.

The next morning investigators will find another Rembrandt self-portrait, this one a much larger oil on panel, leaning against the same piece of furniture that once held its smaller counterpart. The piece was facing in and, due to its dark wood verso propped against the dark wood cabinet, was most likely overlooked in the dimly lit gallery.

The last item taken from the Dutch Room is a small Chinese beaker called a *gu* (pronounced "goo"), which was securely affixed to a drop-leaf table near *The Storm* and held in place with clamps. The subjects take the time to slice away the tablecloth and pry the piece from the table, a tremendous amount of effort to pilfer an object that, by comparison, isn't all that valuable. Years later, their progeny will be able to purchase identical pieces off eBay for a few thousand dollars.

During those two brief trips to the Short Gallery, our subjects take five Degas sketches, mere studies created by the artist in preparation for the final works. Two of the sketches depict jockeys, a fact which will lead to speculation that the thieves liked the ponies. The sketches are smashed out of their frames; a puddle of shattered glass and splintered wood are all that remain.

The last piece taken from the Short Gallery is a finial perched atop the flag of Napoleon's First Regiment. The piece is an imperial eagle, the symbol of Napoleon's divine authority.* It stands about ten inches tall and weighs roughly five pounds. Again, not all that much

* Napoleon replaced the rooster with the eagle, since he believed the rooster was "unfit to represent such a great empire." He may have also made the switch because French schoolchildren probably snickered every time their teacher uttered the phrase, *Vive le coq!*

in the grand scheme of things, unless one thought it was made of solid gold (it's not; it's gilded brass). Our subjects wasted a minute or two removing half a dozen screws from the frame that held the flag, sandwiched between two fine sheets of glazing, presumably before they realized that the finial could be snatched by simply lifting it off the dowel on which it rested. Those half dozen screws, eventually recovered from a sand-filled fire bucket in the corner of the gallery, will spawn an endless stream of theories attempting to tie the Gardner Museum robbery to French ultranationalists and Corsican organized crime figures.

The motion sensors in the Dutch Room register movement at 2:24 a.m. as the subjects make their way back down the staircase to the first floor. It has been exactly sixty minutes since they first rang the buzzer. Before they leave, the subjects visit the Security Office and eject the surveillance videotape from the VCR, thus depriving investigators of those blurry black-and-white images that can only come from a circa-1990 videotape that's been recorded over dozens and dozens of times.

Our subjects also grab the motion-sensor printouts from 12:50 a.m. onward, a pointless gesture since the collection of empty and shattered frames will trace their exact route through the museum like a trail of breadcrumbs. So why take them at all? And is there any significance to 12:50 a.m., the exact recorded time when those printouts were ripped off the printer, given the fact that the subjects didn't enter the museum proper until nearly an hour later?

At 2:41 a.m. the service door briefly opens and closes as our subjects begin the process of loading up their haul. The door opens one last time at 2:45 a.m., and then our subjects are gone.

In just eighty-one minutes, they have committed the world's largest art heist.

* * * *

There was a thirteenth item stolen from the Gardner Museum that night: *Chez Tortoni* by Édouard Manet. The oil on canvas depicts a well-heeled and well-mustachioed gentleman, an impossibly tall top hat cocked jauntily atop his head, sketching at a table inside the Café Tortoni in Paris. A half-empty glass of beer sits next to his sketchpad (or perhaps, optimistically, it's half-full). The only piece not swiped from the second floor, it was taken off the wall in the first-floor Blue Room gallery, and its frame was recovered on a chair inside the Security Office.

That's odd—our subjects never visited the Blue Room that night.

But someone else did.

CHAPTER 2

81 minutes and 22 years

From Ghoulies and ghosties
And long-leggedy beasties
And things that go bump in the night,
Good Lord, deliver us!

—TRADITIONAL SCOTTISH POEM

It's four a.m. on February 10, 2012, and I'm in a hotel room somewhere in Connecticut. Almost every arrest starts off with an early alarm, and this one is no different, even if the goal this morning is to recover the world's most valuable stolen artwork. I silence the alarm and pinball my way through the darkened room to the bathroom purely by memory, the layout memorized even though I've never stayed here before. Every hotel room is identical, a perfect rectangle comprised of a bed, a desk, and a coffee maker, with a perfect square cleaved out for a bathroom. I take a quick shower, using a hotel-size bottle of shampoo that's always an unnecessarily florid amalgam of two discrete ingredients, one of them always edible. (This particular morning, in this particular hotel, it may have been spearmint and lilac.

Or perhaps oatmeal and sandalwood; I can't recall.) I wash off with a tiny cake of soap that's hermetically sealed in a bag you can rarely open with dry hands; simply impossible to accomplish when they're wet. I dry off and get dressed.

It's game day, so to speak, and my morning routine differs greatly from the ritual most other guests of this hotel will undertake in a few hours' time. I holster my service pistol, a .40-caliber semiautomatic Glock, then strap on handcuffs, two extra magazines of ammunition, a knife, and an impossibly small FBI badge (which bears an uncanny resemblance to a piece of foil-wrapped chocolate). I take one last glance around the room to make sure I'm not forgetting anything, leave a couple of singles for housekeeping, and then take the elevator down exactly one floor—the lazy man's route to the lobby. I rouse a bleary-eyed night clerk from the back room, get a printout of my bill (one night, no incidentals, tax-exempt for official government business), and then search the darkened parking lot for my Bureau car, known by its clever portmanteau as a Bucar.*

I squeeze the door-lock button on the key fob and a black Ford Fusion honks and flashes a few spots away, momentarily bathing the lot in muted fall colors of burnt orange and crimson. The exteriors of these hotels are equally identical to their interiors—two-story travel lodges parked hard against a highway access road, typically sandwiched between a moderately priced chain restaurant and an all-night gas station, the latter being the location where I'd filled up my Bucar last night and grabbed a bag of Skittles. The gas station serves an important role in this American landscape, tethering the whole lot to an endless stream of itinerant travelers, and preventing it all from simply drifting off into the scrubland beyond that yields, little by little, to the inexorable creep of suburban sprawl.

Thirty minutes later and it's still dark out, but already a light fog has settled on the parking lot of a Dunkin' Donuts in the small

* Our federal acronym partners use the more generic terms *G-Ride* or *G-Sled*.

Connecticut town of Manchester. I drove down from Boston last night so I could be the first one here for the briefing, since the ageless FBI maxim, *never be late to your own arrest,* heeded by all but a brash young Special Agent Johnny Utah, rings true. Whenever possible, these early-morning briefings are held at or near a Dunks, and the logic is manifest: hot coffee, plenty of parking, and a bathroom. I buy a few dozen Munchkins and a cardboard box full of coffee. The former is a treat but the latter is obligatory and comes accessorized with a sleeve of paper cups, sugar packets, thimbles of creamer, and a clutch of stirrers. I grab a fistful of napkins and head back out to the parking lot.

Already a few other agents have begun to filter in, and by five a.m. the lot is filled with a collection of late-model, somber-toned FBI sedans and SUVs. They cluster around my Bucar, the nucleus of this briefing. The scene is illuminated by the glow of amber parking lights; the sounds are the low rumble of diesel engines nestled inside Evidence Response Team trucks, the chirrup of morning birds, and the easy banter of agents, their volume rising with the sun.

I assemble the makeshift coffee buffet on my Bucar's hood, warm from the engine and coated with a fine sheen of morning dew. The heat keeps the coffee hot, but the moisture wets the paper bag holding the creamers. Once refreshments are in place, I start the process of informal greetings and thanks. Both are genuine. When it's one of my cases, it's always a profound feeling to know that everyone else who got up at this godforsaken hour is here to help me. Unlike most other briefings, however, I know very few of these agents. While a few guys from my squad took the long drive down from Boston last night to join me, today we're in Connecticut, and that area of responsibility, or AOR (we are, truly, an agency of acronyms), falls to the New Haven division. This is an away game, and I'm meeting most of the two dozen or so agents and professional support for the first time. (And everybody gets a Munchkin!) There is a comforting familiarity to this group, regardless of which field office I'm visiting, and everyone looks roughly the same—the mildly tactical interspersed with the full-send warriors, the amount of Velcro and snap clips directly proportional to years of service (it declines steeply over time). The unifying habiliment for this group is the identical body armor, olive-drab with FBI emblazoned in bright yellow. Almost everyone holds a coffee, either contained in one of the paper cups I supplied or ensconced cozily in a tactically hued and transcendentally expensive thermos.

I see one familiar face, Jamie Lawton, a New Haven agent who works organized crime, known as OC. Jamie and I met in the wake of 9/11, when we were both temporarily assigned to Logan Airport in East Boston. At the time, many of us wondered how Jamie, a New Haven agent, ended up in Boston after 9/11. It was hard to pin him down on that one, but suffice to say he was born and raised in the suburbs of Boston and somehow managed to finagle a few months back home.

Back in February 2010, my search for the world's most valuable stolen artwork had led me to Bobby Gentile, a.k.a. the Cook, a rotund and balding used-car salesman from Connecticut. At the time, I ran his rap sheet and found some pretty decent arrests, though he never served significant time and the charges were from many years prior. But when I ran his name through our internal database, known as Indices, I found a litany of organized crime references. Typically, the lack of a recent criminal history equates to a lack of recent criminal activity, unless one is extremely cunning. And Bobby Gentile was extremely cunning. From my research, I learned that Gentile was once the bodyguard for a Boston mobster who was arrested for selling two kilos of cocaine to an undercover FBI agent. And although Gentile was present for many of the meetings leading up to the coke deal, he never opened his mouth, so he never got indicted. Instead, he was still selling used cars and plotting crimes in Hartford while his associates were stockpiled in a number of federal prisons sprinkled up and down the East Coast, eating bologna sandwiches and making license plates.*

* Full disclosure: I've never met a prisoner who actually made license plates, but I've heard they still do somewhere.

This is why I called Jamie. To me, the real mark of a good agent is not how many arrests you've made or cases you've solved but how many contacts you have, that interwoven catalog of cell phone numbers you can summon in an instant or pass along to others. It's a good feeling when an agent on the squad calls out, "Does anyone know anybody at [insert random police department here]?" And I can answer back, "Yep, Detective [insert random Irish or Italian surname here]. Good guy, tell him I said hi." My work phone contained something like four hundred official contacts, and one of them was LAWTON, JAMES T. (FBI) (NH), shortened to just "Jamie."

When we first spoke, I told Jamie that a decade earlier, one of my subjects from Boston may have handed off some very valuable stolen artwork to Gentile. Did Jamie know him, by chance? Dumb question—of course, he knew Gentile, or at least knew of him. Jamie has an almost encyclopedic knowledge of the sprawling netherworld of organized crime in New England, its internecine conflicts and outrageous betrayals. Ask Jamie some innocuous question about some random mobster and be prepared for a dizzying monologue about how this guy knew that guy who clipped the other guy after kicking up to that guy (this was the abridged version). One of these individuals will invariably be referred to by Jamie as a *chooch*. I still don't know exactly what a *chooch* is, but I've gleaned its meaning contextually.

For years, Jamie has doggedly pursued these mobsters, attempting to make headway in a criminal environment where "nobody saw nothing" and witnesses' heads have a tendency to simply fall off, unassisted. As an organized crime agent, Jamie was forever working toward that elusive goal: a prosecutable Racketeer Influenced and Corrupt Organization case, better known by its salsa instructor–sounding acronym, RICO. In its broadest sense, a RICO case involves a group of individuals who come together for the purpose of committing criminal activity. To make a RICO case, the criminal activity must fall within a list of specified predicate acts, such as loansharking, murder, extortion, or even transporting stolen property.

Jamie is always a little disheveled; he's preternaturally tardy, and in what may be the greatest affront to a law enforcement officer, he doesn't drink coffee. But he's also one of the sharpest agents with whom I've ever worked and worthy of the highest praise that can be bestowed upon a cop: If my kid was kidnapped, I'd want Jamie to get the case.

Luck was in short supply on this investigation, but we did have a little bit here: Jamie had an informant, known in Bureau parlance as a confidential human source, or CHS, who knew Gentile. Like most OC sources, his main job was to act as a sounding board, gleaning disparate puzzle pieces of intelligence about racketeering activities and reporting the information back to his/her handling agent.* It's the OC agent's job to try and fit all of those puzzle pieces together. When the last piece of the puzzle finally fits into place, if it ever does, it depicts a RICO prosecution. If it looks like a Thomas Kinkade lighthouse, then something went terribly wrong.

In addition to passively receiving intelligence, sources are sometimes proactive. So when Jamie's source reported that Gentile had offered to sell him prescription drugs, we directed him to start making controlled purchases from Gentile and his partner, Andy Parente, owner of Clean Country Cars, a used-car lot on Franklin Avenue in Hartford that nestled cozily amongst a string of low-slung brick apartment buildings and Italian delis. Over a five-month period, our source made multiple purchases of Dilaudid and OxyContin from the pair. Deals typically were conducted inside the dingy office that served as Clean Country Cars' world headquarters. Of vital importance for us, however, was the fact that one of those deals took place at Gentile's Manchester residence. This is the reason for all of these extra bodies today; in addition to having two teams execute simultaneous arrests of

* CHS reports have always been gender neutral, even before it was fashionable. Sentences will contain pronoun amalgams like *his/her* and *s/he*. The gender nonspecificity is intended not to be politically correct but to protect the source; by obviating gender, the pool of potential snitches infiltrating a gang is not halved.

Gentile and Parente, a third team will be executing a search warrant at Gentile's house, located about a mile away at 69 Frances Drive.

It's now five thirty, and the arrival of a marked Manchester police cruiser is my signal to start the briefing.

It's always the same:

"All right guys, if we can bring it in for a minute." I pause while the arena forms. "First of all, I'd like to thank you all for getting up so early to help out on this..." And so it continues. Daybreak creeps in stealthily as the briefing continues; shadows dissolve and details emerge, and faceless shadows become real agents. Real agents with spouses and kids back home. The responsibility of sending these agents into danger is one I don't take lightly and accounts for some of last night's tossing and turning in that generic hotel bed with all of those comfy pillows.

I pass around a stack of operations orders, or OPORDs, a comically large tome stapled at the corner with one of those heavy-duty staples (normal case = normal staple; Big Case = Big Staple). This is definitely a Big Staple case. I try and sprinkle in a few laughs here and there and stay self-effacing and humble as I read through the OPORD, a document that over my twenty-nine-year career has grown from three pages to twenty (and still counting). Perhaps the Bureau's greatest acronym of all is CYA.

I read the FBI's Deadly Force Policy verbatim and then I'm done.

"All right guys, let's move out."

* * * *

The drive from the staging area to our standby position never varies, a serpentine procession of vehicles negotiating the sparse early-morning traffic, blue lights used sporadically and judiciously to move through intersections and keep the train intact. Late last night I put Gentile to bed, meaning I drove past his house to ensure that he was home, or at least ensure that his ancient blue Buick was parked in the driveway. It was. On the way to the Dunks earlier this morning, I repeated the process to make sure it was still there. Still there. From personal experience, I can relate that there are few incidents more embarrassing than leading an arrest team up to a front door at six a.m., only to learn that your subject isn't home. And if there is one day in a year when he leaves early to catch a flight or go fishing, it will be the one day in the year you didn't put him to bed the previous night. Hence, one of the most-quoted adages in law enforcement: *Don't be that guy*.

Waiting to execute an arrest is a unique sensation; it's tedious inertia tempered with dynamic energy. The transition between the two is immediate and often capricious, so you sit in your car, enduring the monotony, expecting something to happen at any second. And right now, we're a block away, waiting for Gentile to leave his residence and drive off; that's when we'll arrest him. It will also be the signal for the other team to knock and announce at Parente's front door. Up until that moment, however, we sit and wait, staring at his house as full daylight arrives.

When I was an operator on the SWAT team, sitting in the back of a black-paneled van, staged a two-minute drive from the target, the nervous energy of the pre-arrest ritual was palpable. All of us clad in tactical gear, a study in olive drab, fidgeting endlessly with equipment and joking with each other, the banter casual and easy but tinged with an undercurrent of nervous energy. And always with an eye on the green digital clock on the dashboard as it crept towards 6:00 with excruciating lethargy. Six a.m. marks the FBI's proscribed wake-up call, and the alarm goes off with cruel efficiency. When the seven in 5:57 suddenly grew appendages and became an eight, the routine radio chatter in my earpiece would cease, anticipating the twin commands: the first being the on-scene commander handing off operational control to the subordinate SWAT team leader, and the second being an acknowledgment of that order and the thrice-repeated command to move from Phase Line Yellow (the last stepping-off point to the mission) to Phase Line Green (the front door).

"Romeo-1 to Zulu-1, you have command and control."

"Received, Zulu-1 has command and control. Execute. Execute. Execute."

I used to joke with my teammates that if we could bottle the sensation of Phase Line Yellow, the street value would be extraordinary. It's an ineffable amalgam of excitement and fear, exhilaration and trepidation; Christmas morning and Halloween night at the same time.

But now, it's just Jamie and me, sitting in his nondescript Impala, daytime running lights overridden, with both of us needing the bathroom (Jamie not as much, since he doesn't drink coffee), waiting interminably for an old man to limp out of his house and have his day ruined.

Finally, I see the front door open and watch Gentile step out.

"All units, subject coming out the front door," from an agent over the radio.

I key the mic. *"That's him; that's our guy."*

Jamie quickly calls the other arrest team leader and gives the go-ahead to arrest Parente.

I watch as Gentile lumbers down his driveway, an aluminum cane in one hand and a perceptible hitch in his step, slowly making his way toward the Buick.

Have you ever watched a seventy-six-year-old man get into his car? Perhaps waiting in a Walmart for some septuagenarian's parking space to open up? The wait is excruciating. Truly excruciating.

Finally, after an eternity marked by regular radio updates advising that the car is *"still stationary,"* Gentile starts to move.

"Brake lights on, starting to back out."

Jamie drops the transmission into drive, foot pressed firmly on the brake.

"Setting up to go west. On the move."

We start a slow roll down Frances Drive, Gentile's Buick momentarily obscured by the hard left-hand curve of the street.

Other units: *"Received; standing by at Keeney."*

"We got him. North on Keeney."

"Redballed at Wetherell. Stand by. Fresh green; we're moving." The light turns from red to green and Gentile continues northbound.

We fall in behind another Bucar as we tail Gentile, closing the distance to effect a car stop. Unlike a "no-burn" surveillance, where it's preferable to lose the subject rather than get made, at this point we're all in. And as Gentile makes his way over the I-384 overpass, I give the order:

"This is good here; light him up."

The Bucar in front of us immediately erupts with a cascading staccato of blue lights secreted behind taillights and a heavily tinted rear window. Our Impala does the same.

Gentile pulls over.

I walk up to the driver's side door as he rolls down the window.

"Hey, Bobby, I need you to step out of the car; you're under arrest." The casual command is based on familiarity, the end product of hours of face-to-face conversations we've had over the past two years; conversations in which I entreated him to cooperate and he pretended to know nothing. Our first one took place in March 2010 at his attorney's office in Hartford, sitting across from each other in a nondescript conference room with a well-polished table (the tables are always well polished). Despite offers of immunity and a multimillion-dollar reward, Gentile feigned ignorance, even when confronted with some pretty convincing evidence to the contrary. And the prevarications continued for the next two years, which is why Gentile is now stopped on a highway overpass this morning, car doors akimbo, surrounded by FBI agents.*

I help him out of the car, a compliant but awkward dance as he unspools from the Buick. As Gentile finally gets upright, he teeters a bit and reaches for his cane. Technically, that three-foot length of lightweight aluminum could be construed as a weapon, but I'll take my

* I avoided the trite literary device *armed FBI agents* or *heavily armed FBI agents*. Of course, we're armed; we're always armed.

chances. I walk him around to the trunk of his car, away from traffic, and give him a thorough pat-down. Gentile may be old, but anecdotal intelligence about his storied history in the mob tells me that even a guy pushing eighty can still squeeze a trigger. And I've made his life so miserable over the past twenty-three months that if he could get off one clean shot, it would probably be aimed right at me. Actually, he'd probably shoot Jamie. In the Good-Cop, Bad-Cop gavotte that played out before Gentile, I was the Good Cop; I was the one with enticing offers of rewards, immunity, and anonymity. Jamie was the Bad Cop. Jamie's always the Bad Cop.

Based on Gentile's ample girth and limited mobility, I handcuff him to the front. He is, by decades, the oldest person I've ever arrested. Paul McNamara, a Connecticut state trooper assigned to Jamie's squad, pulls up in an unmarked Crown Vic and I gingerly place Gentile in the back seat. He exhales with an audible whoosh of air as he sits back. I stretch the seat belt across his belly—way, way across his belly—and then climb in beside him for the short journey to the US courthouse in Hartford.

I try to make small talk with him, or at least the closest thing to small talk one can make when your small-talk partner is wearing handcuffs. Nothing substantive; just small talk.**

It's somewhere around the interchange at I-384 and I-84 when Gentile starts breathing heavily, the tempo increasing at an alarming pace.

"Bobby, you doing okay?" I ask, my tone betraying genuine concern.

He gives a half-hearted nod that does little to reassure me. I make eye contact with Paul in the rearview mirror, and he shoots me a quizzical look that reads: courthouse or the ER?

** Contrary to how it plays out in the movies, law enforcement officers rarely provide a subject with their Miranda warnings at the time of arrest. I'm always amused by cop shows that depict the protagonist reading the bad guy his rights, all the while interspersing random insults and obscenities and, perhaps, even a head slap. Unless you want your subject to avail himself of your generous offer of an attorney, Miranda is provided later, after everyone has had a chance to cool down. Get him a cup of coffee and a Danish first; then we'll talk.

I soft-pedal the arrest, using palliative words to calm him down, minimizing the looming criminal justice process that lies ahead. My fear, however, is palpable; it's a fear associated with the knowledge that perhaps the last man on earth who knows the whereabouts of the Gardner Museum paintings is having a fatal coronary. I have a macabre vision of me performing CPR on the shoulder of I-84 during the morning rush, screaming, "*Where are the paintings?*" between chest compressions, the whole scenario playing out in perfect rhythm to the Bee Gees.

Perhaps it was my soothing tone that did the trick, because Gentile begins to relax, his breathing settling back into a routine. I give Paul a nod, and the remainder of the drive—to the courthouse, not the ER—continues without incident.

* * * *

The Abraham A. Ribicoff Federal Building is a brick-and-ugly structure built back in the '60s, that heady period of urban renewal when soulless governmental buildings were the norm. The uglier the building, the more I wonder what it replaced. I have a perverse vision, circa 1960, of a bucolic meadow being plowed under by one of those Mike Mulligan steam shovels, or a wrecking ball arcing into a nineteenth-century Gothic cathedral. All in the name of progress. The building squats low and formidable against its urban backdrop, eight stories of windows grouped in clusters of five that punctuate the dismal façade like one long, monotonous Morse code message: *Raze me, please.* Perhaps at the time there was a perception that the intrinsic homeliness of these buildings would impart a sense of general intimidation and, in doing so, foster in the citizenry a strict adherence to the law. Instead, the structure is simply foreboding, just another one of those modernist government buildings that even gives me a sense of unease, and I'm one of the good guys.

We drive around to the rear sallyport and bring Gentile in through the US Marshals entrance. Three floors up in a granite-veneered cube and we're at the US Attorney's Office and its warren of rooms, each one a bounty of civil service décor and office supplies. General rule of thumb: If the same company that made the couch also made your notebook, then you're in a federal building. Gentile rebuffs my offer of a cup of coffee or something to eat, and we sit him down in the conference room. To make him more comfortable, I remove a cuff and secure it to the arm of the chair in which he lolls. When Jamie shows up a few minutes later, having finally found a parking space, we sit down to start the interview.

The modicum of panic he may have felt in the back seat of the cruiser has been replaced with defiance, and his tone is once again imperious. As with the previous times I've interviewed him, he denies any knowledge about the stolen Gardner Museum artwork. He speaks with a lilting cadence that's almost melodic, rapid-fire denials delivered with conviction, yet the timbre always wispy. And just when I feel certain that surely his voice is finally going to trail off midsentence, he always manages to finish it with a mumbling sibilance and rhythmic tempo as reliable as a gentle ocean wave. It's a voice that demands impersonation, and everyone—reporters, agents, informants, even his attorney—has mastered their own Bobby Gentile impression. He's Hartford's answer to Elvis, *thankyaverramuch*. Gentile concocts his denials in an almost whimsical doggerel, emphatically asserting, as he has asserted so often in the past, that he has never seen the stolen artwork, and he has never heard of the Gardner Museum.

Thirty minutes into this futile exercise, I get a call from my supervisor, Dave Donahue, who also made the trip down from Boston last night. I knew that Dave was out on the search at Frances Drive, and while typically I won't interrupt an interview to take a call, what's presently occurring can hardly be called an interview; it's simply a waste of time.

I answer the phone with a "Hey, Dave."

"Hey, you gotta get over here. We found an old *Boston Herald* with a headline about the Gardner."*

Well, this is interesting. Apparently Gentile, currently sitting across from me and asserting stridently that he's never heard of the Gardner Museum, has a vintage newspaper in his house with banner headlines about the robbery.

"Okay, we're coming over," I reply.

"No, you gotta get over here now," Dave stresses. "There's a handwritten list inside the paper of all the stolen artwork."

I hang up with my supervisor and inform Gentile that we just found a list of the stolen Gardner Museum paintings tucked inside an old newspaper. Inside his house.

"I wanna lawyer," he mumbles.

And with that, the interview concludes. Jamie and I make our way over to Frances Drive; maybe we'll have better luck there.

We do.

---

* Except it sounds like *Gahdner*. Dave was born and bred in Boston, and he has a very pronounced and very authentic local accent. It's a real accent, not an affected one that actors in so many Boston crime movies fail so miserably to mimic. Most native Bostonians, especially those in law enforcement, wear that accent like a badge of honor.

CHAPTER 3

The Ruckus

A part of our heritage has been stolen from us;
it was a barbaric act.
I would characterize it as a tragedy.

—ANNE HAWLEY, March 19, 1990

Dawn arrives a little before six. Act I of *The Gardner Heist* has concluded, and sunrise signals intermission as the house lights come up. Inside the museum, shadows that infested each dark and cloistered recess are evaporating, and sunlight, filtered through gauzy drapes, seeps into the galleries and spills across the tiled floor of the Dutch Room. Undiscernible objects, lying at haphazard angles, slowly begin to take shape: wooden stretchers and stout gilded frames hiding sliced fragments of canvas. They lie prostrate on the floor like redundantly perforated Mafia bosses in a gangland slaying. Instead of blood and shell casings, however, they rest amidst a puddle of broken glass. A cluster of notable bystanders looks on impassively: the Earl of Arundel, the Duke of Modena, and François d'Angoulême, eldest son of France's first Renaissance monarch, King Francis I. Although they must have seen something, none of these witnesses will provide statements.

The museum is silent, savoring these last few minutes of peace before its staid and pristine galleries endure the final outrage of a law enforcement response. The appropriate soundtrack to this ethereal scene would be the rhythmic ticking of a lone clock, except Mrs. Gardner's museum has no clocks. So instead, it's just silence.

Shortly after seven there is a sound, and over time it swells in volume and frequency, its crescendo signaling the start of Act II. The sound is the incessant knocking on the Palace Road service door, and the timpanist is the day-shift guard, attempting in vain to summon her nocturnal counterparts so she can access the museum and get to work. But her efforts go unheeded, for at this very moment Rick and Randy are in the basement, ensconced in duct tape and handcuffed to the viscera of the museum. Rebuffed, the guard finds a pay phone and calls her boss, Larry O'Brien, who makes the fifteen-minute drive to Palace Road.

The scene that will confront the museum's assistant security director is the stuff of nightmares, assuming, of course, one happens to be the assistant security director of a museum.

O'Brien keys into the museum through the greenhouse, an artificial forest nurturing the museum's iconic nasturtiums, those cascading riots of flowering vines that grace the courtyard every Easter, courtesy of Mrs. Gardner. As he moves through the museum, O'Brien finds the watch desk untended and above it, a surveillance camera pointed askance. Unanswered calls give way to empty galleries, and so at 8:02 a.m. O'Brien uses the watch desk telephone to call the Boston Police. The number, laminated and posted conspicuously at eye level, is the same one that Rick should've dialed last night at precisely 1:24 a.m. Within minutes of O'Brien's call, a collection of boxy Ford LTD cruisers arrive at Fenway Court, and for the second time on March 18, men in Boston Police uniforms make their way through the service door, past the mantrap, and into the Gardner Museum.

The cops locate Rick and Randy a few minutes later as they clear their way through the basement. Rick is moments away from rescue when one of the officers has the presence of mind to delay his extrication; Rick remains ensconced in duct tape just a few minutes longer so he can be photographed in his mummified state.

The FBI arrives, including photographer John Green, armed with a 35mm Nikon and many rolls of film. He freezes the tragedy in time, capturing the iconic image of the Dutch Room, its tiled floor littered with the remnants of the robbery and strewn with crime scene tape. That photograph, which has circled the globe many times over, did for art devotees what the humanity-ridden image of the *Hindenburg* conflagration did for blimp lovers. (If you don't care much for museums or dirigibles, then you simply won't understand.)

All morning, a steady stream of FBI agents arrives at the museum. Unlike the steamroller response of local police, all of whom are either on duty or on call somewhere in the city, the pace of an FBI response on a Sunday morning is a little more sporadic. Agents throughout the AOR answer pagers and phones; some still asleep, some in church, and still others in the shower.

* * * *

As law enforcement officers continued to pour into the Gardner, FBI agents and police detectives trailed behind the museum staff as they took stock of the loss. Missing was an eclectic collection of art, stolen from a larger eclectic collection of art, housed in a museum that was itself an eclectic collection of art. The Dutch Room suffered the greatest indignity. The Chinese *gu* was gone, having been pried off the table on which it was secured, it's tablecloth bunched up like an unmade bed. Noticeably absent too was *The Concert* by Johannes Vermeer. The piece depicts what can best be described as a seventeenth-century jam session, with a woman seated at a harpsichord, a second woman singing, and a man strumming the lute. *The Concert* was Mrs. Gardner's first major acquisition, purchased in 1892 at a

Parisian auction house for a mere $5,000. Known for creating paintings within a painting, Vermeer gave Mrs. Gardner her money's worth, for depicted in the background is a rendering of *The Procuress* by Dirck van Baburen, a piece that once hung in the home of Vermeer's mother-in-law in Delft. (In fact, Vermeer liked *The Procuress* so much that six years later, he used it in the background of another work, *A Young Woman Seated at a Virginal.*) The scene portrayed in *The Procuress,* that of a Dutch madam demanding payment from a *Johannes* for her prostitute's amorous ministrations, creates an ironic counterpoint to the one depicted by the chaste women in *The Concert.* By sheer coincidence, *The Procuress* is part of the permanent collection of the Museum of Fine Arts, located just down the street from the Gardner.

As museum staff thread their way through the empty frames and police tape in the Dutch Room, they are struck by the absence of the two large Rembrandts, *A Lady and Gentleman in Black* and *Christ in the Storm on the Sea of Galilee,* arguably two of the finer pieces in the collection. Also missing is Rembrandt's *Self-Portrait* etching. The piece measures just two inches square and, based on its diminutive dimensions, will come to be known as "the stamp" by investigators.

Landscape with an Obelisk is gone. For years misattributed to Rembrandt, it was only a few years before the heist that scholars determined the piece had been created by one of his pupils, Govaert Flinck. This is a noteworthy detail, for if the subjects had researched the Dutch Room's collection using slightly outdated literature, they would've read that this piece was created by Rembrandt. Staff note that the larger Rembrandt oil-on-panel self-portrait, a piece that spawned the idea of creating a museum in the first place, is off the wall but resting face-in against a piece of furniture. There must have been an audible sigh of relief to discover that the piece had seemingly been overlooked in the dark.

Do you notice a pattern? A surplus of the word *Rembrandt* in the inventory of stolen loot, perhaps? Of the six items taken from the Dutch Room, three were Rembrandts and a fourth had been misattributed to Rembrandt until shortly before the heist. And don't forget about the large self-portrait left behind.

As they head into the Short Gallery, museum staff note the loss of five works on paper by Edgar Degas. The works are comprised of unfinished sketches in charcoal and ink, as well as a small watercolor. All that remains of the works is a pile of glass shards resting on a shelf below a broken frame. Eventually, investigators will take note of the fact that two of these works depict jockeys, a favorite subject matter for both Degas and Boston mobsters.

Eventually, the processing of the museum is complete. Crime scene tape is gathered, the photographer has snapped enough pictures, and the crime scene technicians have bagged the dearth of evidence, which consists mostly of broken glass, a handful of paint chips, and the few "latent prints of unknown value" that were lifted from the frames. The FBI agents and detectives head back to their respective offices to write up the reports, and the beat cops fire up those big LTDs and resume patrol.

What the museum staff failed to notice during their assessment that morning was the absence of the Napoleonic finial. In fact, the dearth of Napoleonic finials in the collection won't be noticed until the next day when museum employees—finally able to clean up once the crime scene tape came down—find a handful of screws poking out of the sand inside a fire bucket tucked in the corner of the Short Gallery. Glancing up, they belatedly realized that the eagle had flown the coop. As a result, those inchoative reports about the Gardner Museum heist, wired to FBI Headquarters (known as FBIHQ) and newspapers around the world, listed only twelve stolen items, which explained Monday morning's headlines in The Boston Globe: 12 ART TREASURES WITH VALUE OF AT LEAST $200M STOLEN FROM THE GARDNER MUSEUM.[1]

Two days after the heist, the Gardner Museum's newly minted director, Anne Hawley, stood in the Spanish Cloister, before John Singer Sargent's wall-size masterpiece, *El Jaleo* (which ironically translates as "The Ruckus"), and held her first press conference. She announced the $1 million reward, an astonishing figure at the time, which was "guaranteed by Sotheby's and Christie's of New York and by unidentified private benefactors willing to contribute."[2] Although Anne had been at the museum only a few months, she now found herself thrust into the spotlight as the face of the world's largest art heist.

But in reality, Mrs. Gardner was the face of the world's largest art heist; poor Anne was merely her press secretary.

CHAPTER 4

Barcarolle

If they shall at any time change the general disposition or arrangement of any articles which shall have been placed in the first, second and third stories of said Museum at my death...then I give the said land, Museum, pictures, statuary, works of art and bric-a-brac, furniture, books and papers, and the said shares and the said trust fund, to the President and Fellows of Harvard College.

—LAST WILL AND TESTAMENT OF ISABELLA STEWART GARDNER

Isabella Stewart was born in New York City in 1840, the privileged scion of a wealthy linen merchant. When she was sixteen, the family moved to Paris, where Isabella enrolled in a posh finishing school for American girls. And it was here where she met Julia Gardner, granddaughter to a successful Sumatran pepper merchant (apparently, the Sumatran pepper trade was a big deal back in the day).

The following year, Isabella and Julia visited the Pezzoli Museum in Milan, at the time the private residence of the prolific art collector Gian Giacomo Pezzoli. His frequent travels to Paris had introduced him to the concept of the romantic museum design, which created a cultivated concept of home through a combined collection of artwork and furniture. Pezzoli set to work remodeling his seventeenth-century palace in a historicist manner, with individual rooms becoming galleries in which to showcase different architectural and artistic styles. The essence of a house-museum, Pezzoli's rooms were decorated and furnished in order to match the artwork that hung on the walls. The showpiece of his palace was a central courtyard, designed in the neo-Classical style, with an English-style garden and statuary. In keeping with Pezzoli's wishes, following his death the palace and its contents were converted into a museum. At the time of her visit, Isabella prophetically mused, "If I were ever to inherit some money, I would have a similar house for people to visit and enjoy."

After returning to New York, Isabella accepted an invitation to visit Boston, where she met Julia's older brother, the rakish Sumatran pepper scion John Lowell Gardner (Jack, to his friends). They were married in 1860, and two years later Isabella, now Mrs. Gardner, gave birth to John Lowell Gardner III (Jackie, to his mom). There's a photo of the two of them, Jackie cradled in his mother's arms, with Mrs. Gardner looking down on him with a smile of uncontained affection that seems to belie the traditional decorum so often memorialized in stodgy Victorian photographs. Mrs. Gardner was truly the doting mom. Jackie died in 1865, succumbing to pneumonia, and was buried on March 18, a truly miserable day in the Gardner family's legacy. Mrs. Gardner was inconsolable.

Jack, in a desperate effort to shake his young bride of her crippling depression, whisked her off to Europe, fervently hoping that the architecture and the artwork would bring her back to life, so to speak. The plan worked, and Mrs. Gardner came to fully embrace the ideal of art's restorative powers. She became a prolific and astute collector, ably assisted by her advisor, the noted Renaissance art historian Bernard Berenson, who later wrote that "art was believed to possess redemptive and spiritually elevating qualities." It certainly did the trick for Mrs. Gardner.

In 1896, Mrs. Gardner and her husband purchased Rembrandt's *Self-Portrait, Age 23,* the oil on panel that nearly a century later came this close to being stolen (as I squint at my thumb and index finger, held mere millimeters apart). It was after they purchased this Rembrandt that the Gardners first considered the idea of creating a museum. Because of their shared love of Italy, they visited Venice, Florence, and Rome, collecting the fragments of history that would eventually complement the design of their new museum. They brought back with them a vast collection of architectural details and statuary, culled from a wide swath of time periods.

On December 10, 1898, Jack Gardner "was struck by apoplexy" at the Exchange Club in Boston and died at home hours later. Undeterred by his death, Mrs. Gardner forged ahead with their shared vision to build a museum and just six weeks later, purchased a lot in the Fens, at the time a virtually uninhabited marshland in Boston's Back Bay neighborhood and an intrinsic link in Olmsted's Emerald Necklace. The lot fronted the Fenway, a meandering parkway that snaked through the brackish tidal flats. Fourteen years later, the Fenway would lend its name to a nearby baseball park of some renown.

Undeniably influenced by her visit to Pezzoli's residence-cum-museum many decades earlier, Mrs. Gardner set about designing an edifice worthy of her masterful collection. She hired Willard T. Sears, a prominent Boston architect with a penchant for Gothic and Renaissance Revival styles. Sears, along with his partner, Charles Amos Cummings, had already amassed an impressive list of accomplishments under their collective belts, including the Old South Church at Copley Square in Boston and the Yale University Boathouse.

Sears designed Fenway Court, a Venetian-style palace named after the parkway on which it fronts. The palace's design was loosely based on the Palazzo Barbaro in Venice, one of Mrs. Gardner's favorite spots in Italy. Sears flipped the palace inside out, however, and designed

Gothic porticos that faced an interior courtyard rather than the canals of its Venetian counterpart.

Construction began in 1901, and it was not uncommon to see the iconoclastic Mrs. Gardner perched on a ladder amidst construction debris, barking out orders to workers as they feverishly worked to re-create a slice of Venice in the swampy hinterlands of the Fenway. While Sears's creation does bear an uncanny resemblance to the Palazzo Barbaro, it's the central courtyard, with its colorful gardens and fine statuary, that seems like a nod to the Pezzoli residence. The courtyard has come to represent the Gardner Museum in the same way that *The Storm* has come to represent its collective loss. Enclosed with a glass and steel roof, its garden sprouts greenery and fresh flowers year-round, a manifestation of Berenson's ideal of artistic rejuvenation.

Mrs. Gardner oversaw the furnishing and design of the entire structure and left the fourth floor for her private apartments. In 1888, John Singer Sargent painted a full-length portrait of Mrs. Gardner, a double-strand of pearls encircling her impossibly narrow waist, standing before an enlargement of the tapestry of Italian voided velvet that hangs in the Long Gallery. With its "sensuous display of flesh," Jack requested that his wife not display the portrait until after he died, so she placed it in the third-floor Gothic Room, a private gallery that was not open to the public during Mrs. Gardner's lifetime. She positioned the piece so that it surveyed the beautiful gardens of her courtyard, and she angled two of her beloved Roman busts—the one in the Long Gallery and his comrade in the North Cloister—so that they would gaze longingly and eternally right back at her.

In 1903, Mrs. Gardner held a lavish party on New Year's to celebrate the opening of the museum. The Boston Symphony Orchestra performed Mozart and Schumann, guests dined on champagne and donuts, and galleries were festooned with paper lanterns. Music critic William F. Apthorp described the scene:

No one was in the least prepared for the fairy beauty that greeted [their] eyes; even those who had been privileged to see the court before had never seen it like this...Here, in the very midst of winter, was a "gorgeous vista of blossoming summer gardens."

The Gardner is often referred to as a house-museum; actually, a misnomer, since Fenway Court was purpose-built as a museum, but it possesses an intimacy that evokes Mrs. Gardner's spirit in every gallery. She must have been pleased with her creation, for Mrs. Gardner's last will and testament contained the infamous stipulation dictating that every item in her collection, from the pedestrian "bric-a-brac" to the priceless Titian, must remain fixed in place, a sepia-tinted snapshot frozen in time. Were this dictum to be violated, the whole lot would be liquidated and the proceeds donated to Harvard College. The monumental collection was, for all intents and purposes, uninsured,* but since Mrs. Gardner's will stipulated that even stolen or damaged pieces couldn't be replaced, there was no point in paying hefty insurance premiums.**

The lack of insurance is an esoteric detail about the collection that even an astute criminal might have missed, and one that may have had a chilling effect on any initial attempts to return the stolen artwork. Historically, insurance companies representing victimized museums often act as intermediaries, discreetly negotiating the return of the stolen artwork. And while museums are loath to pay a "ransom" to recover their stolen pieces, paying a modest reward to a consultant who facilitates the recovery is something different altogether.

It's all about perception.

* Invariably elicits a shocked gasp...

** ...well that makes sense.

CHAPTER 5

The Investigation

It is difficult to get a man to understand something
when his salary depends upon his not understanding it.

—UPTON SINCLAIR

The role of an FBI case agent varies with the type of investigation. If it's a typical case, say a bank robbery or an insurance scam, the case agent will typically work it alone, and depending on the type of violations worked and the complexity of any one particular case, FBI agents may carry anywhere from a few cases to a few dozen. Larger and more complex investigations, however, will invariably have a co-case agent assigned. And when an FBI supervisor assigns the world's largest art heist, convention and common sense would dictate that at least two veteran agents be assigned.

Instead, the case was assigned solely to Dan Falzon, a Boston agent with just two years on the job. Dan was a former San Francisco beat cop and by all accounts a solid agent. He responded to the museum from his Beacon Hill bachelor pad and dove into the case headfirst.

I would suggest, however, that a case of this magnitude required a co-case agent—someone to deal with the day-to-day minutiae of managing the investigation, swearing out warrants and serving grand jury subpoenas, briefing executive management, requesting exams from the laboratory, and setting leads to FBI offices around the country and to agents stationed in embassies around the globe as legal attachés, known as Legats. Freed from these necessary but time-consuming administrative obligations, the lead investigator—in this case Dan—would've been able to handle the two substantive objectives of this investigation; that is, identify the UNSUBS* and recover the stolen artwork.

Although it seems like the deck was stacked against Dan, he was resilient. He took on the yeoman's task of getting a major theft investigation off the ground (this is beyond a freight train; think Howard Hughes's *Spruce Goose* lumbering across the channel in Long Beach), demonstrating outstanding organizational skills in the process. In September 1991, the FBI attempted to establish an interagency task force to work the investigation, but "Boston PD and State Police refused due to lack of manpower for same."[1] Although Dan managed the administrative aspects of the case well, it seems that the overwhelming administrative burden left him scant time to fulfill his primary role as lead investigator. As a result, crucial interviews of witnesses and suspects were delegated to agents who knew very little about the case. There are things I would've done differently, had I been assigned the case back in March 1990, but I had a perspective that was not available to Dan back at the time.

* * * *

I grew up in Irvington, a tiny village that hugs the eastern shore of the Hudson River, just north of New York City and just south of the

* In Bureau parlance, an UNSUB is a colloquial portmanteau of the term UNidentified SUBject.

Tappan Zee Bridge, currently referred to by no one as the Governor Mario M. Cuomo Bridge (including the Cuomos). The town was named after our most famous resident, Washington Irving, and many of the historic locations that inspired his stories are sprinkled throughout the area. If you stood in Irvington's riverfront park and looked left, you would clearly see the George Washington Bridge off in the distance, and framed behind it, the Manhattan skyline. I grew up in a creative environment: My mother is a wonderful singer and pianist (and a five-time undefeated *Jeopardy* champion, I might add), and her brother, Jack Fiorito, was a baritone with the Metropolitan Opera company in New York City. My father was a talented artist and onetime art director at J. Walter Thompson. He grew up in Liverpool, the son of Theo Kelly, who was the first manager of the Everton Football Club.* My dad immigrated to New York in 1956, and a few years later he was introduced to my mother. In the early 1970s, he designed the Popsicle logo, that iconic red dot that continues to spread across the frozen treats aisles of supermarkets like measles and helped put me through college.

Although I enjoyed photography and graphic arts growing up, for some bizarre reason I was drawn to law enforcement. There was a book in my elementary school library entitled *Your Police* by George Zaffo, its cover bearing an NYPD cap superimposed over the tented arch of an orange-tinted fingerprint. As a kid, I was fascinated by this book, perusing its monochromatic images of police equipment spread out over royal-blue pages. Aided and abetted by episodes of *Adam-12*, *Your Police* made me want to be a cop, and I kept signing it out, over and over again, until my exasperated librarian implored me to read a different book.

As a teenager, when my friends and I would drive into Manhattan or out to Jones Beach, we'd typically take the Major Deegan Expressway. It's one of the main arteries linking Westchester County to New York

* *Come on you Blues!*

City and Long Island, generally working its way toward Astoria, at least in theory. Like so many roads in the City, you never know exactly when it ends; suddenly, you're just not on it anymore. Along its journey, the Deegan skirts Yankee Stadium as it cuts through the South Bronx, a neighborhood with the dubious distinction of comprising the poorest congressional district in the nation.

In *The Bonfire of the Vanities*, Tom Wolfe described the Bronx as a neighborhood of "fear and otherness" that caused the ruination of its protagonist after he made a wrong turn and ventured into its bowels after dark. Driving the Deegan as a teenager, that feeling of dread was palpable to my friends and me, a Corolla wagon full of suburban kids heading into the West Village or Soho for a Saturday night, fake IDs tucked securely into Velcro wallets. Whenever we took the Deegan, following the sluggish stream of traffic running north to south, I always looked for the square box that jutted above the Bronx horizon off in the distance. It wasn't until I read Wolfe's book that I finally learned that this fixture of the skyline was the Bronx County Courthouse, a stalwart outpost in imaginary enemy territory. Sometimes when we were driving south, and oftentimes when we were driving north hours later, my friends and I would ponder the question, "Can you imagine if we broke down?" It was the stuff of ghost stories around campfires, right up there with *the call's coming from inside your house*. And when we went to a Yankees game, the door-lock button was rigorously checked and rechecked many times before we reached the East 161st Street exit. We were your typical suburban teenagers, insulated from the harsher realities of the 1980s, all the while bedecked in a glut of Swatch watches and upturned teal collars and reeking of Polo cologne.

I studied filmmaking at Boston University, which at the time seemed a likely major given my keen interest in photography. After registering for my freshman classes in the fall of '85, I was accosted outside the student union by a handful of varsity rowers from the crew team, poised beside a strategically positioned eight-man shell. They were hunting for potential rowers, and since I stood just an inch over six feet, I was thusly encircled. I tried out for the team, successfully, and spent the next four years rowing up and down the Charles River. My teammates and I once calculated that during our collegiate years, we rowed nearly two million strokes; the same mechanical motion, varying only in cadence and intensity, executed over and over again. And despite our expectations of a different result, we never did beat Harvard, perhaps proving the old aphorism about the definition of insanity.

Crew is the archetype of teamwork, as evidenced by the sheer number of sales office motivational posters that depict a coxed eight. It requires a selfless reliance on the other seven rowers in the boat, working cooperatively toward a common goal, while simultaneously cursing the coxswain, the diminutive taskmaster who exhorts from the stern. The crew team was perhaps the single most influential activity in my life, and it came to shape my career aspirations. While I'd always possessed this barely latent interest in law enforcement, it was because of the crew team that I first considered doing something more with my life than merely making movies.

To that end, in my junior year I switched my concentration to criminal justice and started taking sociology and law classes, one of which was taught by an off-duty Boston Police detective. To my knowledge, it was my only class at BU taught by a professor with a snub-nosed .38 strapped to his hip. I was fascinated with the course curriculum, but even more so with the exciting war stories told by this seasoned veteran.

I graduated from BU in 1989 with a degree in broadcasting and film and, despite the unfortunate major, still managed to overcome adversity and actually land a job in television production. I was hired by Comedy Central, where I worked as an associate producer for *Short Attention Span Theater*, a segment show comprised of comedy clips that was hosted by a vaguely known stand-up comic named Jon Stewart. Since I, too, was vaguely known, we had a great time working together. One of my responsibilities was finding new talent for Jon's show, culling through hours and hours of horrific stand-up material, searching for little gems of humor in a barren landscape of truly bad comedy, at times a slightly less jocular version of waterboarding. Because our show was renewed in thirteen-week chunks, every three months we all waited with a collective bated breath to hear if we'd been picked up again. If it had, then we were still employed. At least for another thirteen weeks.

Regardless of the perpetual state of job insecurity and the capricious nature of the entertainment industry, it was still a fun place to work. But the urge to do something more than just have fun was growing stronger, and I resolved to pursue a career in law enforcement. In the end, I don't recall which specific event signaled my epiphany and the abrupt career change.

Perhaps it was Carrot Top.

With much hand-wringing and gnashing of teeth, my parents learned of my decision. Actually, the decision was made for me, since I believed then—and still do to this day—that for some people, law enforcement is truly a calling. My ultimate goal was to join the FBI, but when I spoke with a recruiter, she tactfully informed me that my chances were quite slim, as the Bureau was looking for attorneys and accountants; at the time, the need for comedic filmmakers was not quite as pressing. The recruiter advised that I still had some time to punch up my résumé, since the FBI required three years of full-time work experience before applicants were even eligible to apply. All of this was a moot point, however, because the Bureau was in the midst of a hiring freeze.

In an effort to make myself a more viable candidate, I applied to a number of local and state law enforcement agencies, and in December 1992, I was hired by the Metropolitan Transportation Authority Police Department in New York City. It was a historic appointment, as I became the very first associate producer in Comedy Central's brief history to resign in order to become a transit cop.

* * * *

On a bitterly cold morning in early January, I descended into the 86th Street station in Manhattan, surfaced an hour later on Metropolitan Avenue in Brooklyn, and walked the six blocks to the New York City Transit Police Academy on Gold Street. I had reasoned that my four years on crew would have prepared me for the Academy's training regimen, but I was sorely mistaken. While I did well physically and academically, only the recruits with prior military service were prepared for the martial bearing of our instructors and the low-grade hazing that infiltrated every part of academy life. There were about 160 recruits in our class, and the concepts of conformity and shared responsibility was drilled into us daily.

Every morning we stood at attention for roll call, a perfectly spaced dot-matrix rectangle on the Academy's rooftop, dressed right and covered down. Because of the frigid weather, they allowed us gloves, but if even one recruit forgot their pair, then no one wore gloves. On these particular mornings, the instructors would leave us at attention forever, alternating the repetitive commands of "secure you gear!" and "ground your gear!" In clattering unison, we would robotically pick up or drop the black oversize bowling ball bags that contained our class books, gun belts, and side-handle batons. Off to our left, the sun would rise over Brooklyn, barely warming our freezing fingers as it illuminated the synchronized madness. But there was a method to this synchronized madness, as it weeded out those recruits who were unwilling or unable to tolerate the verbal abuse. They lacked patience, a vital character trait in law enforcement, and one that helped us to remain nonplussed and unmoved, despite the insults and harassment we would later experience out on the street.

After six months of training, our Academy class was let loose on the streets of New York (actually, *under* the streets might be more appropriate). Along with NYPD's Transit Bureau, we shared the responsibility of safeguarding New York's massive transit system. Like any decent transit cop, I became adept at subway surfing; that is, riding a train car without the need to hang onto a strap, anticipating the lurching and swinging of the car beneath my feet with both thumbs hooked confidently into my gun belt. I worked for a year in Midtown and Harlem before being assigned to the South Bronx, the same neighborhood Tom Wolfe once described as a wasteland. And after viewing the Bronx courthouse from the protected confines of the Deegan less than a decade earlier, it was almost surreal to actually stand before it, to study it up close and gaze up at its basket-weave façade that rose up from the surrounding tenements.

It was exhilarating to work the city in uniform, either riding the trains or responding to calls in a marked cruiser (in New York we called them RMPs, short for radio motor patrols). I especially enjoyed working nights, akin to riding a roller coaster with the safety bar up; stopping into a bodega on the Grand Concourse for an obscenely caffeinated cup of Café Bustelo; or eating at the *cuchifritos* on East 161th Street, which had the best pork carnitas in the city. I mastered tactics that weren't trained in the Academy: Upon entering a store, I would quickly scan the aisles and make eye contact with the clerk, lest I unwittingly interrupt a robbery. It's a reflexive habit that I still practice to this day. And while there was certainly no shortage of criminals on my beat, I learned that the majority of people in these communities were law-abiding and supportive of the police. They welcomed our presence, and their major criticism of law enforcement was that there weren't enough of us around. Throughout my career, I've worked in some really dangerous neighborhoods, but that same message always resonated: Overall, people are good, and they support the police.

I quickly learned that cops are funny. This surprised me, especially considering that my last place of employment had the word *comedy* in its name. There's an acerbic cynicism about police work that translates well into gallows humor. In reality, it's a coping mechanism, one that helps prevent law enforcement officers from internalizing the violence and misery that surrounds them, deflecting the sadness and pain that is inherent in the job description. The age-old formula is true: Tragedy plus time equals comedy, except in law enforcement there was no need for the variable of time. And the humor always lies in the delivery, an ironic indifference that's always in stark contrast to the grim circumstances surrounding the dark punch line. While much of the humor is too inappropriate for print and would seem callous and insensitive when taken out of context, there is an editorial bemusement that permeates the job, an ongoing social commentary, temporal and scathing, and always delivered with impeccable timing.

In my first command, one of the guys on our shift was universally referred to as Mango, even though his nameplate said CRUZ. When I asked my field training officer about it, he explained that years earlier, Cruz had submitted a burglary report, and he had typed in the narrative: "*Man go into the store, take the merchandise, then man go out.*" And that's how Officer Cruz became Mango. To everyone. At roll call, the sergeant would assign Mango to a post. The humor lay in the assimilation; Cruz became Mango, with a grudging resignation that was devoid of comment or protest.

In January 1995, my partner, Terry McGrory, and I were working the 2-Sam sector in the Bronx when we received a radio call of a dog hit by a train near 163rd Street and the Grand Concourse (a location pronounced in radio jargon as "*1-6-3 and the Conk*"). Terry and I arrived on scene and found a stray dog lying alongside the tracks, a malnourished beagle-shepherd mix with a broken and degloved hind leg. I radioed our dispatcher to summon the ASPCA, who would respond and mercifully put her down. But as we waited, I couldn't break eye contact with this dog, whose warm brown eyes implored me to do something. So I radioed my patrol sergeant and requested him to respond to the scene:

"*2-Sam, 2-Sergeant, 10-85 my location, 'kay.*"

When Sergeant Dan Reinmuth's cruiser wheeled into the yard a few minutes later, I asked him for permission to drive this dying stray to the animal hospital across the river. He wavered, understandably, since Terry and I wouldn't just be leaving our sector, we'd be leaving the entire borough, and calls were beginning to stack. Most supervisors, if not every single other supervisor, would've denied the request, and with good reason.

"All right," he relented finally, "but put a muzzle on her. I don't want you getting bit."

Since the dog was barely conscious at this point, there was little chance of that occurring, but I wasn't going to press my luck. As we searched for something to use for a muzzle, Terry offered up the floral scrunchy that held back her hair. I placed it over the stray's shivering muzzle and lifted her into the back seat of our cruiser. With Sergeant Reinmuth's farewell entreaty—*"don't get into an accident!"*—we crossed the Harlem River and sped down FDR Drive to the Animal Medical Center on East 62st Street. I carried her inside, and a nurse waved me straight through to an examining room, where I left her with the medical team. I stood by in the waiting room, monitoring the radio and trying to clean the blood and dog hair off my uniform.

A nurse came out shortly to tell me that although they could save the dog, because she was just a stray they would have to put her down. With zero time to ponder the ramifications, I blurted out, "I'll adopt her." The nurse smiled warmly and said, "I was hoping you would." And then someone asked me for my credit card.

One month and three surgeries later, Annie finally came home. She was named after Anna Karenina, the titular Tolstoy character who threw herself in front of a train. And while her medical bills equated to almost a third of what I made that year, she was worth every penny. That November, I received the Animal Medical Center's Heart of Gold award for rescuing Annie. The previous month, I'd received my appointment letter to the FBI, and since I'd already left for Quantico, Sergeant Reinmuth, the patrol sergeant whose forbearance had made Annie's rescue possible, accepted the award on my behalf. Over the course of my career, the Heart of Gold was, by far, the award of which I'm most proud.

It was with mixed emotions that I'd turned in my shield. Although I was excited to join the FBI, there had been a sense of camaraderie and fellowship in the police department that I hadn't experienced since my days on the crew team.

On Sunday, October 15, 1995, I entered on duty to the FBI, known as my EOD. Earlier that morning, I tossed a duffel bag and two suits into the back seat of my '87 Jeep Wrangler and aimed south, over the George Washington Bridge. Halfway across the Hudson, I stole a quick glance to my right and took in one last look at Irvington off in the distance, recognizable by the square of its waterfront lumberyard that juts out into the river. As I crossed into New Jersey, I thought that if my life was being written in book form, then this drive to Quantico would be the start of a new chapter.

Or at least a chapter break.

CHAPTER 6

The Start of a New Chapter

There is no greater folly in the world than for a man to despair.

—MIGUEL DE CERVANTES, *Don Quixote*

I went with a new chapter.

After merging onto the Jersey Turnpike, it was a straight shot all the way to Quantico. My forty-nine classmates and I comprised NAC 96-02, which translated as the FBI's second New Agents Class of the 1996 fiscal year. Later that night, we rose from our desks, in unison, and were sworn in as the newest Special Agents of the Federal Bureau of Investigation.

Quantico was an incredible experience. Three years earlier I'd gone through the Transit Police Academy, surviving six months of excoriation and vilification for committing even the slightest perceived infraction—standing at attention for hours, alternately picking things up and putting them down. But Quantico was different; despite the lack of vituperation, there was more expected from us, especially with the academics. Two test scores below an 80 and you were gone; the same went for firearms. And when a classmate was dismissed, the alacrity of their departure was shocking.

It usually occurred out on the pistol range as we were facing new targets. The first to notice the impending arrival of our class counselor would give a nudge to the others, and we would look up-range, watching him close the distance to us like a thunderstorm moving across the plain. Conversation ceased, and all eyes watched as he moved down the line. The collective fear was palpable; the wait excruciating. *Eeny, meeny, miny…* While it seemed capricious and arbitrary, we knew that it wasn't; a classmate had transgressed the rules or failed to keep up. *Moe.* The counselor's selection finally became known, and a classmate received an economical tap on the shoulder. There would be a whispered message and then, *poof,* they were gone. There were no goodbyes, no hugs. When we returned to the dorms after lunch, our classmate's room would be empty, the bed stripped bare, that blue plastic college-grade mattress serving as a cautionary tale. *Study hard and shoot straight, kids!*

As Orders Night approached, we filled out our wish list, an optimistically prepared document that ranked all fifty-six field offices in order of preference. Boston topped my list, with San Juan ranked fifty-sixth. Some classmates gambled with reverse psychology, reasoning that the Transfer Unit would send new agents to their least-favored offices; for this reason, they strategically downgraded their top choices. ("*Whatever you do, don't send me to Honolulu, Br'er Fox!*") Orders Night occurred roughly halfway through the Academy, and it was an event not to be missed. Our instructors ringed the periphery of our tiered classroom as if it were the Colosseum, awaiting the lions. They shared in the ecstasy of high picks realized and commiserated in the agony of the lows.

When my turn came, I opened my orders and was actually speechless for a moment. "Boston," I announced to the class in a hoarse whisper.

And the classmates who begged for a good roasting over the briar patch?

Mostly, they got roasted.

We graduated in February 1996, a ceremony that seemed almost surreal, the culmination of a long-held dream. My credentials, known ubiquitously as creds, were presented to me by Louis Freeh, the only FBI director to have ever served as an agent and, in my opinion, without peer (an opinion shared by most veteran agents). After the ceremony, we had a small reception with family, and they served up a vanilla cake with GOOD LUCK NEW AGENTS CLASS 96-2 spelled out in blue icing. This was, I believe, the last free thing I ever received from the FBI (RECEIPT FOR PROPERTY ISSUED: CAKE; ROUND, VANILLA; ICING; BLUE-COLORED).

In keeping with some bizarre Bureau tradition, immediately after the reception concluded we were unceremoniously hustled out the door. Since we'd already vacated our dorm rooms, we changed from suits into casual travel attire in an unused classroom, all the while being exhorted to leave by our counselors. We said hasty goodbyes, checked out our SIG Sauer 9mm pistols from the armory, and were summarily evicted from Academy grounds. I stopped off in New York briefly to collect Annie from my parents' house, and together we headed off to Boston (her first time). We moved into a condo on Beacon Street, a crosswalk away from the Charles River where I once rowed those nearly two million strokes, and just a few blocks from Fenway Park. I always found this ironic, since Annie used to live just a few blocks from Yankee Stadium.

Just like her dad, her allegiances were divided.

* * * *

The day after I arrived in town, I reported to the Boston field office. I was a first office agent, or FOA, a term used to signify the new guys, since the Bureau historically transferred agents from their first office after three or four years of service. I came into the FBI after a lengthy hiring freeze, however, and the costs associated with onboarding a tidal wave of new agents had left little money in the budget for routine transfers. I escaped the mandatory transfer policy and, as a result, Boston would be my first and only duty station. Nearly twenty-nine years later, I would retire from the FBI as an FOA.

Because of my prior law enforcement experience, my first squad assignment was the Providence Resident Agency, or RA, in Rhode Island, one of the four states covered by the FBI's Boston division. RAs are smaller, regional offices that are sprinkled throughout the country, ensuring that every community has an FBI presence. Because they have fewer agents (two-man RAs are not uncommon), the work demands are higher and the oversight is lower. A new agent assigned to the division's main office, known as headquarters city, or HQC, will typically spend much of his or her two-year probationary period on the applicant squad, conducting background investigations for prospective Bureau and White House employees. As a new agent in the Providence RA, however, I hit the ground running.

Within a month of graduating from Quantico, I got my first real case. It involved a con man who used counterfeit bank checks to purchase more than $2 million in computer equipment, all of which was delivered within a proscribed two-day window to a nondescript office in Providence. This was back in the days when you could still pay the UPS driver for merchandise upon delivery, the antiquated concept of COD. On the third day, the UNSUB skipped town, and a day or two after the first checks began to bounce, his victims began calling the FBI. I hastily swore out my first search warrant at the US District Courthouse in Providence, and after it was signed, we hit the UNSUB's place of business. As expected, it was nothing more than an empty room in a converted textile mill, rented with bogus identification and paid for in cash.

About a month later, some of that fraudulently obtained computer equipment began popping up for sale on something called the World Wide Web, and I was finally able to identify my UNSUB. His name was Andrew Leppo, and he lived in Randolph, a commuter town on the southern fringe of Boston's Route 128 belt. He was the son of a notorious Boston mob lawyer named Marty Leppo, and Andrew had the poor judgment to sell that stolen computer equipment out of the basement of his father's law office.

On July 31, 1996, I executed the second search warrant of my career at the Law Firm of Martin K. Leppo & Leppo. And that's how I first came to meet Marty Leppo. After the team made entry downstairs, I ascended a narrow staircase that opened directly into Marty's office, where I found him chatting casually with his son, Carl (the second Leppo in Leppo & Leppo). I handed him a copy of the warrant, which he scanned quickly and tossed on his desk with a dismissive shrug. After Marty instructed me not to speak with his son, I returned to the basement and we set to work, seizing nearly $2 million worth of fraudulently obtained property. I ended up charging Andrew federally with bank fraud and trafficking counterfeit checks. The following year, he pled guilty in US District Court in Boston and was sentenced to twenty-eight months in prison.

I didn't know it at the time, but Marty Leppo represented many of the individuals associated with the Gardner Museum heist, people like Carmello Merlino, Myles Connor, Billy Youngworth, Bobby Guarente, David Turner, and Stephen Rossetti.

I thought I was done with Marty Leppo.

But that was before I inherited the Gardner case.

* * * *

After two years working in Providence, I was transferred to Boston's HQC and assigned to Squad C-5, an economic crimes squad, where I specialized in telemarketing fraud cases. This was in the days before emails and texting, when con men actually called their prospective victims on the telephone like real fraudsters, not like those lovelorn Nigerian princes who fire off emails from inside their lavish palaces. And in a forgotten era when spam was still known only as a canned luncheon meat and perhaps a tagline in World War II documentaries, the victims answered the phone. My subjects would purchase lists of potential victims, often culled from those cardboard boxes positioned next to cash registers at pizzerias or delis, the ones that read *Enter your name for a chance to win a 1996 Ford Mustang.* And back then, a lot of gullible people did just that. There was no Mustang, of course, and everyone who dropped their name and number in that box would soon receive a glut of phone calls from telemarketers—perhaps even one of my subjects—informing them that they were big winners. They won, all right, and not just the Mustang; these victims won prizes from contests and lotteries they didn't even recall entering. They just had to pay some minimal taxes before the winnings could be released. Outrageous claims made; checks mailed.

Those pitiful victims who fell prey to my subjects earned a coveted spot on a "mooch list," a veritable shooting gallery of victims who'd already proven themselves sufficiently vulnerable to a good scam. These unfortunates would then receive calls from the denizens of "recovery rooms," a motley assortment of "lottery officials" and "FBI agents" who could recover their losses…for a modest fee. And so it went, with these professional victims being exploited over and over again. After we got involved, my subjects would have the audacity to advise their victims that it was the FBI's involvement that was preventing them from receiving their Mustang. This prompted hang-ups when I tried to contact the victims to find out why they didn't show up for court.

The cases were always interesting, often frustrating, but not all that exciting. Most of the investigations I worked were opened with the name of the subject already identified in the case title; the tricky part was proving that the subject's actions amounted to a crime. In order to charge a crime, we had to first prove that our subjects had the specific *intent* to commit a crime, one of the essential elements of fraud statutes. It's not a crime to be lousy at business, which was invariably their defense. ("*I'm not a criminal, I'm just an idiot.*" Well, you're half right.)

When I finally made the case, even the arrests—which represented the culmination of investigations lasting months, or even years—were often anticlimactic. If one of my particularly well-heeled subjects heard that the FBI was poking around, the assistant United States attorney, or AUSA, assigned to prosecute the case would invariably get a call from a defense attorney bearing a twofold message: First, under no circumstances is their client to be interviewed; and second, if an arrest is forthcoming, their client would prefer to self-surrender at the courthouse. Sadly, many of the AUSAs with whom I worked would honor this self-serving request and allow the defendants to show up at the courthouse with their attorney at a time that was mutually convenient for everyone. The arrest comprised no more than meeting the subject on the courthouse side of the magnetometer and escorting them the short distance to the US Marshals office.

While this practice may seem counterintuitive, it's really not when you consider that most AUSAs will not spend their career in public service. They'll work at the US Attorney's Office for a couple of years and get their ticket punched, so to speak, before entering private practice. Once there, they'll use the skills they learned as federal prosecutors, coupled with knowledge gleaned about how agencies like the FBI conduct criminal investigations, in order to become a more effective defense attorney. As a result, many AUSAs don't want to antagonize a white-shoe defense attorney lest it hurt their employment opportunities down the road.

There were a number of occasions in my career when I sat on the witness stand, being cross-examined by a defense attorney with whom I'd previously worked at the US Attorney's Office. During these occasionally excruciating exchanges, I would have a brief second to reflect on how we used to be comrades, working together for the common good; now, I'm listening intently as my every word is parsed and dissected, interpreting questions that are phrased with intentional ambiguity and obfuscation in an attempt to portray my every action and motivation in a nefarious light.

The irony of the white-collar self-surrender often rested with the criminal histories of the subjects whom I investigated. Economic crimes comprise, by definition, a lack of violence, yet the same cannot be said for the subjects. When I opened a case, it was de rigueur to run a newly identified subject's criminal history. Invariably, their rap sheet would reveal a litany of serious felonies, including a number of violent crimes, that demonstrated the parabolic nature of criminality: Career offenders, facing draconian prison sentences if they accrue just one more violent-crime conviction, often turn their attention to economic crime. With its misguided reputation for encompassing rarified criminals with advanced degrees and higher social status, the punishment was more of the slap-on-the-wrist variety. As a result, committing fraud was a viable and more profitable alternative to a maximum-security prison. It was galling to see these potbellied felons at sentencing, appearing sufficiently rueful and repentant as they addressed the court whilst stuffed into ill-fitting sport coats like sausages and wearing short, fat ties that lent them an uncanny resemblance to Oliver Hardy.

A victim in my first case, a computer reseller from Sunnyvale, California, provided his life savings to the aforementioned son of that prominent Boston defense attorney. He tearfully admitted to me that he would rather have been robbed at gunpoint. "If the guy stole my wallet, he would've gotten what, a hundred bucks?" he reasoned. "This guy took everything I had." That sentiment later made for a memorable victim impact statement at Andrew Leppo's sentencing, but it still didn't get the victim his money back.

* * * *

In December 2000, I finally got my long-awaited transfer to Squad C-6, working violent crimes and major offenders, a program known in the FBI as VCMO (pronounced "vick-mo"). The squad was an interagency task force comprised of agents, state troopers, and detectives from the Boston Police and a handful of other local agencies. We were colloquially known in the office as the Hollywood Squad, since many of our exploits were sexy enough to make the evening news and local papers: bank robberies, armored car heists, vehicle pursuits, and fugitive apprehensions. These were the cool cases, the ones that made me want to be an FBI agent in the first place. And ever since I got my transfer to HQC, I'd been vying for a coveted spot on Squad C-6. I volunteered to help out on their search warrants and surveillances, and whenever an overhead page notified the task force of a bank robbery in progress, I jogged down to the squad area and offered to assist. So when a vacancy finally opened up, the squad's reticent and taciturn supervisor, John Trahon, at least knew my name.

Rather than suits, we wore hoodies and jeans, and if the relaxed dress code wasn't reason enough to want a transfer, there was another huge benefit to working VCMO: self-surrender was not an option. We arrested our subjects, thank you very much. These were violent offenders committing violent offenses, with many sufficiently egregious enough to merit a SWAT mission. A courthouse self-surrender with a continental breakfast just wasn't on the table.

The number of pending investigations differed dramatically, as well. Whereas my economic crime caseload had consisted of perhaps a half dozen complex investigations, I had at least five times as many cases on Squad C-6. And unlike my white-collar crime cases, almost all of these were opened as UNSUBS. Despite the squad's good-natured reputation in the office of being comprised of Neanderthals and knuckle draggers, the work was anything but. In addition to proving the case, we first had to identify the subject who committed the crime. It was that extra step, the *whodunit* part of the crime, that drew me to VCMO work in the first place. And while one of the cases we worked on at the time was a long-term investigation into a crew of deadly armored car robbers from Boston's Charlestown neighborhood (a fictionalized account of this real-life crew would be depicted in the movie *The Town*), the cases were mostly quick hits that rarely stayed open for more than a few ninety-day file review cycles.

And almost two years to the day after arriving on Squad C-6, my supervisor assigned me the Gardner Museum case.

CHAPTER 7

A Very Cold Case. And Very Big.

Ah! well a-day! what evil looks
Had I from old and young!
Instead of the cross, the Albatross
About my neck was hung.

—SAMUEL TAYLOR COLERIDGE,
The Rime of the Ancient Mariner

I'd first heard about the Gardner Museum robbery when I was a recent college graduate living in New York, probably a week or so after it occurred. I was at the American Museum of Natural History on the Upper West Side, gazing up at the giant blue whale suspended from the ceiling, when I overheard two elderly ladies discussing the details of a monumental art heist that had just occurred in Boston.

Heist. It's one of those words that commands attention. Use it in a sentence in a crowded elevator, and someone will invariably listen in. Naturally, I couldn't help but eavesdrop on their conversation and listened as one woman related to her friend a fabulous tale of fake police officers, outrageous subterfuge, and stolen treasures.

And here it was, a dozen years later, and I just got the case.

Until the implementation of a computerized database system, which arrived a few years after the Gardner robbery, FBI files were in paper form. When a new case was opened and assigned to an agent, written as *O+A*, the very first document, known as a serial, would be two-hole-punched at the top and slipped into a cardboard jacket, skewered in place with two steel prongs. When the file became too fat to be safely secured with the bent-over prongs, Volume II commenced, although most cases rarely merited a second volume. Each squad had a set of file cabinets that held the hundreds of pending cases for that particular squad, and the whole lot was managed by file clerks known in Bureau parlance as rotors, named after the rotary file cabinets over which they governed. Newspeak eventually changed their job title to Operational Support Technician, or OST, but we still called them rotors.

No agent wants to inherit a case; typically, they're either unsolvable or there isn't an AUSA willing to prosecute. It's common for agents to shop their cases door-to-door at the US Attorney's Office, moving down the carpeted hallway like vacuum cleaner salesmen, hoping to fund an AUSA who'll bite. These forlorn cases float from one agent to the next, until eventually the statute of limitations expires; that is, the deadline for prosecution, which is typically five years for most federal crimes. Once the statute has expired, the case can finally be administratively closed. Days before a new agent arrives on a squad, the supervisor typically polls the senior agents to surrender a case or two for the new guy. And that's how a brand-new agent manages to inherit a full caseload of crap.

The Gardner was no exception. Prior to my tenure, it was a moribund case that nobody wanted. The only difference with this cold case was that pesky statute of limitations, as there is no expiration date for possessing stolen property. The reasoning is logical—if there was a firm deadline for prosecution, thieves could conceivably hold on to stolen property for five years and a day, then claim it as their own.

They could register a stolen car at the DMV or sell a stolen painting at auction. Since the statute of limitations for the possession of stolen property never expires, theoretically the Gardner case would remain open indefinitely.

Yet despite all the challenges, I really wanted this case. And I was intrigued by the biggest challenge of all: the title. The Gardner Museum heist was still carried as UNSUBS. It was the ultimate whodunit.

My first task was to get an idea of the scope of the investigation. Typically, the squad rotor (the file cabinet, not the human) contains every volume of a particular pending case. But due to the sheer size of the Gardner investigation, all but its most current volumes had been relegated to the Closed File Room down on the fourth floor. It was an area rarely visited by most agents, but one which I got to know quite well. Rolling stacks of cabinets extended the entire length of the room, containing a comprehensive collection of all of Boston's historical FBI cases, arranged numerically by classification. It was surprisingly easy to find the Gardner case, classified as an 87A matter (interstate transportation of stolen property), since it took up nearly an entire file cabinet, sandwiched between other vintage theft cases, many of them ensconced in sepia-tinted file jackets that dated back to the days of J. Edgar Hoover.

And there it was, at gut level: the Gardner case.

Dozens and dozens of volumes, each one sated to bursting with documents, with its successor to the left and its predecessor to the right, representing the manifestation of twelve years of FBI investigation into the heist. I stepped back for a moment to take it all in: twenty-five linear feet of intelligence—about two feet per year, divided every inch or so by a cardboard jacket. It was completely overwhelming. I'd seen big cases corralled into three or four volumes, perhaps five or six, but this was madness. Where to start?

Well, Volume I. I began sliding files out of the stack, and with each pull the volume numbers decreased until I found the very first

Gardner Museum case file. I plucked Volume I off the shelf and signed it out on an index card, an atavistic nod to my halcyon days when I'd sign out *Your Police* in my elementary school library over my librarian's feckless protestations.

Back at my desk, I started my review at the bottom, since serials were stacked one on top of the other, a ream of paper impaled twice at its head. It was fascinating to relive the heist from the very beginning, albeit vicariously. Serial number one was the opening memo, with *O+A* scrawled in red pencil on a dog-eared lower-right corner. The memo was "From: Boston, To: FBIHQ," and it detailed in broad strokes the audacious tale of two UNSUBS who robbed a local museum by posing as police officers and inveigling the night guards. As I continued to peruse the subsequent serials, the emotions of those first days following the robbery were tangible: confusion, disinformation, and the simmering exasperation that there was very little to go on. Police sketches of the UNSUBS, so mundane and ordinary, illustrated both with and without their bushy—and possibly fake—mustaches. A flurry of leads to other field offices, requesting information on any known art thieves who may fit the general description. And the crime scene photos, always haunting, freezing for eternity a moment in time and capturing the latest affront to the social contract; just a slight pull in the threads that weave together the sweater vest of civilization.

I continued to leaf through the serials. Boston was receiving information daily from other field offices and Legats: snippets of intel, rumors from informants, and assorted nonsense. A litany of documents littered the case file: communiques to and from FBIHQ, known as Airtels, which memorialized ongoing efforts in Boston; letterhead memorandums to outside agencies, known as LHMs; and the ubiquitous and infamous Reports of Investigation, known as FD-302s and referred to simply as 302s. Each document was stamped with a precedence, and the Bureau has three: IMMEDIATE, PRIORITY, or ROUTINE. All of the initial Gardner communications were marked IMMEDIATE.

It's fascinating to review old 302s, regardless of the case, and read their recounting of some historic crime event, always delivered in the Bureau's inimitably dry and pedantic narrative. The very nature of the 302—*just the facts, ma'am*—ensures that even the most thrilling event will be recorded in a manner destined to make it seem dull. Flowery prose is kept to a minimum, and you won't find many exclamation points in a 302, regardless of how badly a sentence may have merited one.

And all of this information, both incoming and outgoing, was duly recorded by Dan Falzon, the Gardner's first case agent. The few "latent prints of unknown value" that were collected from the crime scene were run through the Automated Fingerprint Identification System, or AFIS, as well as through international crime databases. I considered this a necessary but futile step in the investigation—the UNSUBS were obviously crooks, and while more sophisticated crime-fighting techniques like DNA were still in their infancy back in 1990, the concept of catching bad guys by comparing their known fingerprints to questioned samples was familiar to anyone who'd ever watched an episode of *Dragnet* or *T. J. Hooker*. In my opinion, even inept criminals knew enough to wear gloves during a robbery so they wouldn't leave prints.

And more to the point, when the UNSUBS first entered the museum, Abath observed that at least one of them *was* wearing gloves, so it's reasonable to assume that his partner was also wearing a pair. I doubt they would've removed their gloves prior to handling picture frames and opening doors. And since I found it unlikely that the subjects would've pulled this one off bare-handed, I was surprised at the amount of effort that was expended to run these meaningless prints through databases, over and over again. It came as no surprise to read that the recovered prints—which most likely belonged to members of the museum's conservation staff—yielded no meaningful results.

As I reviewed the file, I read that within days of the robbery, the office stood up a video review station in the squad area, where teams of agents scoured every second of the surveillance images contained on the sixteen VHS tapes that were recovered from the museum's security office, the ones left behind by the subjects. Considering that these tapes encompassed at least fifty hours of video, divided into a multiplex system, it was a monumental task. The review took days to complete and ultimately generated no leads and left no lingering questions.

In those first weeks of the investigation, FBI agents and Boston detectives tracked down and interviewed all of the Gardner Museum employees, yet it was readily apparent that in addition to scant clues, there were even fewer meaningful leads. As with any major investigation, a glut of useless tips poured in from well-intentioned cops and civilians worldwide, and anyone capable of committing a robbery of this magnitude was duly noted and investigated thoroughly.

Eventually, I finished Volume I, after taking copious notes and littering the edge of the file with a riot of multicolored sticky notes.* Now it was time for Volume II. This pattern continued until my desk, along with the shelves above it, were cluttered with teetering stacks of case files bearing crenellated margins of Post-its. It was through this process that I learned about the case and began to form my own nescient opinions about what really happened that night.

In September 2005, Anthony Amore was brought on as the new director of security at the Gardner. Anthony was the third security director with whom I'd worked, and while his predecessors were intelligent and well qualified, their primary focus had been on the protection of what remained in the collection, as opposed to the recovery of what had been lost. They dutifully forwarded to me any tips they received about the heist, but they were not investigators. Anthony was an investigator. After serving as a special agent with the Federal Aviation Administration and earning his master's degree

* I had a personal system for categorizing noteworthy documents, and their level of importance was based on the color of the sticky note.

from Harvard, Anthony became the director of the Transportation Safety Administration at T. F. Green Airport in Rhode Island before heading to Boston to become the TSA's assistant federal security director at Logan.

In addition to upgrading and improving the security posture at the museum, Anthony was conducting his own investigation into the theft, all the while coordinating his activities with me. For tipsters who didn't feel comfortable contacting me directly—either due to a general intimidation inherent with speaking with the FBI or because of concerns regarding their own criminal exposure—the Gardner Museum presented them with a viable alternative to where they could report their information. And since the reward was being offered by the museum and not the FBI, it made direct contact with Anthony even more attractive. I was fine with that, as long as the intelligence was being disseminated, and for his part, Anthony diligently wrote up his reports and forwarded them to me for incorporation into the case file.

There were severe limitations with this arrangement—specifically, the intelligence flowed in only one direction. Anthony didn't work for the FBI, so I wasn't permitted to reciprocate with any details contained within the case file. It was a frustrating arrangement and one that hindered the pace of the investigation. In the summer of 2011, I spoke with Rick DesLauriers, at the time the Special Agent in Charge, or SAC, of the Boston FBI, and lobbied on Anthony's behalf. In a conventional criminal investigation, the need to preserve the integrity of a pending case is paramount, since any deviation from protocol may jeopardize the integrity of the case if it goes to trial. With the Gardner investigation, I argued, the statute of limitations regarding the theft itself had long since expired, and for years the FBI had been working the case primarily as a recovery effort. I reasoned that the sharing of intelligence between the Bureau and the museum was crucial to achieving this goal.

Rick had the foresight to weigh the benefits of my request, and ultimately authorized the sharing of case details with Anthony, unencumbered by the traditional restraints and regulations imposed by the Bureau. This unconventional arrangement worked well—exceedingly well—and as a result, the FBI and the Gardner Museum were in a position to freely share intelligence about tips and theories without having to play some silly game of charades. (*First word…sounds like… Rembrandt…*) Once Anthony had access to relevant details about the case, the revived investigation quickly gained momentum.

* * * *

For Christmas in 2010, my mom got me *An Object of Beauty,* a novel by actor and comedian Steve Martin. It was the perfect gift for someone who was fascinated both with art and the author. It wasn't until I got well into the book that I realized that one of its ancillary plots involved the Gardner heist, and one of the characters was a fedora-wearing FBI agent leading the investigation. *Hey, that's me!*—minus the silly hat. I reached out to Gretchen Koss, a good friend of mine from college who worked in the publishing industry. Gretchen knew Steve Martin's publicist, and after making a few phone calls, she let me know that I'd soon be getting an autographed copy of his book. A few weeks later, I feverishly tore open a crime fiction novel–shaped FedEx package that had arrived in my mailbox, postmarked from New York. I eagerly flipped to the title page, imagining what pithy and irreverent quote Steve Martin had written for the real-life FBI agent who worked the Gardner Museum case, the one he had so cleverly depicted in his novel.

And there it was:

To Geoff,

All Best,

Steve Martin.

Well, it was succinct, I'll give him that. Still a big fan, regardless.

* * * *

As I continued to dive deeper into the Gardner investigation, I experienced the practical difficulties of working on a cold case while still juggling a full caseload of violent crimes. In the Bureau, the Gardner heist was polarizing, and over the years I worked for supervisors who either loved the case or hated it; rarely was there middle ground. The former were indispensable, advocating for the case and running interference from the latter, who were frustrating impediments. They believed that Bureau resources should not be wasted on recovery efforts for what amounted to a mere billion dollars in stolen property (if you're reading this book, I'm hoping you're firmly entrenched in the former's camp).

A number of years ago, I was introduced to Boston's newest SAC, and when he learned that I was the case agent on the Gardner Museum investigation, his warm salutation was delivered in the form of a question: "Let me ask you something: With all the crime going on in the world today, why are we wasting our time looking for some old pictures?"

My respectful response was words to the effect that while it was certainly his prerogative to close the case, he should probably first speak with Headquarters. And then there was no more talk of closing the case.

* * * *

So why is the FBI wasting its time looking for some old pictures? It's a fair question. As a career violent-crime investigator, I fully understood the need to balance what amounts to essentially stolen property. It's an awful lot of stolen property, to be sure, but it's still just stolen property. I'm cognizant of the fact that property theft takes a secondary role to violent crime, especially terrorism matters. On the afternoon of 9/11, I was dispatched to the Hilton at Logan Airport to interview the next of kin of passengers who were aboard Flight 11 and Flight 175. These interviews were conducted immediately after family members received confirmation that their loved ones had, in fact, been on one of those doomed flights. Two of the salient questions I asked that day were the name of their loved one's dentist and a description of the clothing they had been wearing. I've thought back to these questions many times over the years, almost quaint in their naivety; in those first hours, there was this woefully ignorant assumption that perhaps we would be able to identify victims at Ground Zero from dental records and articles of clothing.

A dozen years later, I responded to the finish line of the Boston Marathon and witnessed firsthand the carnage wrought by two well-placed pressure cooker bombs. Three days later, I was at the crime scene in Cambridge minutes after MIT Police Officer Sean Collier had been executed, and a couple of hours after that I was in Watertown, ducking gunfire and searching through suburban backyards for Dzhokhar Tsarnaev.

In the first few years that I was working the Gardner, our squad was still investigating that Charlestown armored car robbery crew. One of their first jobs occurred in July 1996, when they shot and killed an armored car guard in Somerville, Massachusetts, over a box of coins,* and nine years later, I responded to a Citizens Bank in Quincy, just moments after they shot a guard pointblank with an AK-47 as he was unloading cash onto his hand truck. The bullet severed his femoral artery, and when I arrived on scene, the parking lot smelled like a sweaty handful of pennies. As I surveyed the carnage, my initial thought was that no one could have survived that much blood loss, but he did, thanks to the elementary school nurse who responded from the Catholic school across the street and applied a tourniquet to his leg.

Throughout my career, I became adept at ducking crime scene tape while sidestepping congealing puddles of thick arterial blood, so yeah,

* Coincidentally, this was the same day I executed the search warrant in Marty Leppo's basement, and I vividly recall the tense radio traffic over my Bucar radio as I was transporting the seized evidence back to the office.

I get it. I understand that the quest for stolen property—regardless of its historical or fair-market value—must be tempered with our responsibility to keep America safe.

But it's not just stolen property; it's much more than that. It's an integral part of our cultural heritage. It represents who we are as a people and it defines us as a civilization. History has proven repeatedly that the destruction of cultural heritage is an essential element of genocide, and one that has been intrinsically linked to atrocity crimes. Through the years, the gratuitous destruction of cultural heritage has been used by oppressive regimes to weaken the resolve and identity of particular groups and eradicate their existence. Without a link to the past, it's reasoned that these cultures lose their future. In response to the systematic destruction of cultural heritage sites and cultural property by the Nazis, in 1949, Article 53 of the Geneva Conventions was passed to prohibit the "intentional or gratuitous damage to undefended cultural heritage by invading or occupying forces," and the Additional Protocols of 1977 specifically prohibit attacks against cultural property.

This is important stuff. Art and cultural property theft was an aspect of crime unknown to me before I was tasked with the Gardner Museum investigation back in 2002. In fact, very few in the Bureau gave much thought to preserving cultural property. That state of blissful ignorance changed on April 9, 2003, when a US-led coalition of armed forces entered Baghdad and toppled Saddam Hussein's government. The previous day, with the imminent threat of invasion looming, employees of the National Museum of Iraq had fled their beloved institution, taking with them more than eight thousand cherished artifacts; with precious little time to act, they could grab only the most portable objects at hand. On April 10, looters broke into the National Museum and over a scant thirty-six-hours stole more than fifteen thousand artifacts and destroyed countless others. This wholesale destruction of the museum is generally regarded as one of the worst acts of cultural vandalism in modern history.

With US forces firmly ensconced in Baghdad, and grim reports of the museum's looting unfolding in the media, the FBI realized belatedly that it was sorely lacking in the art crime department. While rank-and-file street agents have been working art crimes for decades under the auspices of major theft investigations, the FBI had never formed a unit specifically designed to address the esoteric crime of art and cultural property theft.

It was for this reason that in the fall of 2004, twelve years after the world's largest art heist, the Bureau finally created the Art Crime Team. When I saw the canvass for applicants, I'd been working the Gardner case for nearly two years and had already formed relationships with some of the notable figures who comprised the Bureau's ad hoc art unit, including Bob Wittman, a Philly agent who was the impetus behind assembling the team. I reached out to Bob, who encouraged me to apply.

In January 2005, the Art Crime Team's inaugural training event was held in Philadelphia. There was just a dozen of us, a random sampling of agents from around the country, working a random sampling of violations, and the occasion was memorialized in our first team photo, taken that week at the Barnes Museum. It's your typical group photo, except some of the agents' faces are blurred out because they worked undercover, effectively making it your typical FBI group photo. As with many aspects of the Bureau, there often exists a certain kind of alchemy when disparate groups of agents with vastly different backgrounds are thrown together in a bell jar to see what happens. Philly was the bell jar. In those early days of the team, we toured local museums, met with conservation experts and curators, and examined historical case studies. And thus began my tutelage into the rarified world of fine art.

Along the way our annual training became more sophisticated, with an emphasis on legal instruction into the nuanced laws pertaining to cultural property, especially the preservation and repatriation of Native American artifacts. We received regular training from the Smithsonian

Institution on the proper handing, collection, and storage of fine art and cultural artifacts. Even more important than learning what to do, however, was learning what not to do. As an example, in the FBI, it's standard practice for agents to ascribe their initials and date on any item of collected evidence. The reasoning is sound; if questioned on the witness stand about a particular item of evidence, those Sharpie-induced scribbles will validate the fragile chain of custody that every defense attorney attempts to tear asunder. But since scrawling graffiti on ancient artifacts of cultural patrimony is generally frowned upon in the museum community, the Art Crime Team had to come up with other methods that satisfied the legal requirements for establishing a chain of custody without defacing the evidence.

This would be a good time to discuss provenance, that lofty term used in the art world to describe the record of ownership of a work of art or an antique, from its creation by the artist's hand to the present day. Think of it as a chain of custody for the art world. For many collectors, a piece's provenance is as important—if not more so—than the piece itself. The documentary evidence of where the piece was exhibited and sold, which galleries and auction houses it visited, and who owned it—all of these myriad facts are the intangible window dressing of the tangible object. In fact, provenance investigation actually reveals more fakes and forgeries than scientific analysis, and the internet has connected the art world in a manner that makes it much easier for any astute collector or gallery owner to verify the authenticity of a piece of artwork. Bogus exhibitions, galleries that don't exist, and imaginary art collectors simply cannot survive the scrutiny that a simple Google search can bring to bear.

Much of a piece's historical information is displayed on its verso like breadcrumbs, and the trail can be traced by gallery labels, museum accession stickers, and in the case of Nazi-looted art, the notorious stamp of the Einsatzstab Reichsleiter Rosenberg, the task force Hermann Göring created for the looting of Jewish cultural property throughout Europe. These marks, from the whimsical to the repulsive, contribute to a piece's provenance. They tell a story; maybe a good story, maybe a really bad one, but a story nonetheless.

I've always believed that an FBI evidence stamp, affixed subtly to a painting's verso and partnered with an agent's initials inscribed in Sharpie, would only lend substance to the piece's provenance and increase its value.

Having said that, we do not draw on artwork.

It was during my tenure on the Art Crime Team that I learned about the nefarious world of art theft, an education bolstered by my investigation into the Gardner Museum heist. Over the two decades that I served on the team, I recovered more than $100 million in stolen art and cultural property, items as diverse as rare books, fine art, Native American artifacts, and looted cultural treasures.

And cultural treasures can have a very broad meaning.

On February 5, 2017, New England Patriots quarterback Tom Brady's game jersey was stolen out of his locker minutes after the final whistle of Super Bowl LI in Houston. The following morning, images went viral of a forlorn Brady sitting at his locker, a jersey-less duffel bag in his lap, evoking sympathy from everywhere but Atlanta.* Later that week, I received a call from NFL Security, requesting the FBI's assistance to help them locate the stolen jersey. In order for the case to be worked by the Bureau, however, we first had to show that Brady's jersey satisfied the elements of the National Stolen Property Act, in that it:

1. *crossed state lines or international boundaries; and*
2. *possessed a value of at least $5,000*

The latter element would not be a problem, since in the days following the game, a number of notable sports memorabilia collectors estimated that Brady's jersey would fetch at least a million dollars on

* Final score: Patriots 34, Falcons 28.

the open market, well exceeding the $5,000 requirement. Proof that the jersey had crossed state lines would come a bit later.

Over the next five weeks, we were able to track Brady's stolen jersey to the home of a fanatical sports memorabilia collector who lived in Mexico City. On March 17, I flew down to Mexico City and recovered not only Brady's Super Bowl LI jersey, but two other items of stolen sports memorabilia: Brady's jersey from Super Bowl XLIX and Von Miller's Broncos helmet from Super Bowl 50.*

I shipped Von Miller's helmet out to our Denver office and two weeks later, signed over Brady's jerseys to Patriots owner Bob Kraft. After the hand off, my SAC (the same one who once questioned why we were wasting time looking for stolen paintings) posed with Kraft for the press release, a spread of Vince Lombardi trophies laid out before them. Brady gave one jersey to his ailing mother and the other was put on display at Gillette Stadium. Although I never got a thank you from Brady (please don't get my wife started), Miller was exceptionally gracious when he collected his helmet from the FBI's Denver office, posing for photos and sending out an appreciative tweet.

* * * *

Throughout my career, I became adept at assessing museum (and locker room) security, conducting site assessments at cultural institutions in order to prevent theft, as well as postmortems after a theft occurred. I had the opportunity to travel the world, instructing the FBI's international partners in the best practices to prevent art theft. We provided training in countries that were known conduits for looted cultural property, property that had been excavated from hallowed ground in Syria and Iraq by an indentured army of prospectors overseen by the Islamic State of Iraq and the Levant, or ISIL. After a quick cleaning and perhaps some minor restoration, ISIL packaged the artifacts and

* Apparently, for this semi-centennial game, the NFL went with cardinal numbers, since *Super Bowl L* just felt wrong.

shipped them west. Along their frenetic journey, one that began under the temples in Palmyra and in the galleries of Mosul, these artifacts shed their dubious past and reinvented themselves, aided by bogus documentation and a plausible backstory. They finally ended up, pristine and unencumbered, in the rarified air of the world's finest auction houses and art galleries, their sanguinary history expunged.

In 2015, the Art Crime Team placed these galleries, auction houses, and dealers on notice, advising them of the nexus between antiquities of questionable provenance and terrorism financing:

> **Purchasing an object looted and/or sold by the Islamic State may provide financial support to a terrorist organization and could be prosecuted.**

The notice was more of a symbolic gesture intended to educate the industry to the very real perils of buying or selling cultural artifacts with a questionable provenance, and no galleries or auction houses were ever charged with providing material support of terrorism.

As I learned more about museum protection, I formed my own opinions about the security at the Gardner back in 1990. Contrary to what's often reported in the media, the security system at the Gardner was sufficient, and certainly on par with comparable museums at the time. With an array of alarms and motion sensors, the Gardner Museum was well suited to protect its collection. But as is the case with every building that strives to guard itself against things that go bump in the night, its Achilles' heel was the exterior door, the weak point that allows in those things which are best kept out. And because the museum lacked redundancy in their security protocols, that access was controlled solely by one guard in command of the watch desk. He also had the ability to summon help instantly, because tucked right next to that desk was a panic button, a small white box with a recessed black plunger that, if pressed, would call the cops.

But what happens if no one presses the button?

CHAPTER 8

The FBI Doesn't Deal Pot

It is always wise to suspect everybody until you can prove logically, and to your own satisfaction, that they are innocent.

—AGATHA CHRISTIE, *The Mysterious Affair at Styles*

The drive west from Boston is long and scenic. My partner that day is Jesse C.,* a freshly minted FBI agent newly arrived from active duty in the Marines Corps. We chat comfortably on the drive, getting to know each other as we wind our way through the bucolic countryside of southern Vermont. Steely Dan comes on the radio, with Donald Fagan singing of the tribulations and ultimate redemption of a gambler and a killer.

"I love Steely Dan," I mention casually to Jesse.

"Oh yeah? So does my dad."

Ouch. I had just turned forty but suddenly feel very old. At this point in my career I've been an agent for twelve years, which is why I'm driving a late-model Ford Crown Victoria Police Interceptor and

* Last name redacted.

not a beige or avocado-tinted economy sedan that's typically issued to the new guys. Over the years, the major auto makers have devised the most unflattering colors for cars, many of which invariably end up in government motor pools. If you find yourself being tailed one day by a mint-green Ford Focus, you may want to reevaluate your lifestyle choices.

On this very cold and cloudless day in December 2007, as I navigate the gentle curves of Interstate 89 as it cuts through Vermont, I've had the Gardner case for exactly five years and six days. Exactly five years and six days of dead ends and false leads.

The round trip to Vermont from Boston takes nearly seven hours by car, although significantly less in an unmarked Crown Vic. Even so, it still leaves a lot of time for Jesse and me to chat. Jesse is impassive, a pair of sunglasses perpetually perched atop his head and a convivial presence that belies his experience as a Marine combat veteran. Jesse will go on to become one of the FBI's most effective undercover agents, known as UCEs (short for undercover employees), in part because he simply doesn't look like a cop. If you met Jesse in a social setting—trust me, you don't want to meet Jesse professionally—and tried to guess what he does for a living, you'd probably come up with "astronaut" or "stuntman" long before you guessed he was an FBI agent. Which is what makes him so devastatingly effective; with his unassuming bearing and disarming charm, he's just that good. I learn all about Jesse on the drive, especially when the hunt for radio stations becomes more challenging as the elevation increases, the radio's manic display cycling through the FM bandwidth, settling briefly for a moment here and there, before finally giving up.

Getting a crash course in the intimate details of coworkers is one of the unique aspects of this job, since it's commonplace to be thrown together for hours on end with a cop or agent whom you've never met before. You could be paired up on a twelve-hour surveillance with a total stranger, and with nothing else to do but talk, you talk. About life, marriage, kids, career, all the while sipping coffee out of Styrofoam cups and stifling the urge to pee. For some reason these chance encounters always engendered brutal honesty, and topics like bad bosses, money problems, and health issues were fair game. Add in the momentary adrenaline burst when you fling open the car doors in perfect synchronicity to finally effect the arrest, and it's almost poignant when you finally say your rueful goodbyes to this erstwhile stranger with whom you've shared so many intimate details, always with the ubiquitous cop parting phrase: "Be safe!" And like some platonic, vocational version of an ex-lover, over the years the two of you will bump into each other from time to time; perhaps it will be at an arrest briefing for an interagency gang sweep, known as a hobo rodeo, with hundreds of cops and agents milling about a National Guard armory or a high school gymnasium. Or at a crime scene, your eyes meeting across yellow tape and a recently exsanguinated corpse.

Why, it is almost romantic. "*You're looking well.*" "*And you.*"

And now back to the Green Mountain State. Still feeling old and maybe a little intimidated by this brash young agent with the Ray-Bans nestled into his perfect hair, our discussion turns to the upcoming interview, which is the reason for this long drive. Our destination is a coffee shop in Burlington, a college town that sits hard against Lake Champlain, especially in mid-December. We are meeting with Rick Abath, the guard who initiated the world's largest art heist with the simple opening of a door.

Rick was an enigma. As I leafed through the pages of those initial Gardner case files, it seemed so apparent to me that he was complicit in the heist. If this were an Agatha Christie novel, Rick would've been the red herring, the suspect inserted into the story who seemed so obviously guilty that the reader will be stunned to learn that the killer was actually Lord Winston's trusted apiarist. This literary device, of course, differs radically from any episode of *Scooby-Doo* which, owing to time constraints, has only three potential suspects, all of whom sound exactly like Casey Kasem. There is no finely honed sense of tension and misdirection with *Scooby-Doo*; it will always be the most obvious suspect.

Rick was a *Scooby-Doo* suspect and, without the benefit of any meddling kids, appeared to have gotten away with it.

I parked the Bucar and we headed toward the café and its promise of respite from the stinging cold. We found Rick standing out front, stomping his feet to stay warm, awaiting our arrival.

As Rick described it in his unpublished memoir:

"I'd been waiting about ten minutes when I spotted a shiny, black, mid-size sedan with Massachusetts license plates coming down Main Street and parking about a half a block away from me. The two guys certainly looked the part as they stepped out of the car. They had short hair, were clean-shaven, wearing sharp-pressed dark suits and darker sunglasses. I wondered if they were required to dress like stereotypical G-men."[1]

We all shook hands and headed inside to find a table. I had no idea what to expect when I finally met Rick, but I was surprised to find him affable and humble. Five years later, our meeting in Burlington was made public when Rick was interviewed by *The Boston Globe*, where he spoke about our interview, claiming that the FBI "all but accused him of stealing the Manet."[2] I told Rick that we had not been able to eliminate him as a suspect and pointedly asked him if he had taken *Chez Tortoni* off the wall and stashed it somewhere, an accusation he strenuously denied. Rick asserted that he had "absolutely nothing to do with the robbers or the robbery" but conceded that his actions that night certainly appeared suspicious, especially given the fact that just three days prior to the heist he'd given the museum his two-week notice.

While our interview was cordial, in the end it was wholly unproductive. His remonstrations seemed genuine, yet they were emphatically contradicted by his own actions that night and, frankly, by common sense.

All of this certainly added to the *Scooby-Doo* pall of suspicion that had dogged him throughout his life. Add to the mix his admission that while working at the Gardner, Rick used alcohol, marijuana, LSD, and cocaine—and sometimes showed up for his overnight shift drunk or stoned—and the evidence against him was quite compelling.

But herein lies the problem: Rick's apparent complicity was all but ignored by my predecessors. I couldn't ignore it, however; it was just so glaring. And when the statute of limitations for the actual robbery expired in March 1995, any leverage that may have been used against Rick vanished abruptly. I was left with few options other than to have a cup of coffee with Rick and entreat him for the truth.

* * * *

So what really happened?

I believe that Rick knew full well that the robbery was going to occur that night. Once his partner was off doing his rounds upstairs, Rick was in total control. And from his perch manning the watch desk, he had full command of the phones, the cameras, and most importantly, that vital door buzzer. What happened next is neither conjecture nor opinion; it's incontrovertible fact underpinned by the science of the motion-sensor data.

Rick left the watch desk and inexplicably made a return to the Blue Room, a room he'd just visited on his rounds a short while earlier. Once there, he snagged *Chez Tortoni* off the wall. We know this because the motion sensors showed that the subjects never went anywhere near the Blue Room. After the robbery, security experts tested the system and confirmed that the alarms and motion sensors were functioning properly on the night of the heist, thus eliminating any excuse that the subjects had, in fact, entered the Blue Room gallery but were not detected due to defective equipment.

The Manet's empty frame was recovered on a swivel chair in the Security Office. I think that as the consummate partygoer, Rick would've favored the Manet, since it basically depicts a guy sitting in a bar, doodling on a sketchpad and drinking a beer. A painting with this subject matter would resonate with the artistic and tosspot bent of the music school dropout who, by his own admission, often showed up to work drunk. I believe that Rick was freelancing with *Chez Tortoni*; since the museum was getting robbed anyway, he reasoned that perhaps the subjects would be kind enough to grab it for him. After all, Rick had already given his notice—what's the worst they can do, fire him? He left the Manet in the Security Office and continued on with his role in the plan.

If Rick was involved, then he needed to let the subjects know that he was in command of the watch desk. It was vital for him to be the voice on the other end of the intercom when the subjects rang the bell, and not his partner, a last-minute replacement who was filling in for another guard who'd called in sick. For this reason, Rick needed to alert the subjects that the coast was clear for the robbery to commence. He reached for his burner phone to call the subjects but realized it wasn't there. Why? Because this was 1990 and burner phones had yet to be invented. He needed another plan.

If Rick had to signal the subjects, the most expeditious and logical manner would be from the rear courtyard. And the door leading to that courtyard was located right by the Security Office. We know that four minutes after Rick left the Blue Room, he opened that exterior door, and the timing is notable: The walk from the gallery to that door takes about forty-five seconds (I've timed it), yet the walk took Rick four minutes. Four minutes would account for a quick detour by the Security Office to drop off the Manet.

The teenaged witnesses outside the museum reported that the subjects' Dodge was parked alongside the curb on Palace Road, roughly adjacent to the tall metal gate that opened into the rear courtyard. I don't believe that parking spot was accidental. Once outside, Rick was separated from the subjects by only this gate. It's more than a bit convenient that the subjects were parked just on the other side, where even a hoarsely whispered code word would be heard, one uttered just loudly enough to let them know it was safe to ring the bell. And I believe that Rick may have done that, but his message went unrequited.

The reason was obvious to the subjects but not to Rick, whose view of Palace Road was obscured by the gate: The teenagers. For about the same time that Rick was in the rear courtyard, those meddling kids were piggybacking each other down the middle of the street, blithely unaware that their shenanigans were interrupting the world's largest art heist. Whatever Rick's signal may have been—a yodel, a fricative hiss, or even a *"pssst, hey guys!"*—it was futile, since at the same time it was issued, the subjects were staring down those kids and waiting with bated breath for their departure. As a result, they couldn't provide Rick with the confirmation that the robbery was ready to move forward.

Rick made his way back into the museum. Did they get the signal? Were they coming? Without confirmation, he'd likely be confused. So, at 1:03 a.m. he violated protocol and opened the service door leading out to Palace Road. I believe he opened that door because he was still attempting to signal the subjects that he had the helm. Rick would later claim that opening that exterior door was one of the assigned duties for the night shift guards, but that simply wasn't true. All night guards were instructed that after the last museum employee exited the museum, usually about six or seven p.m., the dead bolt should be slid home, and remain in that position until the next morning. It was a policy that was apparently known to every museum guard but Rick—the exterior door to the museum was never to be opened by anyone on the midnight shift.

By 1:05 a.m., those teenagers were gone, racing through the darkened streets of Boston in a mad rush to catch that last train home. Another nineteen minutes passed before the subjects finally rang the buzzer and announced themselves.

What happened next sounds like something right out of a *Choose Your Own Adventure* book:

If Rick should open the door and let the police officers in, turn to page 85.

If Rick should call the Boston Police, there is no book.

I guess we're turning to page 85.

Jon-Paul Kroger, who was Rick Abath's guard supervisor at the time of the heist, was convinced Abath was involved, a strongly held belief that he based on the stolen Manet. "Forget about the duck walk around the motion sensors," Kroger said. "Abath took *Chez Tortoni* out of the Blue Room before the robbers even showed up." The duck walk? Kroger is referring to an anecdotal story about how the night guards would attempt to defeat the motion sensors outside the Blue Room, a contest designed solely to combat boredom. As the story goes, if a guard hunkered low enough and crept around the perimeter of the west hallway, a technique they referred to as a "Chuck Berry-esque" duck walk, he or she could occasionally avoid detection by the sensors, about three times in ten. Of course, there's no practicable reason to believe that our subjects would attempt to duck walk their way into the Blue Room and then exit in the same ridiculous manner, now laden with a large piece of framed artwork.

I'm equally suspicious of what happened after Rick and his partner were herded downstairs to the basement. Throughout my career, I've investigated a number of robberies in which hostages were tied up, and they share a common methodology: They are kept together. This way it's easier to keep an eye on them. The fact that Rick and his partner were tied up as far from each other as the physical constraints of the museum's basement would allow makes no sense. Unless, of course, you may need to speak with one of them during the robbery. Perhaps—and this is purely supposition—it was during one of these subterranean visits when Rick told the subjects that there was a Manet sitting on the chair inside the Security Office, a location they would absolutely visit that night when they popped the surveillance tape out of the VCR.

Taking that VHS tape is intuitive since it contained their images, however poor the quality may have been. But why take the motion-sensor printouts? That makes no sense. The discovery of the handcuffed and bound guards in the basement should be sufficient to prod the museum staff to undertake a quick perusal of the galleries, and even a perfunctory sweep will reveal the empty frames and shattered glass. By midmorning, the subjects' route throughout the museum will be known to all. They couldn't have cared less if the FBI had written confirmation of which galleries they visited that night. Or didn't visit that night.

But someone else would care very much.

Rick knew that his return visit to the Blue Room at 12:53 a.m., as well as his opening of the Palace Road service door eight minutes later, would have been recorded on that humming spool of computer paper as it rolled off the printer. It would offer incontrovertible proof that he was the only human being to visit the gallery that night; it would prove that Rick took *Chez Tortoni* off the wall and thus implicate him in the crime. This would explain why the printouts were taken beginning at 12:50 a.m., which coincidentally was three minutes before Rick's second visit to the Blue Room and eleven minutes before he opened the service door. This is noteworthy, given the fact that the subjects didn't actually enter the museum proper until 1:47 a.m., nearly an hour later. I believe that at some point during the robbery, from his lonely spot in that dark basement, married to an electrical box, Rick entreated the subjects to take those motion-sensor printouts with them, since they showed his complicity in the crime. And the subjects acquiesced; after all, it was in their best interests to keep Rick out of trouble.

Except Rick didn't know about computer memory. It turns out that the FBI didn't need the paper printouts to see who went where on the night of March 18, since we had the computer's hard drive. This was, of course, how investigators first learned of Rick's superfluous trip to the Blue Room gallery and the opening of the service door. In the age of smartphones and personal computers, it's hard to believe that anyone wouldn't know that the motion-sensor data would also be stored electronically, but this was 1990, a time when most college students were still pecking away on typewriters. Jon-Paul Kroger doubted that any of the guards—including Abath—were aware that the data was maintained on a hard drive. In fact, after the heist, Kroger himself was surprised to learn that the computer had captured the activity in the museum that night, since he assumed that all of that information had been lost when the printouts were taken by the robbers.[3]

This crucial piece of evidence was virtually ignored by the FBI at the time, perhaps due to the complexity of the case. The Bureau was setting leads worldwide and dealing with a staggering influx of useless tips and theories that were coming in daily. As a result, shortly after the robbery occurred, Rick was cast aside and all but forgotten by the FBI. I leafed through the case file, anticipating the serial that would exonerate Rick, the one that would provide him with the Agatha Christie alibi or the logical explanation for his woefully incriminating actions that night. Yet that serial would never come. And this is why Jesse and I interviewed Rick in that Burlington coffee shop, and why I continued to hound him about the robbery. Our interactions were always respectful, but never fruitful.

Rick's actions underscored a critical failure of the Gardner Museum's security posture on the night of the robbery. While the museum's security system was on par with similar institutions, it was their protocols and procedures that were lacking. Rather than using a layered security approach, with built-in redundancies, the Gardner's system functioned more like a chain, with each individual link representing an essential part of the whole. If one frizzy-haired link in that chain were to break, then the entire system collapses. And that's exactly what happened on March 18, 1990.

* * * *

To me, the most damning piece of evidence pointing to Rick's involvement is somewhat more existential, and it gets back to the moment when he admitted the subjects into the museum in the first place. It's not the fact that he did it, which could be chalked up to atrocious guardianship, a character trait not entirely out of the realm of possibility for an oft-stoned music school dropout who'd just given his notice. While armchair detectives point to Rick's admittance of the subjects as a veritable admission of guilt, I believe that aspect actually has less to do with his complicity. It's more nuanced than that, and at the same time, glaringly obvious.

The most damning piece of evidence was the Gardner Museum's security policy.

Lyle Grindle was the security director at the time of the heist, and he had crafted a specific policy to be followed in the event that the police arrived, unannounced, at the museum. According to Grindle, all of the security guards who worked the night shift—including Rick—had been warned of this eventuality and had been instructed, in writing, not to admit police officers unless they had been directly summoned by the museum. This was a prohibition echoed by Larry O'Brien, Grindle's deputy, who confirmed that the policy was written into the museum's security manual, which was maintained at the watch desk. And according to Jon-Paul Kroger, Abath's direct supervisor, the museum had implemented security procedures in order to prevent this exact type of crime from ever occurring. Kroger told me that the guards had been trained for this scenario, and he was unequivocal about the museum's policy regarding the unannounced arrival of the police: All of the guards on the overnight shift were instructed to obtain the name and badge number of the officers and then call the Boston Police in order to verify their identities.

In fact, Kroger said, the phone number for Area B-2, the police district that serviced the Fenway area, was printed on a laminated sheet that was posted at the watch desk.

Kroger had trained Rick and was adamant that he had personally instructed him to never open the exterior door during the midnight shift. Kroger had also briefed Rick on the museum's policy regarding the arrival of police officers on the overnight. "Rick was very anti-police," Kroger told me, "and I said to him that this was the one time when he could exert authority over the authorities." Kroger recalled that Rick liked the concept of being able to tell the police that they'd have to wait outside while he confirmed their identities.

Which brings us to that damning piece of evidence.

Our subjects had done their homework. They were aware of the security protocols at the museum. They knew that once they had restrained Rick and his partner, they would have unfettered and uninterrupted access to the museum. And they took full advantage of that fact, spending nearly an hour and a half strolling through the galleries, exhibiting a comfort level that is unprecedented in the worldwide history of museum heists. They knew about the VCR in the security office, they knew that no one would be calling to check up on the guards, and they were aware that there was no dead man switch that had to be pressed in an allotted period of time. They knew that the proximity sensors only alerted internally, and there were no alarms affixed to the paintings that would alert the police if their frames were removed from the walls. The subjects were patient and sanguine, adjectives rarely used to describe museum thieves.

It stands to reason that when they were planning a heist that was premised on police officers showing up unannounced at the Gardner Museum late one night, demanding entry, then the subjects must have researched the policy—specifically, what *will* the overnight guards do if the police show up unannounced at the Gardner Museum late one night, demanding entry? And from this research, the subjects would have learned there was a very specific protocol that had been drilled into the guards during their training and memorialized in the security manual.

So, if the robbery goes exactly as planned, the night guard will call the Boston Police and the subjects will be promptly arrested.

Apparently, their entire plan hinged on the fervent hope that the guard at the watch desk would violate protocol, because if he didn't, then everyone would go to jail.

Yet our subjects did it anyway. They had to have known that the guard on the other end of that intercom would violate protocol; otherwise, they would have stayed home.

* * * *

In or around 2012, during one of our many interviews with Rick, he casually admitted to us that a few weeks after the heist, he conveniently "found" a pound of marijuana in an alley near his home. It was a significant detail which he had neglected to mention to the FBI over the previous two decades. More recently, his ex-wife, Emily North, provided me with some much-needed clarification regarding that found marijuana, and it cast even more suspicion on Rick (if that's even possible). According to Emily, she met Rick in the fall of 1990, when she was a student at Marlboro College in Vermont and Rick's band was playing a gig in nearby Brattleboro. It was around this time that Rick advised Emily that, shortly after the robbery, a pound of marijuana "magically appeared" on the front porch of his Farrington Avenue apartment in Boston's Allston neighborhood. The package, addressed to Rick, was wrapped in brown paper and sealed with packing tape, and Emily specifically recalled him mentioning to her that the package had been dropped off, and not mailed. At the time, Rick posited to her that the pot must have been a gift from the police, as thanks for his cooperation in the investigation.[4]

When I first learned of this patently improbable scenario, it certainly made me wonder if this impromptu gift was related to that parting promise, delivered by the subjects on the night of the robbery:

"If everything goes all right, then you'll get a nice reward in about a year's time."

Rick died in February 2024, depriving us of any revelations about the heist and forgoing any possibility of absolution. And while I always believed there was compelling evidence demonstrating that Rick had some degree of complicity in the crime, the statute of limitations on any criminal culpability on his part had expired seven years before my tenure on the case. And with it, that all-important leverage that could have been used to compel Rick's cooperation.

This is yet another reason why most investigators are loath to inherit a cold case: Too many dead ends.

* * * *

In 2010, Robert Fisher was assigned to the Gardner case, joining his fellow AUSA, Brian Kelly. Rob was a seasoned prosecutor who worked as a Massachusetts assistant attorney general before coming to the US Attorney's Office. Like Brian, Rob grew up in the Boston area, and he brought to the case an enthusiasm that tempered Brian's delicious cynicism. They were both outstanding attorneys, and their offices displayed the fruits of their prosecutorial victories: leaning stacks of poster board trial exhibits, framed certificates of appreciation from a number of law enforcement agencies, and, in Brian's case, a white quill poking out of a coffee mug. When I asked him about its significance, he said modestly that attorneys who argue a case before the US Supreme Court receive a goose feather as a memento of the occasion. Like I said, they were both outstanding attorneys.

When Rob first came on board, twenty years after the heist, he quickly realized that it would've been impossible to get up to speed on every aspect of the case, so he chose to focus on Rick Abath because, as he pointed out, "without him, the robbery doesn't happen."[5]

Over the next six years, Rob and Rick developed a rapport, despite Rick's stubborn reluctance to admit to any involvement in the heist. They exchanged phone calls and emails, and Rob once made the drive up to Vermont so they could meet in person. Rick even sent Rob a copy of his manuscript, *Pandora's Laughter*, and asked him to fact-check details of the robbery so that they were accurately depicted in his book. Of course, fact-checking *Pandora's Laughter* proved difficult for Rob, given the glaringly inaccurate depiction of its long-haired, cowboy hat-wearing protagonist.

"Rick admitted to us that things didn't look good," recalled Rob. "He once said to me, 'Mr. Fisher, when you take me through the minutia from the beginning to the end, then even I have to agree, it doesn't look good.'" But then Rob, a veteran prosecutor, pointed to the paradox of working a case that is too cold to prosecute.

"Okay, so what are we going to do with that?" he posed rhetorically. "Rick admitted that he was the last one in the Blue Room. He was the one who let the subjects inside and knew where the security footage was kept," Rob said. "He admitted to all of that, but at the end of the day he still claimed that he had nothing to do with the robbery. All he could say was, 'I don't have a great explanation.'" Rick was using the tried-and-true legal defense of *that's my story and I'm sticking to it.*

"If you look at the minute-by-minute breakdown of the robbery, the subjects were obviously very comfortable in the museum; really certain that no one had hit that panic button," Rob points out. "They were willing to go down into the basement to tie up the guards. It just reeks of folks that were extremely comfortable, and I think if he were involved, then it would explain their level of comfort in the robbery."

Rob is convinced that the subjects' awareness of the museum's security procedures points to the involvement of an inside person. "A lot of time and effort went into this robbery, and if you knew the protocols, you weren't getting into the museum," he notes. "So yeah, a lot was riding on them just knocking on the door to the museum in the early-morning hours of the eighteenth.

"Rick once said to me, 'I'm just really unlucky the way this looks,'" Rob recalled. "And I told him, 'You're either unlucky or you're involved.'" Rob is somewhat philosophical when he discusses Rick Abath: "You can have bad luck a couple of times a night, but he had it consistently, minute after minute."

* * * *

In May 2017, Anthony and I hosted Rick at the Gardner. It was his first visit to the museum since the morning of the heist. Rick was accompanied by his attorney, George Gormley, and Dick Egan, a retired FBI agent who worked for Gormley as a private investigator. Many years earlier, Dick and I had worked together on the white-collar crime squad; in fact, he even guided me through my first case, when I was investigating Marty Leppo's wayward son. Dick was highly respected, both as an agent and as a supervisor.

As Rick and Gormley were signing in at the security desk, Dick took Anthony and me aside to talk privately. "Listen," he said, "just so you know, George and I both believe this guy is full of shit."

"Gormley basically told me the same thing," recalled Rob, when I related to him Dick's assessment of Rick. "I said to George [Gormley] that we just want the paintings back," Rob said, "and if he had something to do with it, no one is looking to put Rick Abath in prison. So now is probably the time."

"What was his response?" I asked.

"George was like, 'I know, I know,'" he recalled. "That would've been the time for a defense attorney to say, 'You guys are barking up the wrong tree; you're totally wasting your time.'"

"But he didn't?" I asked.

"No, he did not."

* * * *

I recently reached out to Dick and asked for his reflections on the Gardner Museum.[6] He had a unique perspective. As a teenager he attended Boston Latin, the city's flagship public school that sits just across Palace Road from the Gardner. Dick estimated that when he was a student at Latin, he must have visited the museum at least a hundred times, since he and his classmates used to study there after they had been summarily exiled from the Boston Public Library at Copley Square. Dick described the Gardner as a "place of refuge," far from the bustle of the city, and his musings about its collection were influenced by the amount of time he spent there in his youth.

Dick had no illusions about Rick, telling me he was "certain that Rick took the Manet off the wall." For Dick, the only surprising aspect regarding Rick Abath was that he was never indicted.

When I spoke with Gormley about Rick, he was understandably more circumspect. He once represented Rick in a criminal matter, and despite his client's passing, attorney-client privilege was still attached. "He was an honest guy when I knew him," said Gormley, "a different guy than the one working at the museum [back in 1990]."[7]

Gormley believed that Rick was "trying to outlive and get beyond what had haunted him all those years."

CHAPTER 9

"...with negative results."

In lands of myth, a tale unfolds,
Of Sisyphus, whose fate was told,
A burden great, a boulder's weight,
He pushed uphill, his eternal slate.

—ALBERT CAMUS, *The Myth of Sisyphus*

The Bureau uses the catch-all phrase "with negative results" to describe the metaphorical strike-out; that is, nothing to report. There are so many enduring theories about the missing artwork—tantalizing theories that once burned brightly with promise, only to die out with little fanfare. Sometimes they were extinguished with the excruciating lethargy of a dying candle flame, fluttering and spitting in their death throes, and other times with a prodigal burst of light. In the midst of these promising leads, it was nearly impossible to tamp down that tinge of excitement, the thought that today might finally be the day, and difficult to temper any semblance of optimism within the context of a historically failed investigation. At some point, however, the sunk cost fallacy kicked in, and the lead, no matter how promising it may have once appeared, was no longer viable. And so, the Sisyphean task continued—I selected another boulder-size lead and started pushing once again.

In contrast to the promising leads, it was the specious ones that always lingered like an oblivious party guest, especially those that were born from flawed information about the heist itself. One enduring example concerns the police uniforms worn by the subjects. At some point during the social media investigation into the heist, it was reported that the subjects' uniforms were those of security guards and not police officers. This false theory has endured, even making it into an episode of *Last Seen*, an NPR podcast about the robbery. In the episode entitled "Anne Hawley's Best Lead," the podcast discusses an anonymous letter received by the museum back in 1994:

> It offered a piece of information that had never before been made public that attested the writer's credibility: The uniforms the thieves had worn as disguises had not been those of police officers but rather of security guards.[1]

That's a very compelling statement, except it's not accurate. Both the guards and the teenaged witnesses on Palace Road provided detailed descriptions of the subjects' attire, and what they described were legitimate police uniforms, right down to the keystone-shaped Boston Police patches "outlined in gold piping" and dark blue pants with light blue stripes running up the seams. None of them described the uniforms as being those of security guards. I once attempted to research the provenance of this urban legend but abandoned the project. Like the alligators of the New York subways, the origins of this myth have been lost to time.

* * * *

In March 2015, a book came out on the Gardner Museum heist entitled *Master Thieves*, written by former *Boston Globe* reporter Steve Kurkjian.[2] In his book, the author asserts that Louis Royce, described as "one of Boston's best thieves," may have been the mastermind behind the heist. Royce was a career felon from South Boston with an eighth-grade education and a penchant for burglary. As detailed in the book, Royce claimed that back in the 1980s, he attempted to break into the museum in an effort to pilfer *Lamentation Over the Dead Christ*, an oil on panel that's displayed in the second-floor Raphael Gallery. According to Royce, late one night he and an associate stumbled upon a cherry picker that conveniently had been left unattended at a Boston construction site.* He simply hopped aboard the machine and drove it through three miles of darkened city streets to the Gardner. Royce then parked in front of the museum, climbed into the bucket, and ascended to the second floor, banking on the slim chance that the window to the Raphael Gallery would be unlocked. A mere fifteen feet from his goal, however, Royce saw from his suspended aerie that the window was, in fact, securely locked.

Royce's plan was as implausible as it sounds. By the early 1980s, the Gardner had already installed plexiglass on the exterior of the windows, similar to the coverings that protect those windows today. And as far as locks go, the windows are secured with cremone bolts, a decorative yet practical device that locks the window by means of vertical rods that slide up and down to engage with sockets in the casing. And because the bolts run parallel to the vertical mullion, they would be hidden from view from anyone outside, especially if that someone was dangling in the dark from a cherry picker fifteen feet away. And let's not nitpick—the concept of parking a piece of heavy construction equipment directly in front of the Gardner Museum

* Back in 1982, my parents and I visited my sister at Simmons College, located just next door to the Gardner. Overnight, someone broke into our car and stole the radio. Three years later, my bicycle was stolen from outside the BU Boathouse, leaving me with a wheel still firmly secured to the bike rack with a Kryptonite lock. I wonder why Boston thieves bothered with car stereos and mountain bikes back in the '80s when valuable construction equipment was left scattered about the city, unattended and unsecured.

(just below its plunging neckline), in clear view of the Fenway, a heavily traveled and well-lit street, sounds utterly preposterous.

The book claims that when Royce was a teenager and needed a warm place to sleep, he would visit the Gardner Museum before closing time and make his way up to the third-floor Long Gallery. Once there, Royce "squeezed himself under the ornate antique table with a heavy crimson tapestry hanging over its edge, giving him the perfect hiding place" to spend the night.

Royce's name had come up before. From my initial review of the case file, I was aware that back in September 1981, nine years before the heist, the FBI had alerted Gardner staff to the fact that Royce and an associate were discussing plans to rob the museum (no mention of a cherry picker, however). I was also aware that Royce had an airtight alibi, since on the night of the Gardner heist, he was tucked cozily in a Massachusetts jail cell, wrapping up yet another lengthy sentence that contributed to the nearly four decades of his life that he spent in prison.

Some might argue that anyone who "spent most of his adult years behind bars" should be disqualified for the title of "master thief," but what the heck, I was always receptive to new theories, even if they contradicted my own. And although the stolen-cherry-picker-assisted-robbery attempt seemed farcical, a few months before *Master Thieves* was released, I asked Anthony if Royce's claim about sleeping under the Long Gallery table held merit. In response to my question, Anthony suggested that I stop by the museum.

Anthony took me up to visit the third-floor Long Gallery, which holds the "ornate antique table" in question, known as the Civitali Table. While there is, in fact, a "heavy crimson tapestry" draped over its top, Anthony was able to do something that neither Royce nor the book's author could do: He lifted up that tapestry and showed me that the table rests on a set of stubby little feet. Realistically, no one, not even a wiry and undernourished Southie teenager, could squeeze under that table, let alone spend the night there. Royce's credibility had suffered from what amounted to, in my opinion, an obvious fabrication on his part.

After Anthony happened to mention this revelation to a media source, two unusual events occurred. The first involved the opening sentence of the book's online summary, which changed from:

> In a secret meeting in 1981, a *master thief named Louis Royce* gave career gangster Ralph Rossetti the tip of a lifetime [emphasis added].

to:

> In a secret meeting in 1981, a *low-level thief* gave career gangster Ralph Rossetti the tip of a lifetime [emphasis added].

Curiously, the book's title did not change to *Low-Level Thieves*.

The second event was a mysterious change of the location inside the Gardner Museum where Royce claimed to have slept. When Kurkjian was interviewed on NPR's *Radio Boston* on March 12, 2015, he related a story about Royce's nocturnal accommodations at the Gardner that directly contradicted his own book.

In the author's own voice:

> Now, this is an outrageous story to believe. But, when Louis got out of jail in 2007, and I had already started to talk with him, I took him over to the museum. And, as we were walking through, I said to him, "Louis, show me where you slept." He told me he slept up on the fourth floor...There were two big clocks there, and he said, "Those clocks would drive me crazy. You know, tick, tick, tick in the middle of the night." And then he would sneak out in the morning.[3]

I agree completely, that is an outrageous story to believe. If Royce claimed back in 2007 that he slept on the *fourth* floor of the museum, within earshot of two cacophonous clocks, why did the author write that Royce slept underneath the Civitali Table on the *third* floor?

Regardless, it's a moot point—when Louis Royce was a teen, the fourth floor of the Gardner Museum was the private residence of the museum's director, George Stout, and his family. It was never open to the public. I also confirmed that there are no big clocks at the Gardner, nor have there ever been—thanks to the stipulation in Mrs. Gardner's will prohibiting the addition or removal of objects from her collection.

Louis Royce remained firmly off our list of potential suspects.

* * * *

Theories linking the heist to international organizations abound in this case. One notable example centers around the Irish Republican Army and a wealthy debutante named Rose Dugdale. Born in the pastoral countryside of Devonshire, Dugdale rebelled against her privileged upbringing and became a volunteer in the Provisional IRA. As sectarian violence in Northern Ireland escalated in the late '60s, Dugdale whittled away her sizable inheritance to feed the poor and purchase arms for the cause. As her commitment grew, she turned her attention to art theft.

On April 26, 1974, Dugdale, along with three members of the IRA's Active Service Unit, robbed the Russborough House, a Palladian estate nestled in the countryside of County Wicklow. As the tightly bound Sir Alfred Beit looked on helplessly, Dugdale and her crew made off with a trove of valuable artwork, including Vermeer's *Lady Writing a Letter with her Maid*. After the paintings were stashed in a rented seaside cottage in County Cork, Dugdale fired off a ransom note, demanding £500,000 and the transfer of four IRA volunteers from an English prison to one in Northern Ireland. The robbery came just two months after another iconic Vermeer, *The Guitar Player*, was stolen during a late-night smash-and-grab burglary at historic Kenwood House in London.

The following May, Dugdale was arrested, and the paintings, including the two Vermeers, were eventually recovered.[4] Because of Dugdale's radical sympathies, coupled with that ransom note, British authorities logically focused on the IRA; however, at the time it was widely reported in the press that the IRA "consistently" and "vehemently" denied any involvement in the Kenwood House robbery.[5] More to the point, the IRA "knew full well that the British government would not trade terrorists for paintings, regardless of their value," and they sought to distance themselves from Dugdale.[6] "It would be totally ludicrous to attribute that sort of conduct in the U.S. to the IRA," claimed Martin Galvin in 1994, at the time a member of the national executive panel of the Irish Northern Aid Committee in New York. "There's a lot of political and moral support for the Irish struggle in the U.S.," Galvin noted. "It would be pragmatically as well as morally wrong to jeopardize that support."[7]

In September 1984, a decade after the Russborough House robbery, the swordfish boat *Valhalla* left Gloucester Harbor, a rough-hewn fishing town north of Boston made famous by the film *The Perfect Storm,* where the tragedy of a rogue wave was overshadowed only by George Clooney's abysmal efforts to mimic his co-star's authentic Boston accent. The *Valhalla*'s fuel tanks were topped off, which was a good thing, because she was bound for Ireland. And in addition to thirty tons of ice and a hold full of fish, there were more than seven tons of weapons stashed in her forward engine room—Whitey Bulger and his associate, Patrick Nee, had worked hard to gather the materiel that formed the *Valhalla*'s ballast that night.

Two weeks and nearly three thousand miles later, the *Valhalla* rendezvoused with the fishing boat *Marita Ann* in choppy seas and high winds off the coast of Ireland. Under cover of darkness, the *Valhalla* off-loaded her weapons and turned for home.

Unbeknownst to (almost) everyone involved, an IRA commander-turned-informant had alerted the lads at the An Garda Síochána about the operation, and the *Marita Ann* was intercepted by the Irish navy two hundred miles off the coast. Meanwhile, US Customs tracked the *Valhalla* throughout her return journey across the pond; the trawler was seized when she finally arrived back in Boston.[8]

The *Valhalla* debacle did not sit well with Bulger and Nee. After they received a tip from a crooked FBI agent that John McIntyre, a member of the *Valhalla*'s crew, was the informant who had fingered them in the smuggling operation, Nee lured McIntyre to his house in South Boston, where Bulger tortured him over a period of hours before finally shooting him in the head. Bulger then went upstairs to take a nap while his associates removed McIntyre's teeth with a pair of pliers and buried his corpse in the basement. Nee fled Boston but was caught in 1987, three years before the Gardner Museum heist, and ended up serving eighteen months in a federal prison. Ultimately, the entire *Valhalla* plan was a bust, and just about everyone who was involved in the operation was either arrested, murdered, or worst of all, tortured first and then murdered.

Yet despite the IRA's vehement denials about stealing Vermeers, and the abject failure of the *Valhalla* scheme, art sleuths inexplicably attempt to link the Gardner heist to the IRA. In the April 22, 2019, edition of the *Boston Herald*, for example, a banner headline breathlessly asked, DOES THE IRA HAVE THEM? ART SLEUTH SAYS STOLEN MASTERPIECES MAY BE IN IRELAND.[9] In the accompanying article, entitled ART DETECTIVE EYES IRA IN GARDNER MUSEUM ART HEIST, Arthur Brand, a self-described "Indiana Jones of the art world," claimed that after speaking with Irish sources who were in contact with the last remnants of the IRA, he was convinced some of the missing paintings were hidden in Ireland.

The following year, Charley Hill, a retired Scotland Yard detective who once worked in their *Art and Antiquities Unit*, opined that Bulger had given the Gardner artwork to the IRA. Hill believed that the paintings were most likely stashed inside the wall of a house in Dublin, a claim that was very publicly exploited in the BBC documentary *The Billion Dollar Art Hunt*. In the documentary, journalist John Wilson followed Hill around Dublin, "growing increasingly frustrated at all the dead ends" as Hill searched in vain for any promising

Gardner tips. When asked how a billion dollars' worth of artwork could be smuggled overseas:

> **Aha, replies Wilson. He reckons he has an answer: in 1984 Irish-American criminals shipped weapons from Boston to Ireland on [the] fishing boat the *Valhalla*. Why not try the same with art?[10]**

Why not? I can think of two very good reasons. Just ask John McIntyre.

* * * *

Bulger would go on to become an FBI Top Ten fugitive and the subject of the book *Black Mass*, which recounts his rise to power in Boston's criminal underworld. Because of his leadership role in Boston's organized crime network, many considered Bulger to be a prime suspect in the Gardner heist. He wasn't.

During the period when Bulger remained a fugitive, a number of his associates became cooperating witnesses for the government. At the time, AUSA Brian Kelly was prosecuting Bulger and his crew. Because he was also assigned to the Gardner Museum case, his access to Bulger's associates allowed the two of us to thoroughly investigate claims of Bulger's alleged involvement. Brian and I conducted interviews with many of these associates, all of whom told us emphatically that Bulger was not involved in the Gardner Museum heist.

"We sat down with his closest allies, including Stephen Flemmi and Kevin Weeks, and one of the things we always grilled them about was the Gardner Museum. And it was nothing," Brian recalled. "These guys were telling us about heinous murders, drug trafficking, and extortion; they definitely would've told us about paintings." In fact, when Brian and I sat down with Flemmi (known as "the Rifleman" to his friends), he told us that not only did he and Bulger have nothing to do with the heist, after it occurred the two of them were diligently working their own investigation, attempting to identify who robbed the museum so they could get a cut of the proceeds.

As I sat across from this unassuming, bespectacled little man in his seventies, it was hard to reconcile the fact that Flemmi was a vicious serial killer, and at the time of our interview he was serving two consecutive life sentences for his admitted role in as many as fifty homicides, including the murder of two girlfriends (effectively making them ex-girlfriends). To prevent their identification in the event that their bodies were ever discovered in their quicklime graves, Flemmi extracted their teeth with a pair of rusty pliers. And yet here we were, chatting just like a couple of fellas.

Considering the monstrous crimes to which Flemmi had readily admitted, when he told us that he and Bulger were not involved in the theft of artwork, those fifty homicides lent him an air of credibility. "There was a recurring myth in Boston that Bulger had something to do with the Gardner Museum heist," said Brian. "We looked into it very closely and ultimately determined there was no chance he was involved." In an effort to eliminate distractions, in March 2010, Brian publicly announced that Bulger had nothing to do with the Gardner heist.

Rich Teahan was the FBI agent who supervised the fugitive hunt for Bulger. The day after Bulger was finally apprehended in Santa Monica, Rich flew out to LAX and escorted him back to Boston aboard a Department of Justice Gulfstream 550, known simply as a G5 to the cool kids.* Once they took off, Bulger agreed to speak with Rich, and the interview lasted for the entire duration of the six-hour flight back from Los Angeles. "His recollection of criminal activities was incredible," Rich recently told me. "Really high-IQ stuff." And although Bulger admitted to a litany of violent crimes aboard that flight, the former Top Ten fugitive had no information pertaining to the Gardner Museum heist.[11]

In August 2013, Bulger was convicted in federal court on racketeering charges and eleven counts of murder, aided by Flemmi's graphic testimony. For his "unfathomable" crimes, Bulger was hit with

* If I were to use it in a sentence: *The G5 is a Bureau plane I never once got to fly on.*

a double life sentence, plus five years. And while Bulger was eager to provide any information that could have potentially reduced his prison sentence, he denied ever having the Gardner artwork.

On October 30, 2018, just after he shaved off the *plus five years* on his sentence, the eighty-nine-year-old Bulger died in prison. The cause of death was a sock-wrapped padlock, administered liberally by his fellow inmates.

* * * *

Another international theory links the Gardner heist to French ultra-nationalists. The theory posits that the heist was committed solely to repatriate the Napoleonic flag, which hangs below the empty nub where its finial once perched. According to the theory, when the subjects were unable to remove the flag from its frame, they instead settled for the finial as some type of transatlantic consolation prize. (Apparently, they came all the way to America to steal the flag but had to settle for a lousy eagle; that's not much of a consolation prize, given the cost of hotel rooms in Boston.) This persistent theory has been thoroughly debunked, due in large part to the museum's motion-sensor data, which revealed that after ascending to the second-floor galleries, the subjects made a beeline for the Dutch Room. And although one subject briefly entered the Short Gallery a few minutes later, he didn't stay long; in fact, both subjects were never in that gallery at the same time. If the entire purpose of the robbery had been to repatriate Napoleon's flag, shouldn't the Short Gallery have been their first—and perhaps only—stop?

This theory has been bootstrapped by an erroneous contention swirling through the miasmic online world of the Gardner heist that the subjects were unable to get the flag off the wall, as detailed in an August 2018 article from WBUR, Boston's NPR news station:

Although they tried, the thieves were unable to remove the entire flag, which was in a case screwed to the wall of the Short Gallery, so they finally settled for the finial.[12]

Unable to remove the flag? Was it protected by some Zeus-worthy Gordian Knot of security? Hardly. In reality, the flag was secured in a wooden frame that was clamped together by a dozen screws. That's it—a handful of screws. The subjects had already removed six of them—the screws that were recovered in a fire bucket the following day—and so they were halfway done. And even if their hands got tired from all of that unscrewing, the flag itself was sandwiched into its frame by just two thin sheets of glazing, which is a fancy word for glass. Glass of the same variety that protected the Vermeer and the Degas sketches, all of which the subjects so effortlessly shattered into fragments. And finally, the frame itself was screwed into a plaster wall, and while I would never do so, I'm quite confident that if I gave that frame a good, hard tug, it would pull right out of the wall (please, nobody try).

But the idea of a Gallic nationalist conspiracy would gather steam in June 2006, when the French National Police's art crime unit, known as the OCBC, advised the FBI that a well-placed source had reported that a group of Corsican organized crime subjects claimed to have access to the stolen Gardner artwork. The gang was known as La Brise de Mer, named after a café in the port city of Bastia where they held their meetings back in the 1970s. According to the source, the Corsicans were looking for a buyer.

"Why Corsica?" I asked my French counterpart, Lieutenant Pierre Tabel of the OCBC. Pierre's answer, which may have included the French word for *duh*, was obvious:

"They're Corsicans," he explained. "Napoleon was from Corsica!"

Again with Napoleon?

Despite my misgivings, there was no doubt that the Corsicans were, in fact, claiming to have the Boston paintings, a fact borne out through the OCBC's investigation, which included source information they deemed credible. Whether the Corsicans actually possessed the paintings was another matter altogether, but based on this promising—if somewhat suspect—intelligence, we launched a joint undercover operation with the OCBC that was code-named Operation Masterpiece.[13] The source, already vetted and vouched for by the OCBC, was acquainted with Bernard "Sunny" Ternus, a French national living in Miami on a fraudulent visa. Ternus was the Corsicans' contact in the States, so the source introduced him to Bob Clay, an unscrupulous art broker who claimed to have a potential buyer lined up for the Gardner artwork. Since this was an undercover operation, it should come as no surprise to learn that Bob Clay was, of course, an undercover FBI agent, played by Bob Wittman, patriarch of the Bureau's Art Crime Team.

The investigation continued briskly, with frequent meets in Miami and Paris, but as time passed, I grew more and more suspicious of Ternus and the Corsicans. For months, Bob had been asking them to provide proof of life; that is, photographs which would demonstrate that they actually possessed the Boston paintings. But despite his entreaties for proof, none was forthcoming. Originally, we were seeking images of the backs of the artwork, as the information contained on the verso is a closely held secret (since only Anthony and I know what's on the backs, it makes it easier to weed out spurious tips), but after months of waiting, I would've settled for photos of the fronts—anything to demonstrate that these guys were legit. And while high-resolution images of the stolen artwork were readily available online, at the very least we could've sent photos to the lab for authentication.

A few months after the operation commenced, Sunny met two of Bob's clients aboard an FBI mega-yacht in Miami. The clients were a duo of South American drug traffickers whose trophy wives had a penchant for stolen artwork. And other than Sunny, every single soul aboard that craft was an undercover FBI agent. Ternus had been led to believe that the ostensible purpose of this pelagic meeting was for Bob to deliver the latest cache of stolen artwork to his wealthy narco-clients. Bob had invited Ternus to tag along so that he could see, firsthand, how a real stolen art deal transpired. Also, Bob explained, he wanted Sunny to have a little fun.

A few hours earlier, as we made preparations aboard the yacht, I'd been invited by the captain (in reality, an undercover FBI supervisor) to come along on the voyage, posing as a crewmember. As much as it pained me, I had to decline the generous invite. At the time, I was known in a very limited circle as the FBI agent searching for the Gardner artwork, and I'd been interviewed on television and depicted in print media on a number of occasions. I reasoned that if Ternus had researched the Gardner paintings online, he may have stumbled across my photo. I couldn't risk blowing an international undercover operation simply because I wanted to play dress-up and swab the decks. So I demurred and bid them a bon voyage. I stood on the dock instead, and with a good pair of binos, I watched the yacht off in the distance, turning lazy circles in Biscayne Bay on a three-hour cruise. A three-hour cruise.

Onboard, things were infinitely more entertaining. Ternus was plied with Cristal Champagne and chocolate-covered strawberries, proffered in liberal amounts by bikini-clad female agents. Bob handed over to his clients the stolen artwork, which were, in reality, a stack of good-quality fakes I'd signed out of Miami's evidence room. In return, the captain produced a laptop and, after a few furtive clicks, showed proof that the illicit payment had just been wired directly into Bob's offshore bank account. The clients even gave Bob a gratuity, a handful of genuine diamonds that he passed over to Sunny as a sign of goodwill. Like the artwork, the diamonds had been signed out of evidence control, but unlike the artwork, this evidence would not be going back.

Bob's clients were itching to do the deal for the Gardner artwork, and once again the captain produced his laptop, this time to show Bob and Sunny that his bosses' accounts contained the necessary funds. A lot of funds, since the price tag was $30 million. Ternus was intrigued, and in the weeks following the meet he reached out to Bob's clients on more than one occasion, entreating them to engage in a quick drug deal on the side. They stalled, since we didn't want the operation to get sidetracked into a drug trafficking conspiracy.

The operation continued for more than a year, and as it progressed, we came to learn more about our Corsican mobsters. The La Brise de Mer gang was not to be taken lightly, even if their name translated as the Sea Breeze gang (please don't tell them I said that). At the time, an internecine gang war was raging in Corsica, one that would lead to more than a hundred deaths and a handful of beheadings.[14] But despite the tantalizing conversations with Ternus, the optimism that heralded the start of the operation had begun to wane, due to a profound lack of tangible developments.

This is all too often the trajectory of a once-promising lead. It starts out like that rare moment of synchronicity when you're in the car and the windshield wipers are keeping perfect time with the radio. But they're never really in time, and as Roy Orbison continues to sing for the lonely, it begins to feel just slightly off. With each verse, the song deviates more and more from the squishy slap of the wipers, until halfway through the chorus, the rhythm has become syncopated. And by the time Roy's poor, lonely heart finally breaks, the song has nothing to do with the wipers, and now you're just driving through a rainstorm and listening to the radio. That's where we were with Operation Masterpiece; we were approaching the last verse, and the rhythm was faltering badly.

In an attempt to recalibrate the lagging tempo, we introduced our subjects to a Boston mobster named Mike, played to perfection by Michael McGowan, one of the Bureau's most proficient undercover agents. Mike was Bob's boss, and notionally he was there in Miami to voice his displeasure at the lack of progress on the art deal. There was another reason for Mike's presence—he had been inserted to replace Wittman, who had voiced legitimate concerns for his safety and wanted an exit strategy. If Wittman chose to leave the operation, McGowan was ready to step in and take his place.

I recently spoke with McGowan about his involvement in Operation Masterpiece. "I think Bob thought he was really dealing with true OC people over there, and he didn't want to go after that," said McGowan, referring to the Corsican mob. "He liked to work with the art people, not the OC people."[15]

In August 2007, we introduced Mike to our subjects at the Clevelander, a trendy South Beach eatery. He arrived at the briefing dressed exactly how a Boston mobster would dress on a trip to sunny Miami: baggy basketball shorts, a tank top, white tube socks, and Adidas slides. Wittman, more knowledgeable about art dealers than mobsters, was aghast by McGowan's choice of attire and expressed his displeasure.

McGowan countered, "What do you think a real mobster would wear, Bob? A black pinstripe suit with a red carnation in the lapel?"

McGowan approached his undercover cases in a way that ensured that the subjects would never suspect he was an FBI agent. He had once been the undercover on a case involving the Sinaloa drug cartel. During one meet, McGowan initially chose to wear a $5,000 suit but, just before the bad guys showed up, opted to change into a purple velour bathrobe. "They literally made comments later like there's no way this is the FBI because the guy's in his fucking underwear," McGowan recalled. "I tried to push the envelope a little bit. They might've thought I was nuts, but they never suspected I was an agent."

Whether it was the Adidas slides or the fancy yacht ride, whatever we did worked, and the Corsicans were hooked. But rather than sell Bob the Gardner artwork, on August 5, 2007, they robbed another museum instead. The date of the robbery was auspicious, since this was the day my first child was born. At the same moment when I was imploring my wife, Sonia, to push, a group of armed subjects burst into the Museé des Beaux Arts in Nice and made off with four valuable paintings, including two impressionist works by Claude Monet and Alfred Sisley. The Corsicans demanded that Bob purchase the Nice loot immediately, and so three days later I had to fly to Miami in an effort to sort out this latest wrinkle in the investigation, leaving behind a newborn baby and an apoplectic wife. Not only were the Corsicans insistent that Bob must purchase the Nice artwork for $3 million, they wanted this deal completed before they would sell him the Gardner artwork for $30 million.

My suspicions about the Corsicans had been growing for more than year, due in large part to the noticeable absence of an executed deal, or even any tangible proof of life. The Nice robbery, however, was the last straw. It proved to me that the Corsicans didn't have access to the Boston paintings after all. Bob attempted to steer the operation back on track, telling the subjects that while his narco-clients were itching to purchase the Boston paintings, he had yet to secure a buyer for the Nice artwork. Who turns down thirty million dollars for a paltry three? Con men, that's who. But the Corsicans were insistent, which convinced me that they didn't have the Gardner artwork.

Based on this new development, I transferred the undercover operation to an agent in Miami, just as the weather in Boston was starting to turn cold and raw. It's that previously alluded to ocean breeze that does it; it sucks the life out of Bostonians and may account for their perpetual surliness from September through May (the other three months is anyone's guess). With the Boston office out of the picture, FBI Miami took over the case and negotiations between Bob and the Corsicans continued apace.

In June 2008, seven Corsicans were arrested outside Marseilles when they showed up with the stolen Nice paintings, ready to sell them to Bob. They went to trial in France, claiming they were entrapped into committing the Nice robbery, or to quote a contemporaneous headline from *The Daily Mail*: THE FBI TOLD US TO DO IT![16] A jury disagreed and the Corsicans were convicted, receiving prison sentences that ranged from two to nine years. We arrested Ternus in Miami, and he decided to cooperate and take the five years that we offered.

On a blazingly hot August afternoon in Fort Lauderdale, I interviewed Sunny Ternus at the US Attorney's Office. He confirmed my suspicions about the Corsicans when he admitted that they never really had the Gardner artwork. Ternus claimed it was a scam, as his ultimate goal was to get my source to help him obtain a legitimate visa. Yet despite this convincing rebuke of the Corsican mob theory, a year later Wittman wrote about Operation Masterpiece in his book, *Priceless*, positing that Ternus and his associates really did have the Gardner paintings.

Somehow, a thoroughly debunked theory had become very much un-bunked.

* * * *

Over the years, there have been so many dead ends and false leads, flawed theories and endless speculation, running the gamut from the sublime to the ridiculous. Unlike a fugitive of the human variety, my fugitives have thousands of exact copies milling about the globe. (It's not illegal to own a fake; it's only a crime if you attempt to sell it as the real thing.) And for some reason, copies of *Christ in the Storm on the Sea of Galilee* seem to end up on the living room walls of large mansions being offered for sale through online real estate listings. And each occasion merits a call to the FBI tip line. While it's possible that a wealthy but ignorant art collector may have unwittingly purchased *The Storm* at an antiques store, blithely hanging the piece over their fireplace, it's just not likely. Regardless, these tips result in a cordial visit from a local FBI agent who asks to inspect the piece and ensure that it is, in fact, just a copy. The same goes for the copy of *The Concert* that ended up in an antiques mart in Reno, or the copy of *The Storm* that once was depicted in the background of an episode of the Tony Shalhoub vehicle *Monk*.

These tips were harmless, and submitted by well-intentioned individuals who meant well and envisioned the potential of a huge reward. I appreciated that they took the time to call. The same, however, cannot be said for those who thought it was amusing to playfully offer *The Storm* or *The Concert* for sale through online marketplaces like eBay or Craigslist. While these listings were obviously intended as no more than an amusing prank, the tip still needed to be vetted, and an inordinate amount of time and Bureau resources were expended to first identify the subject through their internet protocol address, and then set a lead to have local agents visit their home. Shortly thereafter, I would get a call from the lead agent reporting the same lame excuse: "He said it was just a joke."

I received many tips that were based solely on an apparent resemblance to the police sketches. "Uncle Mort from Topeka" or "my neighbor's ex-wife's nephew in Akron" looks *exactly* like the taller guy in the police sketch. The first question is obvious:

"Was Uncle Mort an art thief?"

"Gosh no; honest as the day is long! He was a plumber, by the way, but I'm telling you, he looks just like that sketch."

Assuming that Uncle Mort doesn't have a criminal history to include offenses like fencing stolen goods or possession of burglarious tools, then I was comfortable putting that lead to rest without the need to fly out to Topeka and meet with Uncle Mort. If it was a close call, I'd set a lead to the local field office and have a couple of agents go out and conduct an in-person interview. But here's the rub: Having the ability to summon agents from around the country to conduct a logical interview was a heavy burden. These agents have a full caseload, and to send them out on a wild-goose chase to track down Uncle Mort, not because I thought there was any possibility he was involved in the Gardner heist but merely because I wanted to check it off my to-do list, was not meeting the needs of the Bureau.

Sometimes conversations with complainants were so vexing as to be almost comical:

> *"And how old is this nephew of your neighbor's ex-wife in Akron?"*
>
> *"Well, let's see; he was born the same month the hostages were freed by the Iranians."*
>
> *"January of 1981? He would've been nine years old at the time of the Gardner heist."*

"Well, I don't know about that, but I'm telling you he looks just like the taller thief."

With just a modicum of common sense, many of these tips were dismissed outright. Potential suspects who were toddlers or septuagenarians in March 1990 (yes, we've gotten both) or were incarcerated on the night of the heist could be cleared with a modest expenditure of effort.

And then there's the Paintings Never Left the Museum theory. Over the years, multiple tipsters have reported to both Anthony and me their theory that the subjects secreted the paintings inside the museum, where they remain today, stashed inside the walls. I would take this groundbreaking tip and send it to the Paintings Never Left the Museum file, a bulky repository containing correspondence from all of the theorists who came up with the idea first. Why didn't we think of that? Actually, we did. In the mid-'90s, the Gardner Museum updated its HVAC system, which necessitated a team of commercial heating specialists to crawl through every nook and cranny of Fenway Court as they installed new ductwork. There were no paintings.

If you're still not convinced, then let's play a game: The object will be to hide thirteen pieces of artwork inside four galleries in a museum, including two paintings that measure four feet by five. They must be hidden so expertly that over the next three decades, the entire staff of the museum won't detect your clever hiding spot.

And did I mention you have only eighty-one minutes? *Go!*

After culling through these impracticable tips and leads, what remained was a very short stack of promising ones. Many of them were quite logical, even if a bit farfetched, and they merited further investigation. These leads would be vetted out, beginning with some initial investigation and culminating with the interview of the suspect.

Assuming, of course, that the suspect was still alive.

In a cold-case investigation, deceased suspects are an all-too-common theme. And if I lacked the opportunity to interview the suspect and provide him with the opportunity to counter the accusations levied against him, it meant that some leads could simply not be closed.

But for those suspects who were still breathing and willing to be interviewed, the interview would inevitably yield a string of earnest denials. And then what? Since the statute of limitations on the robbery expired in March 1995, I was severely limited by how much pressure I could potentially exert against a suspect, since they were no longer criminally culpable. Allegorically speaking, once that sword of Damocles, for five long years dangling above a suspect's head by the wispiest tendril of a horse hair, was sheathed, I lost leverage.

For this simple reason, the carrot was usually more effective than the stick. And if the suspect was not alleged to have been involved in the actual theft, but perhaps merely complicit in holding or moving the artwork over the ensuing years, that carrot could be worth ten million bucks. That's one big carrot.

And then there are the obsessed.

Over the years, I accumulated a list of individuals who posited their oftentimes bizarre solutions to the FBI and the Gardner Museum, solutions that were gleaned exclusively from investigations they conducted from the confines of big, comfy armchairs, aided by the magic of the Google machine. Keep in mind, they're not submitting a tip; they're letting me in on the solution. In fact, to lend them the air of importance they so richly deserve, let's call it The Solution. Tips may be false, but not so with The Solution. The Solution was gleaned from virtual string charts spun from the recesses of their fanatical minds like fine strands of gossamer.

It's dangerous to attempt to solve mysteries based solely on internet research, because these types of investigations allow amateur detectives to pick and choose facts that support a particular theory while simultaneously ignoring those that refute it. As a result, the final product is specious and flawed, nothing more than square pegs crammed unceremoniously into round holes. Every investigation has a guardrail; that is, a series of unassailable facts that are planted firmly in the ground and joined together by the theoretical banister that ties those facts together. Eventually, it terminates at the newel post of the one true solution. Fantastical hypotheses are fine, as long as the theorists who create them don't venture too far off the trail.

Trust me: If you try hard enough, anyone can find a tangential relationship between the Gardner Museum heist and Kevin Bacon. To quote that ubiquitous and rebellious young flourmill dancer, "*Jump back!*"

Every iteration of The Solution follows the same disturbing trajectory, a rocket heading for certain demise. It starts off straight and true and then begins to develop the slightest wobble, losing stability as the center of pressure becomes misaligned with its center of gravity. As it continues on its fatal arc, the wobble becomes more pronounced, and eventually the unbalanced forces cause it to fail. But unlike rockets crafted by the boys at NASA, the Gardner rockets somehow managed to remain airborne, always landing on my desk.

The arrival of an inordinately thick envelope, return receipt requested, stamped as RECEIVED & INSPECTED by the FBI mail room, heralds the arrival of The Solution. No FBI tip line here; they need ample time and space to relate their theoretical machinations. And while it was never the actual theory that bothered me (in fact, the more outlandish the more entertaining), it was the manner in which it was presented, always posited as unwavering fact and imperious in its tone, as in, "*Look what you missed, dummy.*"

Regardless of how plausible or farcical these solutions may have seemed, if it wasn't viable—for whatever reason—I would usually contact the complainant and explain to them why it lacked merit, assuming, of course, that to do so wouldn't violate Bureau policy or jeopardize the integrity of the investigation. For example, with the Paintings Never Left the Museum theory, I'd give them a call and let them know about the HVAC renovation. But if Uncle Mort was locked up at the time, or if we interviewed Uncle Mort and he had a solid alibi (perhaps he was with someone other than Aunt Ginny), I would not divulge that information. The FBI does not reveal details of pending investigations just because someone submitted a tip, The Solution notwithstanding, and they are simply not entitled to an explanation. But to the extent possible, I respected the effort they expended on their theory and I tried to nip it in the bud, so to speak.

This rarely worked. And then the rocket would begin to wobble.

Since they have incontrovertibly solved the case, using nothing but their superior intellect and the search function on their browser (*"Hey Siri, who robbed the Gardner Museum?"*), then the reason why the FBI hasn't recovered the artwork is obviously due to my incompetence, corruption, or both. They believed that I'd rather ignore The Solution than have to admit to the world that I was outsmarted by [insert name of theorist here]. Invariably, the flawed logic manifests itself as an unceasing flurry of letters—to the FBI director, members of Congress, and sometimes even the president of the United States. I say sometimes, because I've had at least one solution linking the heist to President George H.W. Bush and a certain monarch. (*I'm looking at you, Your Highness*) All of these letters eventually made it into my inbox, bearing a provenance of official stamps from various federal agencies and offices. And off into the file they went.

Lacking anything but on-the-job training in the study of psychology and human nature, I can only speculate as to what drives these individuals, these tumbling rockets with unlimited fuel and inertia.

* * * *

While the easily debunked theories are fine, I was always troubled by those nagging and niggling tips that simply could not be eliminated.

None was more frustrating than the strange case of a Boston antiques dealer and petty crook named William Youngworth III. To some extent, Youngworth had the bona fides, in that he was once friends with the notorious Boston art thief Myles Connor (whose name will feature prominently in the next chapter). In fact, when Connor was locked up in the 1990s, he entrusted Youngworth and wife, Judy, to safeguard his multimillion-dollar art collection, which he had secured in a forty-foot box trailer. Unfortunately for Connor, the Youngworths sold off much of his collection for pennies on the dollar in order to feed a prolific drug habit.[17]

Despite past prevarications and misdeeds, however, in August 1997, Youngworth very publicly claimed to a cluster of reporters assembled outside a Boston-area courthouse that he could "broker the return" of eleven of the thirteen stolen pieces in exchange for the reward and Connor's immediate release from prison.[18] There was one condition, though: He wanted immunity from prosecution. Youngworth's stipulation was not without merit, since Donald Stern, at the time the US attorney for the District of Massachusetts, was taking a hard stance on the Gardner case. His office was not offering immunity to anyone who may have had criminal exposure for even tangential involvement in the Gardner Museum heist.

Youngworth, riding a heady wave of potentially being the guy with access to the Gardner artwork, attempted to prove it later that month. Late one night, an associate drove *Boston Herald* reporter Tom Mashberg to a dark warehouse about an hour outside of Boston. Once there, the associate unlocked a storage unit and produced a black cardboard tube, from which he carefully unsheathed a furled canvas. The canvas revealed itself to be *The Storm*, which was described by Mashberg as having been "unrolled from a tube and illuminated by a flashlight."[19] It was only after the somewhat premature and much-rued headline in the *Herald* screamed WE'VE SEEN IT! that a host of art experts came forward to advise that the thickness of the canvas was such that unfurling it like a poster would be simply impossible. The purported Rembrandt was widely dismissed as a fake, and the *Herald* received a fair amount of derision for jumping the gun.

In an effort to rehabilitate his image, Youngworth took Mashberg to the Barn, a ramshackle building in the Boston suburb of Randolph that served as both his residence and a used furniture store. After a brief jaunt inside, Youngworth emerged with a small vial containing paint chips that purportedly originated from one of the stolen Rembrandts.*

The paint chips were provided to the FBI and subsequently tested by McCrone Associates, a scientific laboratory in Chicago that specialized in materials analysis, to determine if they were, in fact, from one of the stolen Rembrandts. The verdict: They were not. Case closed.

Or maybe not.

In late 2003, nine months into my chronological review of the case, I finally came across the paint chip anecdote in the file. I had heard rumors that perhaps those paint chips originated from another piece purloined from the Dutch Room, and so I signed them out of Boston FBI's evidence control and hand-carried them to the Metropolitan Museum of Art in New York City. There I met with Dr. Hubertus von Sonnenburg, one of the preeminent experts on Johannes Vermeer, and left him with the chips for his analysis.

A week or so later, Dr. von Sonnenburg called to provide me with the results of his examination: The paint chips were the color red lake, a pigment crafted from ground-up beetle shells and one often used by the Dutch Masters, including Vermeer. In fact, he used red lake to create the rug that hangs over the left edge of *The Concert*. Hypothetically, if someone wanted to scrape a few flecks of pigment off a painting, the extreme edge of the piece would be a likely location. Furthermore, Dr. von Sonnenburg advised, the peculiar geometric shape of the varnish's cracking pattern, known as craquelure, was similar to the visible patterns on another Vermeer, *Girl with a Pearl Earring*. In Dr. von Sonnenburg's opinion, the paint chips "couldn't be closer" to a Vermeer. He asked me if I knew that there were only thirty-six Vermeers in the world. I did not then, but I do now.

---

* Many years later, after the Barn had been sold off, and to silence persistent rumors that the artwork was still secreted somewhere inside, we conducted two consent searches at that location, the second being an exhaustive ERT operation, using X-ray machines and thermal imaging...with negative results.

Of course, the FBI didn't know any of this back in November 1997, when US Attorney Stern softened his posture and agreed to give Youngworth limited immunity if he produced the Gardner artwork. Youngworth had just begun serving a two- to three-year sentence for possession of a stolen automobile, yet he inexplicably rejected the offer.

Inexplicable, that is, assuming you really had the stolen artwork.

Now back to those paint chips. There was speculation at the time that while Youngworth couldn't be trusted with anything as valuable as the Gardner artwork (just ask his chum, Myles Connor), Judy may have earned that trust. Perhaps Youngworth swiped those paint chips from his wife, who, with her connections in the art world, was brokering a potential deal and looking for a buyer?

We'll never know. Three days after the US attorney offered Youngworth immunity for the artwork, Judy was found in their Randolph apartment, dead of a drug overdose.

CHAPTER 10

Thick as Thieves: A Historical Perspective

And this is what ye have shipped for, men! to chase that white whale on both sides of land, and over all sides of earth, till he spouts black blood and rolls fin out.

—HERMAN MELVILLE, *Moby Dick*

Massachusetts has a number of historical superlatives conjoined to its rich history, especially those that relate to art theft. In addition to hosting the world's largest art heist, the Commonwealth holds the dubious distinction of being home to our country's largest residential burglary, which occurred in Stockbridge over Memorial Day weekend in 1978. This was when David Colvin, a small-time crook from nearby Pittsfield, broke into Michael Bakwin's summer home and made off with seven valuable paintings, including a still life by Paul Cézanne entitled *Bouilloire et Fruits*. There were no alarms; in fact, Mrs. Bakwin wasn't even certain if they'd locked the house before heading out for the weekend. Regardless, it was probably a moot point, since it was common knowledge around town that the Bakwins kept a spare key under the ceramic frog on the front steps. A citadel the Bakwin home was not.

Unskilled and uneducated, Colvin embodied the true reality of an art thief and not the glorified version so often depicted in the movies. And with his haul of stolen artwork firmly ensconced in a black plastic garbage bag, Colvin now faced a dilemma common to the accidental art thief: After one procures their illicit treasures, how does one monetize them? Even back in 1978, a piece as valuable and instantly recognizable as the Cézanne would be virtually impossible to move through a legitimate gallery or an auction house. And Colvin, once fined seventy-five dollars by a local judge for shooting a dog, lacked the wherewithal to find a buyer in that mythical bazaar of subversion known as the Black Market (in the fine arts section, just next to home goods and patio furniture).

And this is how David Colvin became the newest member of an infamous coterie of thugs and ne'er-do-wells who belatedly come to realize the irony of committing major art heists: To anyone but the legal owner, ill-gotten masterpieces are worthless. Bakwin's modest reward of $25,000, which represented the tiniest fraction of the artworks' true value, was still more money than Colvin had ever seen before in his miserable life. And he could've used a portion of that reward to repay the fifteen hundred bucks he'd lost in a card game to Arthur "Lucky" Samson. But to a thief—any thief—getting chump change for swag so valuable just didn't sit right, and so Colvin held on to his booty.

By the following February, Colvin still hadn't repaid the poker debt, and Samson was losing patience. Samson showed up at Colvin's Pittsfield home late one night, looking for his money, and Colvin ended up with the two .38-caliber hollow-points in his gut that ultimately proved fatal.

Shortly before his untimely demise, Colvin had met with his lawyer, Robert M. Mardirosian, a criminal defense attorney from the

Boston suburb of Watertown, in order to discuss a pending federal firearms charges. During their meeting, Colvin showed him the Bakwin paintings and related his plan to try and fence the artwork down in Florida. Mardirosian talked him out of it, and Colvin ultimately left the artwork in his attorney's trusted care. After he was killed, Mardirosian suddenly found himself the beneficiary of a garbage bag full of valuable artwork. Rather than return the stolen paintings and collect the measly $25,000 reward, however, Mardirosian opted instead to hold on to them himself, biding his time for just the right moment to make some serious money.

And did he ever bide.

Mardirosian's opportunity finally began to take shape in 1999, when he reached out to Bakwin anonymously, hiding his true identity through a Panamanian shell company called Erie International. Mardirosian made Bakwin a bizarre and patently illegal offer: He would return the Cézanne in exchange for clear title to the other six paintings. Desperate to recover his beloved Cézanne, Bakwin agreed to what was essentially a ransom demand.

On an unseasonably warm day in October 1999, the clandestine exchange transpired in Geneva, at the law offices of Dr. Bernhard Vischer, a Swiss attorney negotiating the deal on behalf of Mardirosian. Immediately after the contract was signed, Vischer excused himself from the meeting, exited the building, and waited at the curb. A moment later, a white car pulled up and a shadowy figure handed him a black garbage bag that contained Bakwin's beloved Cézanne. Mardirosian's plan was finally coming together.

Five years later, Mardirosian attempted to sell the pieces through Sotheby's of London. The timing was auspicious, since it marked the expiration of the federal statute of limitations for transporting stolen artwork interstate or across international boundaries.

But remember—there is no statute of limitations for the possession of stolen artwork.

When Bakwin heard of the upcoming Sotheby's auction, he filed suit in the United Kingdom. The judge eventually ruled that Bakwin had signed the contract under duress, and the deal was voided. At the same time, Mardirosian was finally unmasked as the mastermind behind Erie International.

In early 2006, I received a call from Julian Radcliffe of the Art Loss Register in London, a private company that represented Bakwin on the Cézanne deal. I sat down with Julian and he related the story of Bakwin and Erie International. At this point, I'd been embroiled in the Gardner case for more than three years, and I was now investigating an art theft that had occurred nearly three decades earlier. By comparison, the Gardner investigation was still in its infancy. Bakwin's stolen Cézanne was another example highlighting the fact that historical cases are a common trend in the world of art theft: Stolen artwork is typically recovered either shortly after its theft or generations later.

So, if you work art theft cases, get comfortable; you're in it for the long haul.

After opening a new stolen property case, I attempted to interview the now-retired Robert Mardirosian, only to have him refer me to his own attorney. Without his admissions about the pieces from Bakwin's collection, it would be difficult to prove criminal intent; that is, Mardirosian's specific knowledge that the artwork was stolen.

In February 2006, however, proving intent got a whole lot easier.

I was commuting into Boston, listening to *Morning Edition* on NPR radio, when Bob Oakes announced that his next guest was none other than Robert M. Mardirosian, who was there to discuss Mr. Bakwin's stolen artwork. Over the next hour, I listened in disbelief as my captioned subject laid out the entire scheme on live radio. Mardirosian admitted to finding the paintings shortly after Colvin's murder and hiding them in a Swiss bank vault before forming Erie International. Mardirosian claimed that he briefly considered returning the artwork to Bakwin but, since they were not insured, decided to hold on to them instead.

The most important takeaway from this interview were Mardirosian's statements which confirmed he had *knowledge* that the paintings were stolen property.

Facing federal charges, and most likely rethinking his decision to confess on live radio, Mardirosian fled to France, where he remained a fugitive for the next nine months. With his passport about to expire, however, he had no choice but to return to the United States, and we arrested him at Logan Airport, just after he cleared Customs. In March 2007, he was indicted on one count of "possession of six stolen paintings, including a rare Cézanne," and in August 2008, Mardirosian was convicted after a four-day jury trial in US District Court. He was sentenced to eight years in prison, a hefty punishment for possessing stolen property. Two years later, I finally returned the last of the stolen artwork to Mr. Bakwin, thirty-two years after they were stolen.

In May 2019, Bakwin's celebrated Cézanne sold at Christie's for $59 million, although I still maintain that based on its infamous provenance, it would've gone for a lot more if there had been an FBI evidence stamp and my initials on the back.

* * * *

It would be helpful to discuss some other historical art thefts in Massachusetts that may provide some insight into the choice of loot stolen from the Gardner Museum. Over the past half century there have been a number of notorious art thefts in the Bay State, and many of the thieves share a common trait: Rembrandt. Thieves love to steal them. And a brief examination of these thefts illustrates how they may have set the stage for the biggest art heist of all.

Massachusetts is home to two of the country's most prolific and successful art thieves of all time, Florian "Al" Monday and the aforementioned Myles Connor.

In May 1972, the nation's first armed robbery of a museum occurred when Al Monday, a career felon with a taste for quality artwork, stole four pieces from the Worcester Art Museum in central

Massachusetts, including Rembrandt's *Saint Bartholomew*. Monday hid the loot on a pig farm just over the state line in Rhode Island, but when a Worcester safe-cracker named Chucky Carlo heard about the score, he simply kidnapped Monday and stuck a gun in his ribs, demanding to know where the paintings were hidden (there is no honor among thieves). Thanks to Monday's largesse, perhaps inspired by the barrel of that .38 poking into his rib cage, Carlo returned the stolen artwork four weeks later and received a generous break on a pending prison sentence. Monday fled to Canada but was arrested two years later and, without having a Rembrandt-size bargaining chip, was sentenced to nine to twenty years in jail. This case showed Boston criminals that Rembrandts could be a viable get-out-of-jail-free card.

* * * *

Myles Connor grew up in Milton, a wealthy suburb that abuts Boston's Mattapan neighborhood. A longtime member of Mensa, Connor possesses an impressive grasp of history and a connoisseurship for fine artwork, especially Asian treasures. He can trace his lineage in two diverging directions, and while his mother's blue-blood roots retreat directly back to the *Mayflower*, his father's Hibernian side is a bit more tangled. Myles claims that his grandfather, William Joseph Connor, was an IRA volunteer who fled to South Boston from Galway after shooting two British police officers. In spite of, or perhaps due to, his grandfather's chosen vocation, Connor's dad was a decorated police officer in their hometown of Milton.

Perhaps it was the concept of competing ideals enmeshed in the Connor family tree that came to shape its enigmatic scion. Myles was a talented musician, and back in the '60s and '70s he was the front man of Myles and the Wild Ones, a successful rock band that played to sold-out crowds at the Beachcomber, a waterfront mainstay in Quincy. But when he wasn't gigging with Sha Na Na or jamming with Roy Orbison, Connor was committing brazen museum thefts and armed bank robberies.

At the age of twenty-two, Connor committed his first burglary, stealing a rare collection of Asian artwork from the Forbes House Museum in his hometown. In 1965, Myles cemented his notorious reputation in the criminal underworld when he escaped from the Hancock County Jail in Ellsworth, Maine, by fashioning a gun out of a bar of soap (yes, that really did happen). The following year, he was involved in a dramatic shootout along the rooftops of Boston's Back Bay neighborhood, trading gunfire with state troopers and Boston cops. In the melee, Connor shot a state police corporal before being struck in the shoulder, spine, elbow, leg, hand, liver, and stomach... well, just about everywhere.

On May 25, 1974, Connor stole five Wyeth paintings from the Woolworth Estate, a sprawling summer retreat for the five-and-dime family that was situated on a thousand acres of shoreline on Cobbossee Lake in Maine. He was arrested a month later when he attempted to sell those stolen Wyeths to an undercover FBI agent in a Cape Cod parking lot. Charged federally with the interstate transportation of stolen property, Myles was looking at thirteen years in prison, but his attorney, the indefatigable Marty Leppo, still managed to get him out on bail. After his release, Connor reached out to a state trooper who was close with his father, seeking some informal legal advice. When Connor asked how he might avoid a lengthy prison sentence, the trooper's response was intended to be hyperbolic:

"Myles, it's going to take a Rembrandt to get you out of this one."[1]

So, of course, Myles got a Rembrandt.

In April 1975, Connor pulled off a brazen daytime robbery of the Museum of Fine Arts in Boston, stealing Rembrandt's *Young Girl in a Gold-Trimmed Cloak*. Now armed with a valuable bargaining chip, he negotiated the return of the stolen Rembrandt and ended up serving a mere twenty-eight months in jail, a fraction of the sentence he was facing. Once again, Boston criminals took notice of the fact that Rembrandts were a valuable commodity. Shortly after his release, Myles assisted the state police in recovering another stolen Rembrandt,

Portrait of a Lady, which had been swiped the previous year from a private residence in the tony suburban enclave of Cohasset.

And in case no one noticed the locals' proclivity for stealing Rembrandts, exactly five weeks before the heist *The Boston Globe* ran a story with the musings of a recent visit to the Gardner Museum:

> I went through the Dutch Room, on whose green damask walls were Rembrandt, Vermeer, and Rubens. Rembrandt…painted a storm-rocked sailing boat, and there he is, doing a cameo as a seasick sailor clinging to a line.[2]

It's interesting to note that the Gardner Museum's motion-sensor data shows that our thieves made a beeline for the Dutch Room, the repository for all things Rembrandt. Also noteworthy is the fact that once they were surrounded by those "green damask walls," they ignored equally impressive works by notable artists such as Holbein, Rubens, van Dyck, and Dürer; instead, they went on a Rembrandt shopping spree. The final tally: three Rembrandts, one piece misattributed to Rembrandt, and another Rembrandt accidentally left behind.

I recently sat down with Myles Connor at the Gardner Museum (fittingly), and we discussed the heist—the one really big score that he never pulled off, yet the one that has become intrinsically linked with his almost mythical résumé of crime.[3] We've spoken many times over the years, and the wiry young rock-and-roller who once scaled Boston rooftops has now become an elder statesman in a rumpled sport coat who leans heavily on a silver-tipped cane.

Myles and I discussed some of his noteworthy exploits, as well as the ensuing dark cloud that seemed to follow him throughout his life. Back in the day, Connor was the white whale to a broad swath of law enforcement officials in Boston, all of whom were vying for the prize of that broad, bright coin nailed to the mast; that is, bragging rights to having landed the city's most notorious criminal. Despite Connor's age, there is still a sparkle in his eyes, and they betray his emotions as he wistfully recounts stories from his past. They narrow in rage when he recalls friends who perjured themselves to convict him of crimes, and they mist over when he recalls adversaries who testified truthfully on his behalf.

We talked about the brazen robbery of the MFA, and he chuckled when he admitted that he received a $10,000 reward for returning the Rembrandt; you know, the Rembrandt that he stole.

When I asked him about Billy Youngworth, Connor told me that they first met at MCI-Walpole, at the time the most secure prison in Massachusetts. We discussed his ill-fated decision to entrust Youngworth with his vast collection of fine art, which Connor estimated was worth $5 million at the time. I asked him if he knew that he was entrusting his art collection to a drug addict.

"Of course not," he spat out with contempt. Obviously, that one still stings.

While he was active as an outlaw, Connor's diminutive stature was offset by his assets, a combination of fierce martial arts skills and a superior intellect that served him well in the prison context. After his release from MCI-Walpole, the prodigal son returned, going back behind bars with his band to put on a show for the inmates. His road manager, Al Dotoli, even managed to smuggle in a couple of strippers who were dressed as roadies (think Jailhouse Rock meets Apocalypse Now).

Connor's candor regarding the Gardner Museum robbery is an interesting counterpoint to those who firmly believe that he pulled it off. He didn't. While he has freely admitted to me over the years that he had every intention of robbing the museum, on the night of the heist, Myles was more than three thousand miles away, locked up in a prison cell at FCI-Lompoc.

Connor related how he and his friend, Bobby Donati, cased the Gardner Museum on a number of occasions back in 1970s, scoping out the alarm systems and taking note of its minimal security. Myles claimed that if he had been able to pull off the heist, he would've held on to the Vermeer and the Rembrandts for a year before returning them to the museum. When I asked if the Gardner heist was carried out according to his plans, Connor nodded, then quickly added, "But I certainly wouldn't have cut the Rembrandts out of their frames."

Over the years, I've asked Connor for his opinion on who he thinks committed the Gardner Museum robbery, and he's been steadfast in his convictions: Bobby Donati.

"Do you still think Donati pulled it off?" I asked.

"There's no doubt in my mind," Connor stated succinctly.

He told me that shortly after the heist, a mutual associate, David Houghton, visited Myles at Lompoc and advised him that Donati had just robbed the Gardner Museum. Houghton claimed that Donati wanted to use the artwork to get Connor's sentence reduced. According to Connor, Houghton also related this information to none other than Marty Leppo, corporation counsel for just about every criminal in Boston.

Connor contends that Donati stole the *gu* for him as a gift, since he collected Asian art.

"He took it because I told him I liked it," Connor said simply.

He opined that Donati took the finial because he coveted it but scoffed at the suggestion that perhaps Donati thought the piece was made of solid gold.

"Donati just liked finials," he explained. Fair enough.

Connor also dismissed the idea that Donati may have buried the artwork.

"He never buried anything," Connor advised. "Anybody with any common sense would not have put them in the ground."

CHAPTER 11

Mello

Of two competing theories, the simpler explanation of an entity is to be preferred.

—WILLIAM OF OCKHAM, *The Law of Parsimony*

Corsican mobsters, French ultranationalists, performance artists, power-hungry monarchs, and crooked US presidents. To paraphrase Occam's razor, keep it simple, stupid. Enough of the myths and the Hollywood sensibilities; the rationale behind the heist has been needlessly glorified to fit a cult of personality worthy of an art heist this epic.

But in the end, it was simply a robbery, albeit an epic one.

Carmello Merlino, known simply to his friends as "Mello," was a Boston mobster with strong ties to John Salemme, the brother of Francis "Cadillac Frank" Salemme, who was the former head of the Patriarca crime family.[1] Merlino had a lengthy rap sheet that went back decades, and by the tender age of sixteen, at least one state judge had already labeled him a "notorious thief." Some people just look bad, and with wide-set eyes tucked under a teetering pair of eyebrows and an arcing slit of a mouth situated above a sharply defined cleft chin, Merlino imbued the very essence of a gangster. You could forgive the judge for his unflattering pronouncement of Merlino based solely on the archetypal appearance of the young man who stood before him in the dock.

Dressing up like cops to commit crimes was old hat for Merlino and his associates. On the evening of August 14, 1962, a US mail truck was traveling northbound along Route 3, the main corridor that links Boston with Cape Cod. On that warm summer evening, the truck was bound for the Federal Reserve in Boston, and nestled in the back was $1.5 million in small bills, the proceeds of a summer's worth of fun on the Cape (that's a lot of mini-golf!). Typically, a haul this valuable would be handled by an armored truck under a state police escort, but either due to budget cuts or discretion (depending on who you ask), the postal service got the ticket for this delivery. The truck was a little behind schedule, owing to an unscheduled stop at a Cape Cod gin mill to slake the postal workers' collective thirsts (yes, they left the truck unattended, even though it was loaded with what amounted to more than $15 million in today's dollars).

As the truck traveled onto a desolate stretch of highway just north of the Clark Road exit in Plymouth, the driver was flagged down by a uniformed Massachusetts state trooper. As soon as the truck stopped, three gunmen—including the trooper—drew down on the guards and relieved them of their .38 revolvers. The guards were hustled into the back of the truck and taken for a ride, eventually being released by the side of the highway near Boston, unharmed.

Although it was the largest cash robbery in US history, after five years of investigation by US postal inspectors and FBI agents, the case had yielded scant evidence. Investigators were certain that John "Red" Kelley, an associate with the Patriarca crime family, was the ersatz trooper who masterminded the heist, and they began to turn up the heat. Kelley later claimed that the cops "harassed my wife and frightened my cats." In July 1967, with the statute of limitations looming, prosecutors finally indicted Kelley, but he beat the case at trial. And while never charged, it was generally known around Boston that Kelley's associate and partner-in-crime, Carmello Merlino, was one of the other two gunmen.[2]

In the end, nobody went to jail, and the concept of "police officers" committing a robbery by means of a credible ruse was by all accounts a rousing success. One can only wonder if the Great Plymouth Mail Truck Robbery, as it later came to be known, planted a seed somewhere deep in Merlino's brain, one that would finally bear fruit nearly three decades later on a chilly night in March.

Which is not to say that he and Red weren't keeping busy in the meantime.

On December 28, 1968, a Brinks truck carrying more than half a million in cash was robbed by a Boston crew that included Merlino and Kelley.[3] The robbery became achingly simple to pull off when the guards stopped off for a drink and left the truck double-parked outside a tavern in the North End (yet another cautionary tale advocating temperance whilst transporting large shipments of cash in Boston). Three years later, Merlino and two of his accomplices were convicted of the robbery, thanks in no small part to the credible testimony of Red Kelley, who ended up becoming a star witness for the prosecution (again, no honor among thieves). Merlino lost his final appeal in 1974 and was sentenced to twenty-five to forty years in a state prison (like a bad penny, one of Merlino's co-defendants was ably represented by none other than the noted Cézanne collector, Robert M. Mardirosian).[4]

When Merlino finally made parole in 1981, he settled down and opened TRC Auto Electric Company, a repair shop in the Dorchester section of Boston. And by "settled down," I mean to say that he operated a lucrative drug trafficking network out of the shop, moving kilos of cocaine which were secreted in auto parts boxes. By 1989, Merlino's sketchy auto parts business had caught the attention of the state police (possibly because a replacement carburetor for an '86 Chrysler cost twenty grand), and the Massachusetts Attorney General's Office opened a drug investigation into TRC. Contemporaneous police surveillance logs identified key members of Merlino's crew who were frequenting TRC, including the aforementioned Bobby Donati, as well as Bobby Guarente, George Reissfelder, Lenny DiMuzio, Charlie Pappas, and David Turner. Prosecutors would later claim that Merlino was making a million dollars a year at TRC, with Turner and Pappas picking up carburetor boxes and selling off their illicit contents at local motels.[5]

* * * *

David Turner grew up in Braintree, a blue-collar suburb of Boston that sits at the confluence of the Southeast Expressway and Route 3. When Turner was thirteen, his father died of a heart attack, a tragedy that left him shaken and withdrawn for months. In high school, Turner excelled at sports and was well liked by his fellow students and teachers; when he graduated in 1985, his classmates prophetically voted him "most unique." There's a yearbook photo of Turner, a wide smile on his face, under the caption, *"You have big dreams of fame."* Based on his conventional upbringing, alumni of Braintree High's class of '85 probably expected to see him at their decennial reunions, a name tag with that smiling face affixed to his lapel, sipping a Bud Light and bragging about that walk-off home run against Scituate.

Turner was friends with Charlie Pappas, another Braintree kid. Pappas's father, George, was a convicted drug dealer who kept a machine gun in his car to "effectuate his transactions."[6] He certainly could've used that machine gun back in October 1981, when he was shot through the eye at the Four Seas Restaurant in Chinatown. George had been good friends with Merlino, and it was through this friendship that his son eventually became one of Merlino's most trusted employees at TRC. Pappas introduced Turner to Merlino, and the two became his "right-hand men" in TRC's thriving drug trade, selling those very expensive carburetors.

In 1985, Turner and Pappas were partying out in Provincetown, an artsy beach community that lies at the farthest reach of the Cape. As the bars closed, a gay social worker named Steve Noon offered to give them a ride back to Braintree. A witness watched as Turner and Pappas climbed into Noon's van and headed off-Cape. Hours later, Noon's bludgeoned body was discovered along Route 3 near Boston. No one was ever charged with his murder, but there was much speculation at the time that Noon may have propositioned the wrong guys.

In January 1990, during a home invasion in Canton, Massachusetts, a woman was handcuffed to a stairway with a gun to her head by two subjects who stole $130,000 in cash and jewelry. Investigators believed the robbery was pulled off by Turner and his associate, Lenny DiMuzio, another member of Merlino's crew. The victim, Andrea Freedman, identified Turner as the gunman and agreed to testify against him.

The following year, while the home invasion case was still very much pending, nearly $50,000 was stolen from two safes inside Boston's Bull & Finch Pub, better known as the inspiration for Sam Malone's *Cheers* bar. Turner was charged with the crime, but acquitted after a jury trial.

In April 1992, the attorney general's drug investigation into TRC culminated with Merlino's arrest for "heading a $1 million-a-year illegal drug distribution ring from his Dorchester auto body shop."[7] Of course, Merlino retained Marty Leppo as his attorney. The investigation ensnared Charlie Pappas, who was also charged with cocaine trafficking. Facing a lengthy prison sentence, Pappas agreed to testify against Turner and joined Andrea Freedman on the prosecutor's short list of witnesses for the Canton home invasion case. Pappas's testimony would be crucial in the state's efforts to convict Turner, but on the day before Thanksgiving in 1995, just a few weeks before the trial was to commence, Pappas was shot eight times on the front porch of his girlfriend's parents' house in Braintree. A highlight of the wounds inflicted on Pappas was the two bullets that ended up lodged in his mouth, noteworthy given the context of his agreeing to testify. After news of Pappas's slaying made the papers, Freedman had second thoughts about testifying.

And once again, Turner walked away a free man.[8]

* * * *

Bobby Donati had a lengthy criminal history that included numerous arrests for arson, armed robberies, and fraud. He was an associate of New England mob boss Vinnie Ferrara and was rumored to be making collections from bookmakers and loan sharks while Ferrara was locked up in Connecticut on racketeering charges. In addition to casing the Gardner Museum with Myles Connor back in the 1970s, Donati was also known as a fence for stolen artwork.

Donati grew up in East Boston but lived in Revere, a working-class neighborhood that abuts Boston to the north. Winding, hilly streets host strands of tightly fitted homes perched on tightly fitted lots. An inordinate number of immigrant masons were raised in those sturdy single-family homes, as evidenced by the inordinate number of facades clad in granite, their pieces fitting together with the intricacy of a soon-to-be-lost game of Tetris. Driveways, barely large enough to park two vehicles, are often flanked with majestic stone lions, sentries standing watch over a paved or graveled front yard. Travel due east and the town drops off sharply at Revere Beach, the panoramic swell of the Atlantic broken up by a narrow thread of shoreline that forms the town of Nahant. Off to the south, obscured by the low rise of Winthrop, sits Logan Airport, and every minute or so the impossibly vast and sometimes impossibly blue sky is bisected by an impossibly low and impossibly large plane, landing gear extended, finishing its final descent into Boston. The low whine of its engines competes unsuccessfully with the cacophony of seagulls vying for space overhead as they scan the beach for dropped french fries, the jetsam of Kelly's, a beachfront institution known far and wide for its delicious roast beef sandwiches.

* * * *

On the afternoon of September 22, 1991, Revere Police responded to Donati's Mountain Avenue home and found "a pool of blood and brain tissue" on the front porch. Although the cops surmised that the wounds must have been lethal, there was no sign of a body. As they processed the crime scene, detectives noted that Donati's home had been broken into and ransacked; it appeared that his killers had been searching for something. It wasn't until three days later that a police officer on routine patrol came across Donati's Cadillac, parked in a marshy area about half a mile from his house. Bobby Donati was found in the trunk; he'd been viciously beaten, stabbed, and virtually decapitated.[9]

At the time of Donati's murder, the state police drug investigation into Merlino and his crew included a court-authorized wiretap on TRC's phones. The morning after Donati was murdered, Merlino was picked up on the wiretap stating:

"I need the pictures real bad…so I can use my camera."[10]

Working under the theory that Donati's killers never found what they were looking for when they ransacked his home, assuming it was stolen artwork, we spent years searching any and all logical locations where Donati may have stashed the artwork prior to his murder. Shortly after Rob joined the case, he joined Anthony and me on a consent search of Donati's Mountain Avenue residence, where we rooted through the basement, closets, and even under the porch, hoping to find a hide that perhaps his killers may have missed.[11]

* * * *

In April 1992, after being arrested in the attorney general's drug investigation, Merlino was returned to the state prison in Concord for violating his parole (apparently, heading a million-dollar-a-year illegal drug distribution ring was a parole violation, even in Massachusetts).

A month later, Merlino very publicly offered to return a stolen painting in exchange for leniency. The painting in question was a portrait of George Washington by Mary Stuart, which had been stolen from the Longfellow Museum in Cambridge back in 1985. At the time, Merlino claimed to have other stolen artwork available to barter, and although he didn't specifically mention the Gardner Museum pieces, there was a flurry of speculation that he may have had access to one very serious bargaining chip. In fact, the *Boston Herald* reported at the time that Merlino and Pappas had offered to trade information on the Gardner theft in exchange for leniency on their pending drug charges.[12]

Bob Sikellis was an assistant with the Commonwealth's Attorney General's Office, and he was prosecuting the drug case against Merlino and his crew. On the morning of June 10, 1992, Sikellis received a call from Patricia Pappas, Charlie's mother, who claimed that she needed to speak with him confidentially about "a very important matter." That afternoon, Patricia sat down with Sikellis at his office inside the John McCormack Building, an inspired cereal box of glass and concrete that overlooked the café where a newly exonerated George Reissfelder once tipped a celebratory Heineken and toasted freedom. (More on that later) During the meeting, which Sikellis transcribed for the case file, Patricia told him that she had met with Merlino the previous night at MCI-Concord and was delivering a message on his behalf.

According to Patricia, Merlino claimed to have something for Sikellis that was "very big and international." Merlino was insistent that no one could know that he was communicating with Sikellis, because "he will be killed if word gets out." When Sikellis suggested to Patricia that Merlino should coordinate this information through his attorney, Marty Leppo, Patricia stated that Merlino "doesn't want even Leppo to know." Merlino was insistent that Sikellis must find a discreet way to meet privately with him.[13]

Merlino ended up taking a four-year sentence on the drug trafficking charges, which was pretty lenient considering the nature of those charges and his past convictions. The stolen Stuart painting was eventually recovered in 1994 and returned to the Longfellow Museum.

Merlino's offer to trade artwork for leniency certainly merits discussion. How many drug-trafficking armored car robbers attempt to barter stolen artwork for leniency? It's not a common theme, since gangsters offering to cooperate typically devise a plan more in keeping with their ilk—maybe they'll offer to testify against an associate, or perhaps they'll divulge the hiding spots of dead bodies or drug proceeds. The fact that Merlino was even in the same milieu of art thieves speaks volumes, not only about his associates but about his proclivities as well.

And more importantly, what of Patricia's meeting with Sikellis? What was the "very big and international" topic to which Merlino was referring? The stolen painting from the Longfellow Museum? That could hardly be considered very big and international, and besides, Merlino had very publicly floated the idea of leveraging the Stuart piece months earlier. And more to the point, Leppo already knew about that deal. No, Merlino was talking about something else, something with international implications that was serious enough to get him killed if word leaked out to anyone, including his own attorney.

We'll never know for sure, but I have a few ideas.

* * * *

As soon as Merlino wrapped up his four-year sentence, he was looking for another score. By 1997, the FBI had already deemed him to be a "person of interest" in the Gardner robbery, based in part on information received from one of his employees at TRC.[14] That employee was Anthony Romano, a part-time auto mechanic and recovering heroin addict who served time with Merlino at Concord. Apparently tiring of bologna sandwiches and wine distilled in a toilet bowl, Romano reached out to the FBI and offered up information regarding a collection of rare books that had been stolen the previous year from the Stone Library in Quincy. Special Agent Dave Nadolski got the case, and with Romano's help, the FBI recovered the books and Romano earned his parole. After his release, he got a room in a halfway house and went to work for Merlino at TRC.

Informants have their own motivations for cooperating with law enforcement. The reasons are varied, but most fall into one of two categories: money or consideration. Money is a powerful motivator, and I've had sources who worked for me for years, providing solid intelligence on their criminal associates, all the while staying out of trouble. By far, these were the easiest sources to operate, as the strictly pecuniary arrangement made them, for all intents and purposes, independent contractors for the FBI. They provided a product—in this case, intelligence—which we would assess for value and then assign a requisite dollar value.

The other motivation for sources is consideration. Their association with the FBI is usually the result of pending criminal charges or—as was the case of Anthony Romano—a desire to get out of jail. They are cooperating with law enforcement not for money but for freedom. These sources are the most difficult to manage, since the relationship is founded on the overarching fact that they couldn't follow the rules in the first place. As these sources await their eventual day on the witness stand, their lifespan is finite and brief. You wring them out like an old sponge, trying to extract as much intelligence as possible before they do something stupid, like get arrested again, and have to be closed. Breakups are usually presaged with a middle-of-the-night phone call from a local police sergeant, advising that they just locked up a guy who "says he works for the FBI."

These breakups are messy ("it's not me, it's you"), and not just for the source but for the agent as well. There's an ancient proverb that goes something like, "If you save someone's life, you are responsible for them forever." It's been misattributed to the Chinese; in reality, it was coined by the first FBI supervisor. Human intelligence is an indispensable aspect of law enforcement, and FBI agents are actively encouraged to recruit, develop, and open sources whenever possible. But there's another ancient proverb, this one definitely coined by a street cop, that says, "In order to gather intelligence on criminals, you need a criminal." When good sources are at their apogee, providing actionable intelligence and staying out of trouble, supervisors heap praise on the handling agent. But when the inevitable finally occurs, and these sources get arrested for assaulting their girlfriends or selling drugs to undercovers, suddenly every FBI boss becomes Claude Rains: *"I'm shocked! Shocked to find that Eight Ball was selling drugs!"*

One morning in October 1997, over coffee and brake jobs, Merlino told Romano that he was planning to rob a Loomis Fargo armored car depot in Easton, a small suburban community situated a couple dozen miles south of Boston. Merlino asked Romano if he knew of anyone with a clean record who could get a job there, so Romano promptly called Nadolski, the FBI agent he worked with on the stolen books caper, and requested a meet. According to Nadolski, "I got Tony some reward money and went to bat for him with the parole board, so he says he's going to tell me something." When the two met, Romano advised Nadolski about Merlino's plan to rob the Loomis Fargo depot.[15]

Nadolski needed to vet Merlino's plan to see if it was legitimate. It's one thing to talk about committing an armored car robbery, but every con dreams about that one big score. In order for Nadolski to make a case on Merlino, he had to prove that it wasn't just talk; he had to prove that Merlino's plans extended beyond the "just talk" stage. In the end, Romano's information was deemed sufficiently credible so that Nadolski received authority from FBI management and the US Attorney's Office to wire up Romano and covertly record his conversations with Merlino.

As the Loomis depot robbery plans continued, Romano told Nadolski that Merlino was also discussing the Gardner Museum artwork. Romano believed that Merlino may have been involved with the robbery because he had an "inordinate interest" in the case. Since the investigation had now pivoted to include stolen artwork, Nadolski brought in Neil Cronin, who had succeeded Dan Falzon as the FBI's lead investigator on the Gardner case. Between the Loomis depot robbery plans and the Gardner paintings, TRC Auto Electric Company, an unassuming auto garage in the middle of Dorchester, had certainly become a focal point for the Boston FBI.

For more than a year, Romano worked as a mechanic for TRC, dutifully reporting back to the FBI the information he'd learned about armored cars and stolen artwork. Nadolski and Cronin even visited TRC and spoke directly with Merlino in an effort to persuade him to return the stolen artwork. Although he denied having possession of the Gardner paintings, Merlino intimated that perhaps he knew who did have them. Negotiations progressed to the point where Cronin even delivered an immunity letter to Merlino, which guaranteed that the FBI would not arrest him if he produced a painting.

As these discussions continued, Romano continued to glean intelligence from Merlino, who claimed to have "seven of the most valuable pieces" from the Gardner Museum and a "beautiful plan" to return them and collect the reward.[16] Merlino seemed uneasy with all of the newfound attention from the FBI and began conducting his illicit business activities on the sidewalk outside TRC, even suggesting that the Feds were surveilling him with "lip readers."

The FBI agents noted that Merlino's good friend, Bobby Guarente, known to his friends as "Unk," was a frequent visitor to the shop. Guarente was a morbidly obese cocaine dealer who spent his weekends in a secluded farmhouse in the backwoods of Maine, mercilessly beating his long-suffering wife, Elene. Monday mornings would find him driving south on I-95, ready for a busy workweek in Boston, where he managed a thriving cocaine operation and worked as a bodyguard. Come Friday, it was back to Maine for two solid days of domestic abuse; three, if it was a long weekend.

In addition to his network of associates in the drug trade, Guarente was also good friends with Myles Connor, yet another example of the bizarre blurring of lines between drug traffickers and art thieves that was so endemic and unique to the criminal landscape of Boston.

David Turner was especially close with Guarente; so close, in fact, that he called him "Dad." Considering the fact that Turner had lost his own father at the age of thirteen, the term was profound.

Romano wasn't the only FBI informant at TRC; Cronin had his own source who was spending time in the shop. Richard "Fat Richie" Chicofsky had been providing information to the FBI since the 1960s, and he frequently spoke with Merlino about the stolen paintings. And while Romano was gathering information about the Loomis robbery for Nadolski, Fat Richie was collecting intelligence for Cronin, neither source aware that the other was also working for the FBI.

Merlino confided in Chicofsky about his plans to return the Gardner paintings. On January 7, 1998, he claimed that he intended to first return *The Storm* and the Vermeer; the following day, Chicofsky reported that Merlino was planning to return the Rembrandt directly to the museum. He believed that Merlino would have Turner kill him or his daughter if anything disrupted his plans to return *The Storm*. "Would you be willing to do something with me, work with me?" Turner once asked Chicofsky, who "was one hundred percent sure Turner was referring to the return of the Gardner Museum paintings."

In March 1998, Guarente was arrested by the Drug Enforcement Administration, the culmination of a six-month operation in which Guarente repeatedly sold cocaine to an informant. At the time, Fat Richie believed that Guarente's arrest was the reason why Merlino was "getting the authorization" to return the stolen artwork—once again, the tried-and-true method of using stolen Rembrandts to make a deal.

After his arrest, Guarente initially agreed to cooperate, and he told the DEA agents a few things about his relationship with Bobby Luisi, a Boston mobster who was running a multimillion-dollar cocaine business out in the Boston suburbs. A few days later, however, Guarente changed his mind, opting instead to take a five-year sentence.

Meanwhile, Romano's recordings showed the FBI that Merlino's plans to rob the armored car depot had moved well beyond the just talk stage. Merlino was putting his plan in place, and he'd already enlisted Turner, along with Guarente's nephew, Stephen Rossetti. During a recorded conversation on January 14, 1999, Merlino gave Romano an update regarding Turner and Rossetti, stating, "You know, they got theirs [firearms] already; things they used before." In that same conversation, Merlino told Romano that Turner had already visited the Loomis depot: "I mean, before we even brought this up...I went out there with Dave...to see the fucking place."[17]

To round out the conspiracy, Merlino brought in his nephew, Billy, another recovering heroin addict with a record of petty crimes that accurately traced the trajectory of an inveterate drug user. Unlike his uncle, however, Billy Merlino was not a hardened criminal, and his role in the conspiracy was essentially that of a gofer.

Their plan was eerily similar to the one used at the Gardner Museum nearly nine years earlier: A Loomis security guard, working as their confederate, would open the door to the facility early one Sunday morning so he could go outside for a smoke. This violation of protocol would allow Merlino and his crew to access the facility. They planned to walk their accomplice back inside with a gun to his head, followed by Turner and Rossetti, then tie up their accomplice and his unwitting partner, take the surveillance videotapes, load up $50 million into a Loomis truck, and head back to TRC.

Billy supplied the hockey bags, which had been stuffed with a veritable arsenal supplied by Rossetti: handguns, an assault rifle, bulletproof vests, walkie-talkies, police scanners, and a functioning hand grenade. Later, a federal judge would aptly describe this assortment as "a grab bag of highwaymen's accouterments.[18] Well put, Your Honor.

Merlino needed an accomplice, so he tasked Romano with finding someone with a clean criminal history who could land a job at the depot. That November, Romano told Merlino he'd found a "gambling fucking degenerate" who had agreed to be their inside man.

Loomis Fargo's newest employee wasn't a "gambling fucking degenerate" at all; in reality, he was an FBI agent named Dave Donahue. I'd first met Dave in 1996, when I was a brand-new agent in the

Providence RA. Dave was working undercover on Operation Plunder Dome, a sweeping racketeering and corruption investigation that targeted Buddy Cianci, the embattled but indefatigable mayor of Providence. At the time, I was Dave's handling agent, which is a fancy term for the guy who secures the undercover's audio recordings and runs errands (in the adult film industry, they're called *fluffers*). Over the years, Dave and I had become good friends and coworkers, and in 2011 he became my supervisor. But back in 1999 he was just the "gambling fucking degenerate."

Dave was used to working deep undercover, so by comparison, this role was a breeze. On the occasions when Merlino and his crew conducted surveillance on the depot, Dave would be inside, waiting for a call from Romano. When the call came, he would open the back door and head outside for a smoke, proving to Merlino that Romano's inside man could be counted on to repeat the security violation on cue, especially on one particular Sunday morning. Dave recalled that Loomis refused to hand out a set of keys—even to an FBI agent—so when he was done pretending to smoke that illicit cigarette (Dave didn't smoke), he would then pretend to key his way back inside to the facility, fiddling his Bucar keys near the lock as the Loomis shift supervisor, watching on a monitor, buzzed him back in.

And from the wood line, Merlino watched.[19]

After all the time that he spent at TRC, Chicofsky had his own opinions about the Gardner heist: He believed it was pulled off by George Reissfelder, Lenny DiMuzio, and David Turner, all of whom were "members of Merlino's crew at the time of the Gardner robbery" and "very active."

They were about to get even more active, if that's even possible.

CHAPTER 12

"Execute, execute, execute"

Dripping water hollows out stone,
not through force but through persistence.

—OVID

Every field office has a SWAT team. In the FBI, the team is a collateral duty, meaning that its operators continue to work cases, with only team leaders assigned full-time. During the summer of 1998, I tried out for the team. Tryouts were comprised of a mentally challenging and physically grueling week at the range and at the track, followed by a panel interview. That September, the senior team leader called to tell me that I'd been selected; I was now part of the latest iteration of Boston SWAT's Green Team.

We spent the next year undergoing New Operator Training, known as NOTS, learning the intricacies and dangers of tactical operations. Training iterations were brutal, spent primarily at the FBI's range located inside Fort Devens, a sprawling reserve military base in central Massachusetts that swallows up nearly four towns. There we conducted firearms training, land navigation and tracking, felony vehicle stops and vehicle assaults, and of course, close-quarter battle, or CQB, which is the technical term for clearing buildings and residences. It is, by far, the most essential and most dangerous aspect of tactical operations.

In December 1999, at the team Christmas party at the Union Oyster House across the street from the office, my fellow Green Team members and I finally received our SWAT certification. We were also assigned to a permanent team, and in my case, I went to Gold.

But on the morning of February 7, 1999, I was still just an FNG, a fucking new guy.

* * * *

It was a few days earlier when my SWAT pager went off, alerting the team of an upcoming mission, known as a warning order, or WARNO. We assembled in the eighth-floor SWAT room, at which time our team leader informed us that the mission was scheduled for Sunday morning, February 7. I took notes as we were briefed:

Carmello Merlino...nephew Billy...assoc. Stephen Rossetti and David Turner...robbery of armored car depot in Easton Sunday morning...

At the time, I was still assigned to the economic crime squad, so these names meant nothing to me.

When subjects are planning to commit a violent crime, like an armored car robbery, for obvious reasons the FBI cannot allow the crime to occur. So, in order to charge the offense, the AUSA wants to see an overt act committed by the subjects, a necessary step which demonstrates that they have crossed the Rubicon. For Merlino and his crew, the die would be cast when they arrived at TRC, located on Dorchester Avenue (known colloquially as Dot Ave), the busy thoroughfare that cleaves through the heart of the eponymous neighborhood. This would be the overt act, and this is when we would make the arrests. During the briefing, we were advised that our subjects would be heavily armed for the robbery, and I specifically recall that the terms *assault rifle* and *hand grenade* were mentioned.

Our team would be split north and south. I was assigned to the south team, and my role would be to intentionally strike and disable the vehicle that would be operated by Turner and Rossetti. High-speed pursuits are notoriously dangerous, and the FBI has long preferred a minor fender bender over a car chase, but the technique is difficult at best, since you have to strike the target vehicle hard enough to disable it, but not hard enough to activate your airbags.

Based on the scenario, I surmised that my Bucar would most likely be totaled, so I tracked down Jamie Marinelli after the briefing concluded. Jamie was one of the newest guys on my squad, and as a result, his assigned Bucar was a high-mileage Buick with faded paint and an abundance of dings. It was well overdue to be surveyed, which is the Bureau term for a Bucar being taken out behind the barn. I knew that Jamie wanted to try out for the team after he got off probation, so I was pretty sure he'd say yes. I nonchalantly asked him if I could borrow his Bucar over the weekend.

Jamie readily assented, but then I felt obligated to provide him with the fine print. After learning that this would most likely be a one-way trip, Jamie still agreed, albeit grudgingly, to sacrifice his Bucar for Team America. I wasn't surprised—Jamie was a good guy. God knows what he would get for a replacement, and anyone who thinks that a new agent's Bucar couldn't possibly get any worse than a high-mileage Buick would be surprised. It really can. We swapped cars for the weekend; he got my comically underpowered but almost-new Oldsmobile, and I took his aging Buick.

* * * *

It's four a.m. on Sunday, February 7. I'm parked in a deserted driveway in Dorchester, across the street and just a little bit south of TRC Auto Electric, a one-story brick trapezoid with minimal street frontage and a long row of garage bays that face an adjacent triple-decker. Considering that Merlino once used the business as a front for a cocaine distribution operation, I'm surprised by the amount of signage drawing attention to the shop. There are a number of bright yellow billboards touting TRC's prowess at sales (obviously), alternator installations, and something they referred to as the "$8.00 Electrical Check Out."

Sitting directly behind me is Larry Travaglia, my partner for this morning's operation. Larry's in the back seat, *Driving Miss Daisy*–style, because it will allow him to rapidly exit the vehicle on either side. Slung around his neck is an H&K MP5 submachine gun, custom-produced for the FBI to chamber a 10mm round. Since I'm behind the wheel, for my own protection I'll have to rely solely on my driving skills and my sidearm, a SIG Sauer P228.

In addition to being teammates, Larry and I are friends. He's one of the mainstays on Squad C-6, and his squadmate, Dave Nadolski, is the case agent for this morning's caper. For months now, Larry has been subtly lobbying his supervisor for my transfer to his squad; in fact, it was at Larry's suggestion that whenever an overhead page alerted the task force to a new bank robbery, I dropped my spreadsheets and financial statements and headed down to C-6, offering to assist.

Although it's quite cold outside, Larry and I are warm in our little cocoon, eager to hatch. The only illumination is the green glow of the dashboard clock and the streetlight on the corner of Leedsville Street, half a block away. In the dark, our Buick looks like all the other cars parked in Field's Corner that night, except for the telltale tendril of exhaust that wafts out of the tailpipe. An hour ago, we had our final team briefing, which is when we learned that last night, Turner had announced to his crew that if they were pursued during the robbery, they would exit their vehicle and "have it out" with law enforcement.[1] That's some food for thought.

It's still quite early, and updates regarding our subjects' activities won't be coming for some time yet. Realistically, we probably could've gotten another two hours of sleep, but instead, here we are, talking about whatever two good friends talk about to pass the time. It had snowed briefly around two a.m., and a light dusting of confectioner's sugar covers the garbage cans and old tires that litter the driveway where we're parked. Soon city buses will churn it into a dirty paste that will cling to their wheel wells and pockmark the sidewalks, but for now it cleanses the city, albeit temporarily, like spray-painting a rusty fence.

* * * *

The composition of the community that surrounds our Bucar that night changed dramatically in just one generation. Once an exclusively Irish enclave, Dorchester has become home to a multiracial and ethnic mix, and the community's newfound Vietnamese influence has encroached on Irish strongholds with a dogged persistence. When I used to drive through the neighborhood with veteran Boston detectives, they would point to a dim sum shop or a hip-hop clothing boutique and tell me about how that place used to be an Irish bakery or a spa (not the health variety; in Boston, it means a convenience store). Conducting surveillances with these old-timers was almost comical, attempting to keep pace with their cryptic radio transmissions: *"He made a left at that place that used to be Jimmy O'Shea's"* or *"He's making a right at the old Shamrock."* Growing up in Boston is like being a part of a very exclusive club, and its members jealously guard the club's secrets and uphold traditions that transcend time.

Having said that, after living here for more than fwah-ty years, I'm still not from Boston.

* * * *

A little before six, the radio begins to chatter. It's been virtually silent for hours but suddenly comes to life as the surveillance team, known as the Special Operations Group, or SOG, begins calling out the driving habits of Carmello Merlino. The surveillance plane, known by its call sign, 700, cuts a lazy and eternal figure eight above, calling out Merlino's left turns and right turns, advising us when he's red-balled, and estimating his speed as he makes his circuitous way toward TRC. And toward us. As 700 calls out familiar landmarks, I think of Merlino as he navigates those predawn streets of Boston, unaware of the scores of FBI agents above him, behind him, and of course, directly in front of him. He must be nervous; even a career con has to feel those ubiquitous butterflies. It's game day for all of us. Merlino turns onto Dot Ave, and the distance to TRC diminishes block by block. He finally pulls into the lot and parks.

Our team leader comes over the SWAT radio channel:

"North Team, execute, execute, execute."

As Merlino exits his vehicle, a black-paneled van, lights off, rolls up alongside him. The side door slides open and a clutch of black-clad operators silently pull him into the van. The door slides shut and the van pulls away.

"Subject in custody."

"10-4. Hand him off and reset."

Merlino, having been searched and handcuffed, is passed off to agents from the task force, stationed about a block away. The van stages for the next subject, which happens to be Carmello's nephew, Billy. Again, surveillance calls out his arrival at TRC. Billy sees his uncle's car in the lot, but it's still dark inside TRC. Confused, he crosses Dorchester Avenue to use a pay phone on the sidewalk.

"North Team, execute, execute, execute."

And once again, a black-paneled van, lights off, rolls up alongside him. The side door slides open and Billy is swallowed whole. The door slides shut and the van pulls away.

"Subject in custody."

"10-4. Hand him off and reset."

During this second arrest, an elderly Asian woman is trudging down the sidewalk, probably heading to work, and witnesses a kidnapping. She increases her pace noticeably and hurries off down the street. Hours later, as we debrief the mission, one of my teammates, Mark Karengekis, will make a profound observation.

"Sometimes it's a good thing when a black van rolls up and plucks someone off the street," he muses. "Makes people think about what they're doing wrong in their own life."

Mark, in addition to being an outstanding drug agent with a wry sense of humor, has an unenviable proclivity for totaling Bucars, often intentionally during high-speed pursuits and felony traffic stops. Like enemy planes painted on the fuselage of a fighter pilot's jet, one of the wags on his squad memorialized his many Bucar accidents with paper silhouettes of cars taped to the cabinet over his desk (one merely damaged vehicle was represented by half a car).

Above us, 700 dryly reports the movements of Rossetti's red Honda Accord as it's drawn inexorably to our location, so I drop the transmission into drive and press down on the brake pedal. My pulse quickens, and I have a kaleidoscope of butterflies fluttering in my stomach. My role in this arrest is really dangerous, since I have to impact the front right wheel of a moving vehicle, disabling it completely and pushing it onto the sidewalk. The timing is crucial. If I'm late to the X, which is roughly just across the centerline of Dorchester Avenue, they'll squirt through. If I'm early, I'll get broadsided on the driver's door, which is adjacent to my left hip. Adding to the tickly butterfly feeling in my tummy is the fact that the occupants of this vehicle, both likely wearing body armor and heavily armed, have vowed to "have it out" with law enforcement.

As the Honda moves slowly through the intersection at Field's Corner, one block south, I creep forward, a running back in my goal line stance, anticipating the *Hike!* And it's from this vantage point where Larry and I watch the Honda cruise right past us, heading toward TRC.

"Wait, wasn't that it?" I ask Larry.

For whatever reason, the execute order never comes, and so I reverse the Buick back one car length and we wait. As 700 calls out their outbound travel, I shift the car into park and relax the tiniest bit. There's an antique merry-go-round on Martha's Vineyard called Flying Horses that I used to ride as a kid. As we wheeled around on horseback, the goal was to grab a brass ring from a dispenser. If you missed it, you had to wait an entire revolution to get another shot at it. That's what we were doing now—waiting for the next revolution to grab the brass ring.

We later learned that when Turner and Rossetti drove past the darkened TRC, they were confused to see it deserted, despite the presence of the two vehicles in the lot. As they pulled away, unmolested by the SWAT team, they decided to return to Turner's Chevy Tahoe, parked just over the Naponset River in Quincy, and off-load the three duffel bags which contained their arsenal. After disarming themselves, Turner and Rossetti headed back to Dorchester, all the while under the watchful eye of 700.

As they near TRC once again, I slip the Buick into drive and creep up to the sidewalk, and once again, Larry and I watch the Honda cruise past our vantage point, heading north. Too many cooks. Because they dumped their arsenal, there was confusion in the chain of command regarding whether they should be arrested unarmed, a confusion that wastes at least a dozen precious and excruciating seconds. One dozen precious and excruciating seconds later, the team leader finally comes on the radio and issues the command to stop the vehicle.

I wheel out of the lot and punch the accelerator. Unlike my underpowered but fuel-efficient '98 Oldsmobile, this Buick was manufactured in the waning era of full-size sedans. And despite the abundance of natural numbers on the odometer, she still has a decent amount of power left. But by virtue of our position as the southernmost vehicle in the configuration, Larry and I are now running last. Dot Ave stretches out straight and true before us, and I can see a line of SWAT vehicles blocks ahead of us as we close the distance. 700 calls out a "*Right on Savin Hill*" and a hundred yards ahead of us, I watch the line of Bucars peel off Dorchester Avenue, still attempting to make visual contact with Turner and Rossetti.

"Go straight!" Larry yells seconds before I'm about to make the same turn onto Savin Hill Avenue, a narrow street that cuts over the expressway and heads toward the waterfront campus of the JFK Library.

"But they made a right!" I protest.

"Trust me, go straight!"

Larry knew something that no one else on the team knew, including me: After Savin Hill Avenue winds through its eponymous neighborhood, it merges onto the southbound lanes of Morrissey Boulevard. If we jump onto the expressway, Larry explains, we can get ahead of them. I make a sharp right onto Columbia Avenue, the old Buick slewing sideways on the wet roadway, and then nudge the wheel onto the ramp for the Southeast Expressway. It's still quite early on a Sunday morning and traffic is light, which is fortuitous, because the only emergency lighting in this particular Bucar is a revolving blue light that's enthusiastically called the Fireball. It plugs into the cigarette lighter, an atavistic holdover from the days of Kojak. (come to think of it, so is the cigarette lighter) Regardless, even if traffic had necessitated the need for a blue light, it was lying on the floor on the passenger side, well out of my reach as we raced down the sparsely traveled expanse of highway. We curl around the first exit for Neponset Avenue and come to a stop on the median that separates the north and south travel lanes of Morrissey Boulevard. I grab for the curly tail attached to the blue light, reel it in like a fishing net, dropping it onto the tufted velour seat beside me as we get ready to finally grab the brass ring.

I key the mic on my vest, just under the FBI patch: *"700, where's the vehicle?"*

"Southbound, passing the car dealership" was the monotone reply. Always a monotone. Surveillance pilots and dispatchers always sound bored; it has a calming effect on those of us in the field.

I look out the passenger window and see the Honda, with Rossetti behind the wheel, maintaining the speed limit. As they pass in front of us for the third time today, this time right to left, I make a sharp left and tuck in behind the Honda as the rest of the team attempts to catch up to us like a retracting Slinky. I see Rossetti's eyes flicking up to the rearview mirror, studying the two guys in the Buick with body armor and flight suits, itching to go. In our comparatively undersized

Buick, Larry and I will leave the vehicle stop to the larger SUVs, and so I follow behind Rossetti, our eyes meeting in his rearview at regular intervals.

The cavalry finally arrives and we fall back a bit. And when an Explorer tucks in behind them and a Suburban pulls up on their left, Rossetti floors it. I flip on the siren, plug in the Fireball, and drop it on the dash. It emits an anemic cobalt glow as it rotates slowly, its poor little motor grinding away. At a crosswalk, Rossetti swerves right and drives up onto the sidewalk, the tires leaving wet black strips in the fine dusting of melting snow. Rossetti and Turner are hemmed in by a chain-link fence on their right and a Suburban on their left; they have nowhere to go but straight. And so they go straight. The sidewalk, with a rough edging of chiseled granite, is at least a foot higher than the roadway (apparently, they don't make sidewalks like they used to), so I gun the Buick around the Suburban, looking for a break in the curb. At the entrance to the Devine Hockey Rink, the sidewalk tapers down to meet Morrissey Boulevard, so I slide the car sideways and mash the brake pedal to the floor, effectively blocking the sidewalk. Rossetti is forced to stop.

Larry and I both scramble out of the Buick on the driver's side (see, that's why Larry sits in the back), and I draw my SIG Sauer 9mm. We move up on the vehicle, my eyes fixed on Rossetti. I see nothing else, the pristine example of tunnel vision.

Rossetti shows no emotion, other than a dispirited look on his face that betrays little. He slowly raises his hands like a blackjack dealer leaving the table and then freezes. My SIG is trained on Rossetti with my strong hand as I pull on the door handle with my left. It's locked, so I unsheathe my expandable baton (known affectionately as an expandable metal pipe) and strike the corner of the window, just like we've been taught. The window explodes in a cascade of uncut diamonds that land in a puddle at Rossetti's feet. (Hours later, I would still be plucking shards of glass off my flight suit and body armor as we debriefed the mission.)

I holster my SIG and drop the baton as Larry and I tug Rossetti out through the space where there had recently been a window. After we handcuff him on the pavement, still placid and compliant, I glance up and watch as Turner is extricated by my teammates, using the more conventional and far less physically taxing through-the-open-door method. And that was the day I learned that after the window goes, reach in and hit the door unlock button.

This was one of my first SWAT arrests, and overall I did a pretty good job, right up until I cut off the Honda. At that point, we should've hunkered down and stayed down. Later, Larry and I would be chided by our team leader for exiting our vehicle after the stop. The reasoning was sound—when we popped out of the Buick, we were essentially downrange from Turner and Rossetti. Had there been a firefight, our teammates had better not miss.

* * * *

Merlino and his crew were charged with conspiracy, an attempt to violate the Hobbs Act (simply defined as a robbery that affects interstate commerce), and possessing a firearm during a crime of violence. Turner and Rossetti were also charged with being felons in possession of firearms and an explosive device.

On September 25, 2001, just a few weeks after the 9/11 attacks, opening arguments were heard in the case of *United States v. Carmello Merlino, et al.* Over the next five weeks, the defendants claimed that they were entrapped into the Loomis robbery scheme in an effort to force their cooperation with the Gardner Museum investigation. On October 24, the jury voiced their disagreement and the whole crew was convicted. According to one juror, "I felt the Gardner had nothing to do with it…I believe that the other jurors didn't either." And thus spoke the jurors.

"The government pulled a real fast one," Merlino told the judge, right before he was sentenced to forty-seven years in prison. He died three years later. Billy Merlino, Turner, and Rossetti received lengthy prison sentences for their roles in the conspiracy.

They appealed their convictions on a number of grounds, even arguing that the events of September 11 had created an atmosphere that was unduly prejudicial to their right to a fair trial. This motion was denied, as was the argument that the FBI-created scheme to steal $50 million from the Loomis depot was too enticing to pass up, and therefore represented a form of entrapment. Turner argued that he was coerced into the robbery, claiming that the FBI believed that the prospect of a lengthy prison sentence would compel him to cooperate with the Gardner Museum investigation. The issue of entrapment was dismissed by District Court Judge Richard Stearns and further dismissed by the First Circuit upon appeal.[2]

As Judge Stearns unequivocally stated: "Let me stress, however, that I agree that the fact that the government creates a crime is insufficient 'without a lot more' to make out a due process violation."[3]

CHAPTER 13

"The Location Died with Bobby"

G is for GEORGE, smothered under a rug.

—EDWARD GOREY, *The Gashlycrumb Tinies*

Quincy Market is a popular tourist spot in Boston, and its close proximity to the harbor betrays its original intent as a thriving marketplace for fishmongers and wholesalers. Its current iteration is a collection of seafood restaurants, souvenir shops, pushcarts, and a lot of Irish pubs. (And did I mention Irish pubs?) The market is comprised of three long, seemingly monolithic blocks of granite, anchored at their western edge by Faneuil Hall, a Revolutionary-era building where our forefathers fomented insurrection.

From there it's a short walk across Congress Street to city hall, an unfortunate heap of concrete slabs, prosaic and utterly charmless, which rest forlorn and unloved upon a desolate and barren expanse of brick known as the Plaza. It demarks the southern boundary of the West End neighborhood, a historic section of the city that was razed in the late 1950s under the intoxicating auspices of urban renewal. Hundreds of historic buildings, including the Scollay Square Theatre and the site where Alexander Graham Bell made the first telemarketing call (*"Mr. Watson, are you happy with your long-distance service?"*), were demolished to make way for City Hall Plaza and a carbuncle of brutalist monstrosities known as Government Center. It was here that the FBI maintained its Boston field office, up until the move in 2016 across the harbor to our new digs in Chelsea. The only vestiges of the West End's original architecture that remain are a sprinkling of the lucky few buildings that survived the wrecking ball, as well as the occasional historical marker informing passersby of what they missed.

It's 2015, and I'm sitting in a second-floor law firm at Quincy Market, upstairs from Durgin Park, the iconic restaurant known for its intentionally rude waitstaff (not to be confused with every other Boston waiter). I've been summoned here by my host to meet with his client, a client who claims to have information about the Gardner artwork. Dare I say it, but I'm always the tiniest bit optimistic when an attorney reaches out, since I've always maintained that if someone has truly relevant information about the stolen artwork, they'll be savvy enough to retain an attorney to negotiate on their behalf. In fact, whenever I interviewed someone who claimed to know nothing about the stolen artwork (*"Geez, guys, wish I could help you out. Believe me, I'd love the ten million"*), my parting advice was always the earnest suggestion that they consult with an attorney who can act as their intermediary. It's one of the rare exceptions in my career when I actively encouraged suspects to lawyer up.

The client today is Paul Calantropo. He looks like a jeweler, which is not all that unusual considering he is, actually, a jeweler. Calantropo's piercing eyes seem to appraise me from across the table, possibly assessing what I'd fetch on the open market. He works in the Jeweler's Exchange Building, an eight-story warren of tiny shops overlooking Downtown Crossing, a bustling pedestrian thoroughfare located just a few blocks away from where I'm currently sitting.

According to Calantropo, six weeks after the Gardner heist, Bobby Donati came into his shop looking to sell the Napoleonic finial. Calantropo claims that as soon as Donati unwrapped the gilded eagle, he immediately recognized it as one of the thirteen pieces stolen the previous month from the Gardner Museum. At the time he quipped, "Jesus, Bobby, why didn't you steal the *Mona Lisa?*" However enticing that finial may have seemed, Calantropo passed because the piece was, in his own words, "too hot."

Calantropo told me that he knew the artwork was completely worthless, since "the whole world knew it was stolen."

As I listened to Calantropo speak, I assessed his information. I knew all about Donati and this particular piece. Years earlier, Myles Connor told me that Donati stole the finial because he coveted it, and when they cased the museum together back in the 1970s, Donati claimed that the finial would be his calling card, telling Myles, "The eagle has landed."[1]

But this wasn't classified information. Realistically, if Calantropo had read Connor's book, *The Art of the Heist,* he would've learned about Donati's penchant for the finial. There had been some news stories about it, to be sure, but if Calantropo was lying to me, then what's the point? Is there an angle? If there's one thing this case has in abundance, it's seemingly credible information and viable suspects; the trick was to weed through the prevaricators and the charlatans and try to figure out who's telling the truth. And one part of the process is attempting to ascertain what someone stood to gain by lying to an FBI agent—a federal crime—in the presence of their attorney. At the end of the day, I surmised that Calantropo stood to gain nothing, except perhaps the reward, if his information led to the recovery of the finial. He told a compelling story, and we both shared a similar conviction:

Calantropo believed that "the secret of the location died with Bobby."[2]

* * * *

The Degas sketches. Their theft was just so random. If our thieves were itching to grab a work on paper, they could've stolen Michelangelo's *Picta*, a charcoal sketch that hung a foot or so away from the Degas sketches and was worth at least $20 million. I'd long theorized that the Degas sketches, two of which depict jockeys, may have been stolen because the subjects liked horse racing, And Bobby Donati certainly liked the ponies. Maybe even a little too much.

In May 1979, Donati pled guilty in Boston federal court to fixing horse races at a half dozen racetracks up and down the East Coast, effectively bribing jockeys to hold back their horses.[3] One of his codefendants was Howie Winter, who at the time ran the notorious Winter Hill Gang (named after a neighborhood in nearby Somerville, not Howie). Winter was convicted in the scheme a few months after Donati and was sentenced to ten years in prison, allowing Whitey Bulger, one of the key figures in the *Valhalla* weapons-smuggling scheme, to assume control of the Winter Hill Gang.

If one were to accept Calantropo's contention that "the secret of the location died with Bobby," then the maddening goal of this worldwide scavenger hunt was to find that location. Given Donati's penchant for horse racing, we took a hard look at Suffolk Downs, a horse track that straddles the city line dividing East Boston and Revere. Donati spent a lot of time at the track, and we'd heard vague rumors that the artwork may have been hidden there at one point. The tip became even more intriguing when I learned that two months before the heist, the track was closed for renovations; it wouldn't reopen until 1992. With horse stalls and stables stretching across more than two hundred acres, I surmised that the closed racetrack would've made a great place to stash stolen artwork.

In September 2015, we descended on Suffolk Downs, once again assisted by the Evidence Response Team, and conducted another search that ultimately proved fruitless. The theory had held promise, a sentiment echoed by *The Boston Globe* three months later when they reported on our endeavors:

> There had been this rumor that the paintings had been kept there for a brief time after the robbery...a Suffolk Downs employee claims the racetrack, closed for renovations from 1990 to 1992, was a favorite meeting place for criminals and wannabes.[4]

Like so many other searches conducted in this case, it was conducted with voluntary consent, meaning that the property owner was under no legal obligation to allow the FBI to search their premises. Over time, consent searches became routine as we attempted to exhume the final resting place of the Gardner artwork. I've crawled and squirmed through too many triple-deckers, those ubiquitous multifamily dwellings that blanket the Boston landscape—gumwood trim and oval portraits of the Virgin Mary, rosary beads and doily-covered brown furniture, ceramic figurines and nicotine-stained wallpaper, and musty back staircases that spiral down to dirt-floor cellars with coal chutes and decomposing furnaces, their tangles of ductwork rooted firmly into the low ceilings overhead. I've sifted through the detritus of family histories, searching for hidden nooks and loose floorboards, wriggling into sweltering attics and banging my head on low rafters, the hot smell of dust and pine tar, plaster lathe illuminated by my flashlight and small attic windows with their bright squares of Boston neighborhoods peeking through sharply angled shafts of dust motes. I would emerge from the shadows soaking wet, pulling strands of cobwebs out of my hair and tucking in my shirt.

It's interesting to note that over the years the rate of consent for these informal searches hovered right around one hundred percent. Apparently, everyone would like the FBI to unearth a billion dollars in stolen artwork from their property. Especially when it comes with a $10 million reward.

Two short months after the Suffolk Downs search, we were at it again. This time it was a consent search of a Boston-area residence that once belonged to a Donati relative. Our searches focused on areas where Donati might have secreted the artwork before his death, typically attics and basements. During this particular search, the basement was nearly empty, save for a homemade floor-to-ceiling cabinet, which measured about five feet wide and was secured by two plywood doors. Inside that cabinet sat four shelves, spaced equally apart and resting on wooden cleats. The shelves were removable, as was the cabinet's cardboard back. When we removed the shelves and the false back, what remained was a cavity between the cabinet and the basement wall, about four inches deep. And scattered on the ground in this cavity were dozens and dozens of silica packs, those desiccants that come with home electronics to keep them dry and mold-free. The dimensions of that hide, about five feet by seven, and four inches deep, would've been more than sufficient to store a pretty decent stack of very large paintings.

What else would a gangster store in a hide that size? It wasn't sized correctly for drugs, and besides, there would be no need for the desiccants. A very likely explanation would be artwork. Large artwork. It was another dead end, but one that bolstered the theory that Donati was involved in the Gardner heist.

Two more locations down...how many more to go?

* * * *

On October 14, 1966, a railroad guard was shot in the head during a botched robbery at Boston's South Station. Two robbers fled the scene with less than twenty grand as their victim bled out on a catwalk above the train platforms. This robbery proved extremely unfortunate for George Reissfelder, an unemployed laborer from the Jamaica Plain section of Boston who had recently confided to his girlfriend that he was planning to commit a robbery in South Boston. After she heard about the South Station robbery, she told her father about Reissfelder's plans, which prompted an immediate call to the Boston Police.

Later that day, the cops arrested Reissfelder, who happened to be carrying a .22 revolver at the time. That was unlucky. And when the railroad guard died two months later, Reissfelder's run of bad luck continued as the charges were upgraded to first-degree murder.[5] In Suffolk Superior Court the following July, a jury deliberated for just eleven hours before returning guilty verdicts for both Reissfelder and his codefendant, William Sullivan. Although the jury recommended the death penalty, the judge was more merciful and instead sentenced Reissfelder to life at Walpole State Prison.[6]

In May 1974, just seven years after his conviction, Reissfelder and another convicted murderer, Robert Beauchamp, escaped from prison. And while images may come to mind of Reissfelder and Beauchamp wriggling through half a mile of sewage pipe and standing triumphant in a rain-spangled cesspool of redemption, their escape was markedly easier: They simply failed to return from a one-day furlough.[7] At the time, the Massachusetts Department of Correction had a program that allowed inmates—even convicted murderers—to leave prison for a day or two, as long as they promised to come back. Perhaps no one—not even the inmates—loved the Commonwealth's furlough program more than the Republican Party, and in 1988, it would have dire consequences for then-Governor Mike Dukakis, who was running for president on the Democratic ticket against George H. W. Bush. The Republicans ran campaign ads featuring Willie Horton, a convicted murderer from Massachusetts who had kidnapped a young couple, murdered the man, and then repeatedly raped his girlfriend, all while out on a Dukakis-approved furlough. After Horton broke his pinky-promise, the Bay State rethought the much-derided furlough program, opting instead for the staycation.

After Reissfelder's "daring" escape, he fled to Florida but was arrested three years later in Jacksonville when he attempted to pass a bad check. During his arrest, Reissfelder pulled a gun on the arresting officer and it discharged, wounding the cop. Facing the prospect of his two prison sentences running consecutively, Reissfelder took the fifteen years that the Duval County DA was offering for attempted murder.

Firmly ensconced back in a Massachusetts prison, Reissfelder continued to maintain his innocence regarding the South Station robbery. His run of bad luck was about to change, however, when his codefendant, dying from leukemia, confided to his priest that he'd never even met Reissfelder prior to the trial. The deathbed confession was enough to overturn Reissfelder's conviction, thanks to his legal team, which included future US senator and presidential candidate John Kerry. In August 1982, amidst a swarm of reporters, Reissfelder was released from custody. As he strolled out of the Suffolk Superior Courthouse, his sister-in-law, Donna Reissfelder née Mauras, told a reporter, "In a way, this whole thing is like a fairy tale. You wait and wait, and then it happens."[8] Riding the feel-good Reissfelder wave, even the parole board in Florida granted him an immediate parole for his attempted murder conviction.

Reissfelder was finally a free man.

His first stop was a café in City Hall Plaza, where he downed a celebratory Heineken amidst a throng of reporters. According to *The Boston Globe*, Reissfelder was "fascinated" by the "concrete bunker-style City Hall building" and the "crescent of Government Center" that had replaced the old Scollay Square.[9] This proves my earlier point about the Plaza's brutalist architecture—it was jarring even to someone whose last residence was a maximum-security prison. After finishing his beer, Reissfelder traveled to the Randolph home of his brother, Richard, where a sheet hanging out front proclaimed, "Welcome Home Uncle George."

At the time, Richard told the press that his brother wanted "to get right back to work, get a license, get a car and get his life squared away."[10]

A few years later, Reissfelder finally got that car.

* * * *

George Reissfelder was a member of Merlino's crew, and the surveillance logs from the attorney general's drug investigation showed that he was a frequent visitor to TRC around the time of the heist. Recall that the FBI informant Richard Chicofsky would later tell his handler, Neil Cronin, that Reissfelder committed the Gardner heist with Lenny

DiMuzio and David Turner. And while Reissfelder closely resembled one of the UNSUBS depicted in the police sketches, without much more to go on, he languished on an ever-growing list of potential suspects.

But all that was about to change.

In 2008, Anthony Amore received a letter from Robert Beauchamp, the other half of the 1974 escape duo that never became known as the infamous "Didn't Come Back from Furlough Gang." Still serving out his murder conviction, Beauchamp was an inmate at MCI-Norfolk, the state's largest medium-security facility. He claimed that he and Reissfelder were once lovers and that Reissfelder even admitted to him that he pulled off the Gardner heist. After Beauchamp was finally apprehended and transferred back to Massachusetts in 1987, the two men were in regular contact. Beauchamp claimed that between 1987 and 1991 George frequently visited him in prison. He also claimed to have knowledge of an address in Maine where Reissfelder may have hidden the art. And speaking of Maine, when Anthony first spoke with Beauchamp, he asked Anthony to research information about a murder victim named "Marks."

When Anthony and I interviewed Beauchamp in 2009, he told us that shortly after the heist, "George told me he hit the jackpot." Beauchamp claimed that Reissfelder confided that the Gardner artwork was stashed "in the wall of a house up in Maine."

Jailhouse tips are nothing new, and just about every inmate tries to leverage some kind of information—real or imagined—to get a break on their sentence. But the new information about Reissfelder was interesting and worth a second look. I reviewed Reissfelder's criminal history, since past brushes with the law can often yield clues about illegal proclivities. His record showed a drunk driving arrest in Boston back in November 1989, just four months before the heist. A simple arrest for OUI.

What was he driving?

I asked one of the Boston detectives on my squad to pull a copy of the archived arrest report, known as a 1-1, and there it was, in that inimitable, blotchy microfiche black and white; arguably one of the biggest clues yet in the investigation:

When George Reissfelder was arrested four months before the Gardner Museum heist, he was driving a red 1988 Dodge Daytona.

According to those teenaged witnesses on Palace Road, this was the exact vehicle used in the robbery. The arrest report listed a New Hampshire license plate on the vehicle, and it turns out that Reissfelder had registered his Daytona up in the Granite State, which is why this crucial clue had been missed by my predecessors. I began researching the vehicle, attempting to track it down.

And then things got really strange.

According to Massachusetts motor vehicle documents, Reissfelder coincidentally sold that Daytona six days *before* the heist at a used car lot in Springfield, about two hours west of Boston. Yet the new owner didn't register the vehicle until nine days *after* the heist. Who waits two weeks to register a car? It seems likely that Reissfelder and his partner hadn't planned on being seen by those teenagers outside the museum, and after they got made, Reissfelder had to get rid of his beloved Daytona, even though it was only two years old. But since he'd already been seen behind the wheel, it wouldn't do him any good to sell the car after the heist; no, George needed to find a used car dealer who could predate a bill of sale.

This might explain the fifteen-day gap between the vehicle's date of sale and its eventual registration. I suggest that the Daytona wasn't really sold until the end of March, after the heist, and the need for an accommodating used car dealer might explain why Reissfelder had to make the long drive out to Springfield to sell his car. (In case you're wondering, there are plenty of used car lots in Boston.)

One of the most vexing mysteries about the subject's vehicle was its obvious color discrepancy. Two of the teenaged witnesses got a really good look at the car as it was parked on Palace Road that night, and they both accurately described it as a Dodge Daytona. In fact, one witness was positive that it was a Daytona because a recently released movie featured a similar vehicle.* And while the witnesses nailed the hard part and accurately described the make, model, and year range, they differed wildly on the easy part; that is, the color. One witness claimed it was gray while the other was certain it was red.

For years, this inconsistency was enigmatic, and my investigation into the provenance of the Daytona only furthered the mystery. Reissfelder's arrest report from November 1989 listed his Daytona as red, as did the Massachusetts sales document, known as an RMV-1, which was prepared when he sold the car. But when the vehicle was finally registered two weeks later, it was titled as gray.

The riddle was finally solved by Reissfelder's sister-in-law, Donna, when she told me that George's beloved Daytona was two-toned, red *and* gray. It turns out that in 1988, Dodge offered the Daytona in a two-toned configuration, red over gray.

In 2008, Reissfelder's brother, Richard, an upstanding citizen with a distinguished thirty-two-year career in the Army, visited Anthony at the museum. Richard was adamant that his brother was not involved in the heist and wanted to clear his name.[11] Anthony asked Richard to take a look at images of *all* thirteen stolen pieces, not just ones that were typically publicized in the media, pieces like *The Storm* and the finial.

As Richard perused the images, categorically dismissing each one, his head dropped when he finally came upon the Manet. As Anthony described it, Richard "jumped in his chair and tears formed in his eyes" when he saw *Chez Tortoni*. "My brother had that painting," Richard admitted to Anthony, albeit grudgingly. He advised that six weeks after the heist, Richard saw *Chez Tortoni* in Reissfelder's Quincy apartment. "I know I saw it in his possession," Richard claimed. "I'm

* *My Blue Heaven*, starring Steve Martin and Rick Moranis and released in 1990, features a 1985 Dodge Daytona. Ironically, or perhaps fittingly, in the movie Martin plays an Italian mobster being hounded by a persistent FBI agent.

really disappointed to have to admit I saw that painting."[12] In fact, Richard and Donna helped Reissfelder hang the piece over his bed. Donna recalled the piece specifically and advised me that as they were hanging it, Reissfelder was jumping up and down on the bed and joking around. She said it was the last time she saw her brother-in-law happy. Donna advised that when she was in his apartment, she saw what looked like another painting leaning against a dresser. The piece was wrapped up, so she could only describe its size:

Donna estimated that it was "about 2½ feet tall and almost square but not quite."

The Concert is 28½" x 25½".

About 2½ feet tall and almost square but not quite.

Armed with this new evidence, Anthony showed Rick Abath's partner, Randy, photographs of Reissfelder. Randy gave a "thumbs-up" and stated that Reissfelder's photos "come the closest, maybe even right on, for the shorter thief."[13]

Reissfelder was last seen on March 9, 1991, when he was surveilled by the drug cops at TRC. Two days later, exactly one week shy of the first anniversary of the heist, Merlino called the Quincy Fire Department to report that he hadn't heard from George all day and was concerned for his chum's well-being (perhaps Merlino's biggest crime was that he cared too much). According to a Quincy Police report, when first responders arrived at Reissfelder's Brooks Avenue apartment, there were two subjects already there: "Carmello Merlino... owner of TRC Auto Electric" and "Dick Joyce of Quincy...a friend."[14] Lacking other means of entry, fire department personnel forced their way into the apartment through the kitchen door and found Reissfelder dead on the floor of his bedroom, clad in a pair of dungarees, a shirt, and socks. Officers found a crack pipe, a rolled-up dollar bill, and a "glassine bag of white powder" on the kitchen countertop, as well as three handguns in the bedroom. As for the nature or cause of death, the responding Quincy police officer scribbled a question: *"drug overdose?"*

The Norfolk County Medical Examiner's Office ruled that the cause of death was an "acute overdose from cocaine." While Richard acknowledged that George used drugs, he stated that his brother was scared to death of needles, lending credence to his firm belief that Reissfelder was murdered with a "hot shot"; that is, poisoned with an intentional drug overdose.

It's noteworthy that after the cops and firefighters left with Reissfelder's body, Merlino had unsupervised access inside his apartment. A source later advised me that it was during this time when Merlino removed two Gardner Museum paintings from Reissfelder's apartment and moved them up to Bobby Guarente's house in Maine.

Richard claims that after Reissfelder's death, *Chez Tortoni* "was gone when I went to the apartment." He provided a Boston reporter with his own opinions about what happened to the Manet:

"I think that the day he died, the art was taken by those bums who killed him."[15]

* * * *

Lenny DiMuzio was a Merlino associate who was also hanging around TRC at the time of the heist. Along with Reissfelder, Fat Richie believed that DiMuzio may have been one of the participants in the heist, and while one could argue that DiMuzio closely resembled one of the UNSUBS in the police sketches, that proves little.

DiMuzio was a Vietnam veteran from Rockland, a blue-collar town about thirty minutes south of the city. He was last seen by his sister on March 29, 1991, less than three weeks after Reissfelder's death, and his wife officially reported him missing two days later. On June 11, 1991, Boston Police found DiMuzio's decomposing and bullet-riddled body in the trunk of his Chevy Impala in East Boston, tucked under a bridge overpass near the airport.[16]

In March 2015, a number of news agencies reported that the FBI had officially announced that the Gardner Museum heist had been committed by George Reissfelder and Lenny DiMuzio, although I was never quite sure how they got this information.[17]

* * * *

Jimmy Marks was a bartender in Lynn, a small city located just north of Boston that's (somewhat) affectionately referred to as the City of Sin, owing to its historical reputation for high crime and vice.[*] Marks was a small-time hustler who worked in the local drug trade and dabbled in the strip club business. In October 1961, when Marks was twenty-two, he was arrested for theft and malicious damage of a hotel room, and within a few years, he'd moved on to bank robbery. (Considering the amount of cash that was stolen from Boston banks back in the day, it's a wonder why local crooks did anything else.)[18] When he wasn't tending bar, Marks loved to gamble, and he even owned a stake in a racehorse. He was very close with Merlino associate Bobby Guarente and his wife, Elene, and he used to help care for her horse when he stayed with the Guarentes at their remote farmhouse up in Madison, Maine.

In 2010, Anthony and I spoke with a woman in Lynn who once dated Jimmy Marks.[**] She told us that a few months after the heist, Marks boasted to her that he had two of the stolen Gardner Museum paintings, and as she was sitting in Marks's third-floor apartment discussing the artwork, he gestured in a way that led her to infer that the paintings were hidden above them in the attic. In the tumultuous year following the Gardner heist, this lack of discretion could have deadly consequences; as Anthony pointed out to a local news reporter, "it's a bad move to be talking out of school about the Gardner artwork in early 1991."[19]

---

* Contrast this dubious moniker with Plymouth's, located about fifty miles down the coast, which coined the nickname *America's Hometown*. Plymouth proudly sports the town's nickname on their police cruisers; Lynn does not.

** She wishes to remain anonymous.

On the night of February 20, 1991, Jimmy Marks became the City of Sin's sixth homicide victim. Marks had just returned from Guarente's place in Maine, and as he stood on the front porch of his Broad Street triple-decker, fishing his house keys out of his pocket, he was shot twice in the back of the head with a double-barrel sawed-off shotgun. Witnesses observed a lone gunman, dressed in dark clothing, make his escape over a nearby fence.[20] Lynn cops responded to the scene and found Marks lying face down in a pool of blood, right next to the two suitcases he'd brought back from his trip to Maine. Homicide detectives noted that the light bulb on the front porch had been unscrewed, leading them to describe the murder as a "classic mob-style hit."[21]

At the time, Lynn's police chief surmised that there was very little to go on. However, investigators quickly learned that this wasn't the first time Marks had been targeted: The previous October, a Lynn cop on late-night patrol had observed a suspicious male subject changing clothes in the shadows near Marks's apartment. When the officer stopped to investigate, the subject fled, scaled that same fence, and disappeared into the darkness. He left behind a duffel bag containing two guns, one of which had been equipped with a silencer.[22]

Eleven days after the murder, homicide investigators were following up some leads at a local diner when they observed one of Marks's associates talking with two male subjects. One of them was Guarente, and the other was a Connecticut mobster named Bobby "the Cook" Gentile. The two had arrived at the diner in a vehicle registered under Gentile's alias, Bob Gino. Although there wasn't much to this interaction, detectives still made a written note of their observations in the case file.

* * * *

In the year following the Gardner Museum robbery, three subjects with connections to the heist had been brutally murdered, and one died under very suspicious circumstances. It seemed that being associated with the heist could be hazardous to your health. And it would be reasonable to conclude that these violent murders could have had a chilling effect on anyone who harbored aspirations to provide information about the stolen artwork.

1991 was certainly a busy year for the Gardner.

CHAPTER 14

Bob's Your Uncle

For the moon never beams, without bringing me dreams
Of the beautiful Annabel Lee;
And the stars never rise, but I feel the bright eyes
Of the beautiful Annabel Lee;
And so, all the night-tide, I lie down by the side
Of my darling—my darling—my life and my bride,
In her sepulchre there by the sea—
In her tomb by the sounding sea.

—EDGAR ALLAN POE, *Annabel Lee*

Always a day late and a dollar short. We belatedly came upon solid information that seemed to link Merlino (dead), Guarente (dead), Reissfelder (dead), DiMuzio (dead), and Donati (dead) to the Gardner heist. If you think of a cold-case investigation like a giant hedge maze, then we were running out of viable paths that didn't lead straight to a wall of junipers.

But then in September 2009, a new path revealed itself.

I was sitting at my desk when my supervisor, Randy Jarvis, charged out of his office and dropped a tip sheet, known as an FD-71, onto my lap. "Hey, this just came in," he advised. Prior to the Bureau, Randy had been an officer in the US Army, stationed in Panama, and before that, a defensive end in college. He was still solidly built, with broad shoulders and a finely cropped head of hair. Between his military bearing and athletic prowess, Randy was in a perpetual state of kinetic motion, quivering like the filament in a light bulb just seconds before its prodigal energy consumption caused it to explode. Whether it was a felony car stop or certifying time cards, Randy did everything with a boundless aggression that made the rest of us feel like we were somehow lagging behind.

This was a routine 71, and most supervisors would treat a routine 71 as, well, routine. It would make its way through the eternal stack of papers that rose out of a supervisor's inbox like well-yeasted dough. The bottom corner would be dog-eared, initials would be scratched in red pencil, and eventually it would be forwarded along to the squad secretary; days later, the 71 would finally make its way into my mail slot. But that wasn't how Randy did things, which is why he bucked convention and made the short walk out into the squad area to personally deliver that 71.

Information contained on a 71 is sparse by design, a bare-bones recitation of facts, delivered succinctly and without undue adornment. This complaint was no exception, and the narrative briefly detailed a call from the complainant, referred to as the –C-, who claimed that her uncle once possessed the stolen Gardner artwork. It concluded with "NFI," the ubiquitous Bureau shorthand for "no further information." The –C-'s name was Christina Conlon,* and she lived in Maine.

Conlon. Didn't ring a bell.

I called the number and introduced myself to Christina.[1] During our conversation, she told me that she had just watched a news story about the Gardner heist. As we spoke, I scribbled down a few notes, probably a bit distracted as I scrolled through emails. According to

* Last name changed.

Christina, after the Gardner story aired, she told her husband that the paintings had been missing long enough. "Besides," she told him, "everyone's dead." And so the next day, she called the FBI.

It was her desultory manner that I found so intriguing; a simple recitation of facts that precipitated her call, delivered in a rote, take-it-or-leave-it style. I still wasn't fully convinced, owing to her unrecognized surname, but her tone made me curious enough to know more. When she told me that her uncle had at least three or four of the stolen Gardner pieces at his house up in Maine, and that she had personally seen them, I asked for her uncle's name.

"Bobby Guarente."

I stopped scrolling through emails. Christina had my full attention.

* * * *

Christina Conlon grew up in Maverick Gardens, a public housing project in East Boston, historically one of the tougher neighborhoods in the city. The projects embodied the failed super-block designs of the postwar construction boom, with a seemingly random assortment of three-story brick barracks scattered like LEGOs in a haphazard configuration that interrupted the natural flow of the neighborhood's streets and sidewalks. For Christina, life at Maverick Gardens was a sink-or-swim mentality, both literally and figuratively. She learned to swim at a young age, seconds after her older brothers first tossed her off the dock into Boston Harbor, directly under the flight path into Logan Airport. At low tide, Christina and her siblings would dodge jellyfish as they swam out amidst the rotting husks of dock pilings and scattered cobblestones of Belgium granite, the remnants of the city's seafaring past. The blocks were used as ballast on clipper ships that once plied their way across the Atlantic; once they reached Boston, the blocks were jettisoned overboard as the ships' holds were replaced with more profitable cargoes of cod, timber, and rum.

When Christina was eight, her mother committed suicide. With her father still in prison, the task of raising Christina and her siblings fell to their Uncle Bob, who had just finished a seventeen-year prison sentence for bank robbery. "We didn't have a lot to do with my uncle," she said. "We knew him, of course, he was our uncle, and he would swoop in and drop off things." Christina is charitable when she talks about her mother's suicide. "I don't understand why she killed herself," she says, "but I know that it was difficult trying to do the right thing with all of these kids." Her father's death garners less sympathy. "My father was such a womanizer, you know, he died on my sixteenth birthday, by the way. That little shit couldn't wait until the next day, you know?" she hissed. "He had to stick it to me one more time."

Although an ex-con, somehow the corpulent Guarente managed to receive full custody of the kids, and the adoption garnered a houseful of cousins for his own daughter, Jeanine. After a brief stint in the affluent Boston suburb of Winchester, the whole gang moved up to an isolated farmhouse in Madison, Maine. If you map the drive, it's about three hours. But for Christina and her siblings, that farmhouse was about a million miles away from Maverick Gardens. And despite the hardships of growing up poor in an East Boston housing project, life with Uncle Bob was far worse. "He just did not like me, and I don't know why," she says. According to Christina, her uncle "wanted to be right, wanted to be in control, wanted to be mean." Her brother thinks that perhaps Guarente's enmity was directed toward Christina because she reminded him so much of his late sister, Christina's mom.

She wasn't the only one to incur the wrath of Guarente; he was physically and verbally abusive to his wife, Elene. When Christina was thirteen, she interrupted one particularly brutal incident of spousal abuse by jumping on Guarente's back. In response, he swung around and stuffed a gun in Christina's mouth before throwing her down a flight of stairs. After this incident, Aunt Elene fled for Massachusetts—albeit briefly—and took Christina with her. Although the two weren't particularly close, Christina believed that Elene "felt bad for me and would go to bat for me sometimes when it was unfair." Like some Downeast version of *Thelma & Louise*, they put that Madison farmhouse in the rearview mirror of a battered Oldsmobile 88 and headed south. Christina started her freshman year in Revere and almost made it to tenth grade before being summoned back to Maine by Uncle Bobby. I asked Christina why Guarente made her return to Maine, considering the fact that he didn't seem to like her very much. "He wanted to put it out that he was like the savior, you know, like I did this for my sister and the kids."

Christina related an incident that occurred after she returned to Maine: As she was getting off the school bus one day, she saw her uncle lying face down in the driveway as a swarm of DEA agents searched their yard. "They were looking for guns, digging on the property. Imagine coming off the bus? I was so embarrassed. I mean, I was an athlete. I was a good kid," she said. "This was my uncle."

"I knew very early on that I didn't want any part of the crazy," Christina said. Her sister, on the other hand, simply idolized Uncle Bob. "You know, my sister and Jeanine, they kind of went around like little Mafia princesses," she said, referring to Guarente's daughter. Christina was not impressed with mob life and had no aspirations to be a gangster's moll. After she had her first daughter at the age of twenty-one, she moved back to the farmhouse, but she knew it would be a short stay. "I was tiny, I was small, but I just knew that I would have the last laugh," she said. "I built my first house at twenty-four; that was going to be the big F-U. I was going to do good in the world, and I was going to take care of myself and I was going to raise my children differently. And all those things happened," she said triumphantly, "so that was it for me."

I'm sitting across from Christina, an attractive woman of fifty with wire-framed glasses and a tattoo on her forearm that celebrates her miniature dachshund, Oliver (complete with paw print). Although I will have to take her word for it, she also has "Annabel Lee and the Kingdom by the Sea" tattooed on her shoulder. This one is for her daughter, who could recite the entire poem from memory by the age of five. Christina now owns a successful health-care consulting business and has raised three children well. As she talks about Madison, my thoughts are overshadowed by a visual; it's a visual of Marilyn, the attractive Munster family cousin who lived blissfully unaffected in a creepy mansion filled with caricatures of monsters. The Guarentes truly were *The Munsters,* except without the pratfalls and punch lines.

Christina told me that Guarente's friends were always coming up to Maine to visit for a day or two. Their presence added to an already frenetic household, with children of varying degrees of relativity mingling with some of Boston's most notorious gangsters, many of whom assumed an avuncular familiarity with Christina. There was Carmello Merlino, known to her as "Uncle Mello," and Bobby Donati, known as "Uncle Bozo."

"Uncle Bozo?" I asked.

"Because of his hair," Christina explained. "He was bald here and his hair came out like here and here," she added, gesturing to her own pate.

Donati was hands-down her favorite. "He was very fatherly to me, and I probably loved him the most." Despite the harsh conditions that only a Maine winter can bring to bear, Guarente wouldn't buy Christina a warm coat. "Uncle Bob had plenty of money, but he wouldn't buy me one," so Uncle Bozo ended up buying her a winter jacket, much to Guarente's dismay. During Christina's freshman year in Massachusetts, Donati frequently checked in on her, and she began babysitting his young son, Bobby Jr. She also babysat for the notorious Patriarca mob family soldier Vinnie "the Animal" Ferrara, who coincidentally was indicted on racketeering charges the same week as the Gardner heist. It was a good gig, recalled Christina. "I'd babysit for like two hours and get a hundred bucks and New Kids on the Block tickets."

Bobby Luisi was another frequent guest up in Maine. Luisi was a mob boss in Boston and the son of "Bobby the Blade," an infamous Patriarca family enforcer. On November 6, 1995, Luisi's father and brother were executed at the 99 Restaurant in Boston's Charlestown neighborhood, an event that came to be known as the Four on the Floor Massacre.

Christina recalled that Jimmy Marks was always at the Maine farmhouse and even lived with the family for a period of time. "And then you have 'Bobby the Cook,' who was 'Bobby from Connecticut,'" recalled Christina. She told me that Bobby the Cook and Guarente had been good friends for many years; he used to call Guarente "all the time" and frequently visited the Maine farmhouse. She remembered him as "a really, really good cook. He'd make the Sunday gravy; we'd help him. He was a sweet man."

Bobby Guarente. Bobby Luisi. Bobby the Cook. Bobby Donati—that Madison farmhouse was a veritable cavalcade of people named Bobby.

David Turner was always there, too, visiting his de facto father. Turner was initially introduced to Guarente through Merlino, and the two became very close; so close, in fact, that Christina referred to Turner as her uncle's "pseudo-son." He popped up in their lives very quickly, and while he may have been tight with Guarente, Christina and her siblings never took to him. "Yeah. he's there, but it was weird. My brother never gave a shit about him, you know what I mean? I purposely didn't get close. Was he at my house a lot? Yes. Did I see him all the time? Yeah. But it was weird."

Christina related a scene that unfolded when Hurricane Gloria struck New England back in September 1985. I remember Gloria well; as a newly minted freshman at Boston University, we were all instructed to place masking tape X's on the windows of our dorm rooms.* While the hurricane raged outside, we huddled in our rooms, watching the ceiling lights flicker and drinking an illicit concoction of cheap rum and fruit juice that only vaguely resembled Gloria's namesake drink. Christina's recollections of that storm, which was spent with a dysfunctional menagerie of Boston mobsters riding it out up in

* While I can't speak to its efficacy in protecting us against the elements, the masking tape did make our dormitory look like a giant, one-sided game of tic-tac-toe.

Maine, are a bit more surreal: "I remember Gloria," she said, "Hurricane Gloria. We had a ton of them up there, because they were, you know, running away from the hurricane." As a ten-year-old Christina looked on, an all-pro team of New England mobsters played touch football in the rain-drenched yard. "They also had races down the driveway. It was crazy," she recalled. "They would fight over who was faster. Those fatties would be running down a dirt driveway while it's pouring rain. I can't make it up."

Christina spoke of Uncle Bob and his crew of misfits: "I mean, you're talking about I think the most unintelligent mobsters on the planet. I never understood like, why Uncle Bob didn't have more money," she said. "When he had money, he really had it. But he was broke most of his life."

When Donati was murdered in September 1991, Christina was the first one in the family to hear about it. "I grew up with him my whole life; he was even in my life when my mother was alive." She received a call from a friend who lived on Donati's street in Revere, who told Christina that her uncle was dead. "She didn't know he wasn't my blood uncle. You know how it is with Italians." Donati had already been missing for a couple of days, and his son, little Bobby, had been calling up to Maine, looking for his father. When Christina got the call, the whole family was out shopping, and when Guarente came home, she told him that "they found Uncle Bozo in his car, and he's dead."

As I listened to Christina speak about Donati, I was humbled to hear her speak of him from such a unique perspective, since I'd seen him only in the context of a career hoodlum. But here was Christina speaking fondly of Uncle Bozo, with his bedraggled, clownish tonsure, buying this neglected ragamuffin a warm coat to fend off the brutal Maine winters.

A year or so after the Gardner heist occurred, Christina overheard hushed conversations in the Guarente household about the stolen paintings, but this was never discussed outside the family. "First round,

I think, was when Mello was in jail, and they wanted to use something to get him out; like they wanted to do a trade." This would've been 1992, and the concept of a trade made sense, since Merlino and Guarente were close; so close, in fact, that Merlino gave Elene away at their wedding. And while those initial conversations centered specifically on the Gardner paintings, Christina thinks that later on they may have been discussing an exchange using other stolen artwork. Christina recalled that in 1996, however, right around her twenty-first birthday, discussions about the stolen Gardner artwork became more frequent and profound, and they coincided with regular visits to the Maine farmhouse from the likes of Bobby the Cook.

But when Turner was arrested in 1999, conversations about the Gardner paintings ramped up considerably. "After David got locked up was when the talks about the paintings really started happening, because Uncle Bob loved him so much." Christina recalled that Guarente, Bobby Luisi, and Bobby the Cook would sit around the kitchen table in the farmhouse, discussing plans to barter the Gardner artwork for Turner's freedom, as well as freedom for her cousin, Stephen Rossetti.

"They said that they would want a trade and they said it worked for Mello, so I assumed that they had done this before. That's how my Uncle Mello got out of jail," she added, most likely referring to Merlino's offer of the stolen Longfellow Museum artwork.

"I remember them saying that that's what they were going to do for David," recalled Christina. "And Uncle Bobby and the Cook were talking. They were trying to broker deals. I could hear, but again, I didn't stay very long in there."

When Christina and I first spoke back in 2009, she told me that the paintings had been secreted in a cubby located on the second floor of the farmhouse, above the stairway. I asked her about this recently, and she recalled that "on the second floor, you had this little area, and underneath this area was this closet. And that's where I remember the paintings. I remember them pulling the paintings out of that area."

Christina recalled they were lying flat in this cubby on the slanted floor, which formed the ceiling of the stairway that led downstairs. "The only time I ever saw them was in that cubby," she recalled.

When I asked her how she found the hide, Christina said that at the time, Guarente and Elene were traveling frequently to Florida and leaving the kids home alone. Without much else to do, they passed the time by exploring the expansive farmhouse.

"You were just poking around and peeking?" I asked.

"We all did. We were just kids."

"How many paintings were there?"

Christina closed her eyes and tried to visualize what she saw in that slanted cubby. "I would say maybe four? I just remember there were three this way," she said as she made three diagonal slashes with her hand, "and one this way," as she made an inverse slash.

Although she believed that there were at least four pieces, she could only recall one.

"The only painting I ever remember seeing is the ship. I called it 'the ship.' That's what I called it my whole life, 'the ship.'"

"The ship?" I asked. "That was definitely *The Storm*?"

"Yeah, it was a ship on waves, you know?"

I told her that *The Storm* was Rembrandt's only seascape. "Did you know he painted himself in it?" I asked.

"No," she replied, "and I wouldn't have known that, you know what I mean? Because I didn't know how important they were, to be quite honest."

"It's big, right?" I asked.

"Oh, yeah, like this," she said as she set down her coffee cup and stood up to gesticulate. She stretched her petite arms out wide; first left and right, and then up and down.

That was the one.

As she sat back down and picked up her coffee, Christina went on to describe the piece. "Because I was so young, it was the ship, and you know, my friends watched the Netflix documentary, and they were calling me and they were like, 'Remember that painting that was hanging in your living room?'" She imitated her friends with an exaggerated singsong inflection. "You'd think I would remember that ship being hung in the living room? I just know that's the one I saw, because I know it was 'the ship.'"

Although Christina was confident that Guarente had a number of the Gardner pieces, she was more circumspect when she talked about the heist from whence they came. "The only thing I can't get over is that I can't imagine Uncle Bob being smart enough to pull it off, or Dave or any of them. So that's the only reason why I'm just like, would my uncle try to take credit for something he didn't do? And then store them for someone?"

In 2004, when Guarente's health was failing, it was Christina who cared for him. "I did my due diligence when he was sick, I made all the decisions at the hospital. I made sure he got all the care that he needed." Even though Guarente had treated her so poorly over the years, Christina didn't want to bear any guilt with his passing. "If I didn't do everything that I knew I was capable of doing to help during that time, I didn't know if I would feel guilty, because I was Uncle Bob's least favored child."

I asked Christina what made her decide to contact the FBI back in 2009, adding that I couldn't believe she had actually made the call.

Her face lit up and she smiled warmly. "I couldn't believe I was going to do it either!"

"So why did you call?"

"Okay, so I love art and poetry, and I just thought enough people had died that I knew it would be amazing if they were returned, right? Because her endowment was that nothing could be changed. And wouldn't it be so beautiful to have them back?"

"And you never spoke to anyone else about seeing *The Storm*?"

"I've never talked to anybody except you," she said. "I've never answered another call."

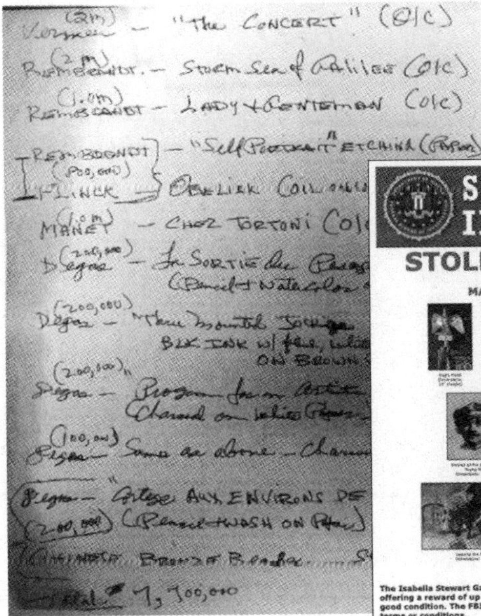

List of stolen artwork found in Bobby Gentile's house. Courtesy of FBI Boston.

FBI missing art poster. Courtesy of FBI Boston.

SEEKING INFORMATION

STOLEN MUSEUM ARTWORK

ISABELLA STEWART GARDNER MUSEUM

MARCH 18, 1990 BOSTON, MASSACHUSETTS

REWARD

The Isabella Stewart Gardner Museum of Boston, Massachusetts, a non-governmental organization, is offering a reward of up to $10 million for information leading to the safe return of the stolen artwork in good condition. The FBI has no involvement in the administration of this reward or any of its governing terms or conditions.

DETAILS

On March 18, 1990, 13 works of art were stolen from the Isabella Stewart Gardner Museum in Boston, Massachusetts. The artwork is valued at more than $500 million, making this the world's largest property crime. Investigation by the FBI has determined that the 13 works of art were separated following the robbery and their location could be anywhere worldwide. Several pieces are believed to have moved along the Eastern seaboard, through the Mid-Atlantic states down south. The FBI is seeking the public's assistance in recovering the stolen artwork.

If you have any information concerning this case, please contact the FBI's Toll-Free tipline at 1-800-CALL-FBI (1-800-225-5324). You may also contact your local FBI office, the nearest American Embassy or Consulate, or you can submit a tip online at tips.fbi.gov.

Field Office: Boston

www.fbi.gov

The infamous service door. Courtesy of FBI Boston.

Palace Road next to the Gardner Museum. Courtesy of FBI Boston.

Above: *The Dutch room. Courtesy of ISGM.*
Left: *Frames on the floor. Courtesy of ISGM.*

Isabella Gardner. Courtesy of ISGM.

FBI press conference briefing. Courtesy of Getty Images.

Carmello Merlino. Courtesy of FBI Boston.

Lenny DiMuzio. Courtesy of FBI Boston.

George Reissfelder. Courtesy of Getty Images.

Bobby Donati. Courtesy of FBI Boston.

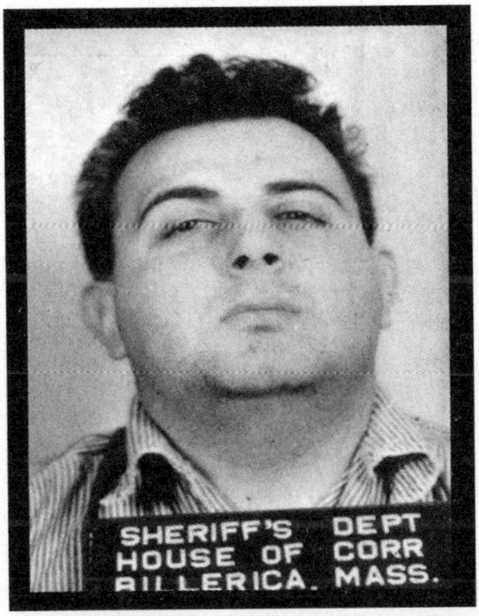

Bobby Guarente.
Courtesy of FBI Boston.

Robert Gentile. Courtesy of The Hartford Courant.

CHAPTER 15

"Almost Square but Not Quite"

Lacey computed that The Concert *was twenty-eight inches by twenty-five inches, and she added three inches all around to allow for the frame and another inch for packaging. Yes, the package was the same size as the wrapped, stolen Vermeer. She was convinced that this was the missing painting.*

—STEVE MARTIN, *An Object of Beauty*

It's February 2010, and Anthony and I are making the long drive to Maine. My time in the Bureau is inversely proportional to the age of my Bucar, and by this point in my career, I'm driving a 2009 Ford Taurus. As we continue to travel north, the deep-blue hood reflects the endless sweep of Maine treetops, simultaneously monotonous and beautiful. We are heading out to Guarente's farmhouse, and in anticipation of our trip, two agents from the Portland Resident Agency have already met with his widow, Elene. I've asked them not to explain why the FBI wanted her consent to search the old farmhouse in Madison; I reasoned that since Guarente had been involved in a myriad of illicit activities when he was still alive, perhaps Elene wouldn't know the reason for today's request. I certainly didn't want to forewarn her that we were traveling to Maine in support of the Gardner investigation.

Elene has already provided the Portland agents with a set of house keys, as well as her signature on the FBI's standard Consent to Search form. Anthony and I meet up with the agents at a Dunkin' Donuts parking lot, where they surrender the keys and the consent form; the latter will go in the case file and the former will soon slide into the lock at 957 Lakewood Road.

At the time of our visit, Guarente's house sits abandoned. It's a forlorn and dilapidated building parked just off Route 201, a two-lane thread of highway that slices through a vast expanse of scrubland and continues all the way to the Canadian border. In fact, the farmhouse is actually closer to Quebec City than Dorchester, and for a group who fancied themselves as big-time gangsters, I can only wonder what Merlino's crew was doing way out in the backwoods of Maine. Christina put it succinctly: "I mean, with their fur coats, you would think they were like Joe Pesci in *Casino*." Yet here they were, scheming and plotting mobster scores in this desolate homestead so very far from Boston.

As I wheel the Bucar into a makeshift driveway, the muffled crunch of gravel further muffled under a thick blanket of weeds, it's hard to stifle a feeling of—dare I say it?—optimism. We're certainly not expecting to find the paintings today, but it seems like we may finally be on the right track. The information from Christina dovetailed with what I already knew about Merlino and his crew, and it's finally provided us with a direction in which to travel. We have, as the tiny Paul Williams once crooned, set a course for adventure.[1]

Guarente's house is white and configured in a traditional cape design, with a front door bracketed by two pairs of casement windows. A brick fireplace is centered on the peak, and a standing-seam roof cascades down to the eaves. We approach the side door, with its seemingly infinite layers of paint split and peeling like the craquelure of an old Vermeer. I see that as a good sign.

I slip the key into the lockset and the door swings opens silently (in the movies, it would've opened with a creak). I have a confession: I love poking around abandoned old houses. The more abandoned, the better. As long as the floor doesn't collapse. I'm fascinated by the decay and degradation as a once tidy home is overwhelmed by the inexorable encroachment of the elements. As the lead investigator on a missing artwork case, it's an avocation that has served me well.

We step inside and the smell is cold and damp, much chillier than the temperature outside. An upholstered couch, mottled with black mold, rests haphazardly on an expanse of pea-green carpet that's matted down with plaster dust and dirt; wide-plank pine floors peek through its threadbare patches. The walls are covered with mottled wallpaper that's water-stained the color of coffee and sloughing off the cracked plaster walls in curling strips of Fruit Stripe gum. The ceiling bows down in spots, reducing the already low headroom as we make our way to the staircase.

Anthony and I climb to the second floor, twisting around to a landing exactly as it was described to me by Christina. To the left I see the door to her bedroom, where a wretched little girl of thirteen once hatched unrealized escape plans. Set into the wall to my right is a small door, about five feet by three, and behind it is a small closet that stretches all the way to the exterior wall. Inside, the right-hand wall is constructed of wide planks that run horizontally. The bottom plank, about ten inches wide, had been removed and lies flat on the floor; had this plank still been secured in place, then the area behind the wall would've been completely hidden.

I get down on hands and knees and peer into the gap, my flashlight illuminating the expanse. I'm looking into the guts of the house, and like an upper GI tract, it's a part only seen by specialists. Horizontal strips of wood lathe alternate with layers of horsehair plaster. Before the advent of drywall, this was the ubiquitous building method; plaster would be slathered onto the lathe strips, oozing into the gaps and hardening to form a bulging "key" that kept the walls from coming down.

In preparation for my upcoming spelunking journey, I strip off my firearm, handcuffs, extra magazine, badge, and cell phone holster, decreasing my girth substantially. I squirm into this cavity, barely, grateful to have Anthony with me in the all-too-possible event that I get stuck. I make it safely through.

I crawl through the space, my flashlight beam playing erratically on the walls and floor. Amidst the beams and the joists and the studs, I spy the slanted cubby described to me by Christina. I crouch low and make my way over to this angled floor, in reality, the ceiling of the stairway Anthony and I recently ascended. Its dimensions mirror those of the stairway below, about four feet wide and three times as long. Amidst all of the antique plaster, however, I find drywall. The incongruity of an anachronistic building material in this antique chamber is striking, like burrowing into King Tut's burial chamber and finding a flat-screen television mounted on the wall. One large sheet has been affixed to the floor joists, and a second, narrower sheet has been affixed along the bottom edge of the first. The resultant ninety-degree angle forms a perfect easel.

And resting on this easel? No, not *The Storm*. (How cool would that have been?) Instead, it's one of those vintage electric football games, the kind with the vibrating tabletop that made the players move about haphazardly on a tin playing field (not quite Madden 2025, but still quite entertaining for the 1970s). While the game itself isn't important, its size is, since it provides some perspective regarding the spaciousness of that hide.

There was more than sufficient space in this cubby to store *The Storm*.

After extricating myself from the claustrophobic space, I rearm myself and we secure the house. Next on the agenda is the short drive into town in order to return the house keys to Elene. Perhaps we can have a quick chat about her now suddenly extremely fascinating deceased husband. As we pull out onto Route 201, I can't help but think about Robert Beauchamp, the inmate who claimed that George

Reissfelder once confided in him that the Gardner artwork had been "stashed in the wall of a house up in Maine."

* * * *

Twenty minutes later, we pull into the parking lot of the Pinewood Apartments in downtown Madison, a cloistered nest of affordable housing units carved out of a dense carpet of forest. The development is formed by a series of long, offset one-story buildings scattered about the landscape with an apparent randomness that was probably calculated. The units are positioned around a central parking lot and joined together by a fine network of sidewalks. Projects like these are the same everywhere, and the only difference between this one and its counterparts sprinkled across the country is the substitution of pine trees for palm trees, or southern magnolias, or cacti.

Our visit with Elene is an impromptu one, precipitated by my recent phone call with Christina. Prior to today, Elene has never spoken with anyone from the FBI or the Gardner Museum. We are hitting her cold, so to speak.

The notional reason for our visit is to return her house keys, and when she opens the door, I introduce myself and present my creds. Elene is cordial, if a bit guarded. She wears a short crop of graying hair that sits over a craggy and deeply creased face, the lines mapping out a difficult life of alternating isolation and abuse. By design, I do not introduce Anthony. Not yet. He stands next to me, reticent, and I'm hoping that Elene believes him to be another agent.

I return the jangle of keys and thank her for allowing us to search the old farmhouse. Almost as an afterthought, I ask if we can chat briefly. Elene opens the door expansively and invites us inside. The air is thick with a pall of cigarette smoke, and a faint whiff of fried food undercuts the cloying stench of tobacco. Over my career, it is a smell to which I've become well acquainted, that of deep-fried cigarettes. Anthony and I make our way across a tract of commercial-grade linoleum and take a seat on the oversized couch that dominates the room.

Elene mutes the television, leaving us with the silent-movie version of some daytime judge show, and then takes a seat on the equally oversized recliner to my right.

We get comfortable, which is surprisingly difficult to accomplish on a sofa as expansive as this one. From years of experience conducting interviews on similarly proportioned furniture, I've learned to perch on the leading edge of the couch. I know that were I to sit back and really get settled, I would sink comically into these marshmallow-like cushions like a crouton in a bowl of chowder.

And now, finally, I introduce Elene to Anthony Amore, the director of security for the Isabella Stewart Gardner Museum in Boston, Massachusetts. The effect is immediate, and Elene's expression betrays her obvious discomfort, since she's now discerned the reason for our visit. This is the first time that the Gardner Museum has been mentioned, and the calculated delay has had its intended effect—if we were playing poker, this is the point where I'd go all in. Anthony hands her his business card as he asks casually, "Have you ever heard of the Gardner Museum?"

Her response is a timid and unconvincing, "No."

"Really?" I counter. I tell her that I find the statement unusual, considering the fact that her husband was once considered a suspect in the robbery. I continue, "He never mentioned anything to you about the stolen artwork?"

At this point, the thin veneer of nonchalance peels off, and Elene reaches for the pack of off-brand cigarettes that rests on the coffee table alongside the remote. A pink disposable lighter clings to the cellophane wrapper like a remora. Throughout my career, I've found that when confronted with difficult situations, people naturally gravitate to their comforting rituals: fiddling with their phone, taking a long, long sip of water, or—as was the case with Elene today—lighting a cigarette.

She begins to cry. Really cry, with real tears, the kind that well up from nowhere and trickle off the precipices of her lower eyelids. With an almost-theatrical shaking of her hand she attempts to light the cigarette that jostles up and down between her puckered lips, endeavoring to marry the flickering flame to the spastic tip.

I ask her why she's crying.

"Because my Bobby had them."

During the pendency of the Gardner investigation, there have been a few occasions that merited a sideways glance. This was one of those occasions. I will not break eye contact with Elene, but when she casts her eyes down to help guide the flame of her lighter to the tip of her quivering cigarette, I steal a brief glance to my left. Anthony matches my widening eyes with his own as his head tilts imperceptibly to the side. I quickly return my gaze to Elene as the cigarette flares to life.

Elene goes on to tell us that her late husband once possessed at least two of the Gardner Museum paintings, and she relates the story with a specificity that seems wholly sincere. When I ask Elene when she saw them, she is able to pin down an accurate time: it was in 2002. She tells us that she is certain of the year because her husband had just been released from federal prison. That day, they traveled down to Bangor because Guarente had to meet up with his federal probation officer. After the meeting, they went straight to the Bangor Public Library, because Guarente wanted to research the value of the paintings. Elene tells us that earlier that same morning, when they were in the driveway of their farmhouse ready to leave for Bangor, Guarente showed her the paintings, which were stacked flat in the generously proportioned trunk of his Oldsmobile 88. Elene was terrified to have them in the car, especially since her Bobby had just gotten out of prison.

When we ask her what they looked like, she can describe only one piece: an oil painting that depicted a seated woman wearing a white bonnet. "It reminded me of *Whistler's Mother*," she says, referring to the iconic piece by James McNeill Whistler. I weighed Elene's information—she had stolen a brief glance at a painting inside the trunk of a car, nearly eight years earlier. All things considered, it was a profound recollection. To conflate a seated woman with another sporting a bonnet seemed not only possible but very credible. In the end, sometimes it's the inaccuracies of recollections that lend them credence.

"How big was it?" Anthony asks. In response, Elene looks over my shoulder and points to a framed poster on the wall, which measures about three feet by two, and says, "About like that." Anthony is scrolling through his phone. "Was it this?" he asks, and shows her an image of *The Concert*.

Elene nods her head and states that there was a "striking resemblance."

As I listen to Elene, I can't help but think of Donna Reissfelder's description of the wrapped painting in her brother-in-law's apartment, the one that went up to Maine along with *Chez Tortoni*:

"About 2½ feet tall and almost square but not quite."

Now the $10 million question. "Elene, what happened to them?" I ask.

Elene tells us that after their visit to Bangor, she and Guarente drove to Portland, where they had dinner with another couple. Halfway through the meal, her husband and his friend left the table and went out to the parking lot while the women stayed behind. They returned a few minutes later and finished an otherwise uneventful meal. Elene tells us that on the drive back to Madison, Guarente said to her, "You can relax now." He answered her quizzical expression by telling her that the paintings were gone; Guarente had transferred them into the trunk of their dinner partner's vehicle when they had excused themselves from the table.

"And who was the man?" I ask Elene.

"Bobby the Cook."

This was now the second time we've heard of Bobby the Cook. When I initially interviewed Christina, she didn't know Bobby's last name, only that he was from Connecticut. Elene doesn't know his last name either but offers that she may have his phone number in an old address book. She extricates herself from the comfy chair and heads into the bedroom. I watch through the doorway as she rifles through a dresser drawer, pulls out a small booklet, and returns to the living room. Anthony and I peer over Elene's shoulder as she begins thumbing through pages, eventually landing on the *B*'s. She scans a few phone numbers and addresses until she finds the name.

"Here it is," she exclaims in triumph as she stabs a name. "Bobby the Cook."

And there it is.

Bobby the Cook. And next to his name is a 203 number, the area code for Connecticut.

CHAPTER 16

Bobby from Connecticut

Behind every great fortune lies a great crime.

—HONORÉ DE BALZAC

That Connecticut phone number came back to Robert Vincent Gentile, better known to his associates as Bobby the Cook. According to his Connecticut driver's license, Gentile was seventy-four and a bit chubby, with a wispy tangle of white hair and a sullen expression. He grew up on Front Street, a community historically known as Hartford's Little Italy. Once the epicenter of Italian heritage in the city, urban redevelopment led to the neighborhood's general decline and caused a mass relocation to nearby Franklin Avenue.

Gentile had a difficult upbringing. He was beaten mercilessly by his father, and at the age of twelve or thirteen, he was hospitalized after his dad hit him over the back with a two-by-four length of lumber. Gentile was raised to be a mason, just like his old man, crafting the swimming pool aprons, walkways, and front steps that graced the wealthier homes of Hartford. As an adult, he still suffered from lingering back problems caused by his father's abuse, exacerbated by the grueling process of lugging heavy stones and working on his hands and knees all day.

By the 1980s, Gentile had retired his brick hammer and trowel and was selling used cars. He owned Gem Auto, a small dealership on Route 5 in South Windsor which boasted a few repair bays and a sparse collection of old clunkers scattered about its concrete pad.

Gentile bought many of those used cars just over the state line in Springfield, a twenty-minute drive from South Windsor. Coincidentally, this was the same city where George Reissfelder once sold his beloved Dodge Daytona. You know, six days before the heist.

Gentile was a mason and a used car salesman.

But mostly, Bobby Gentile was a gangster.[1]

In between laying herringbone walkways and selling Chryslers, Gentile accumulated some impressive criminal charges on his rap sheet, including the possession of illegal firearms, illegal gambling, interstate transportation of stolen property, larceny, and receiving stolen goods. In the 1980s, a rival Connecticut gangster named Frank Zimmitti clubbed Gentile in the face with a pipe and broke his jaw. Gentile vowed revenge, and not long after he got his jaw wired shut, Zimmitti's Cadillac was sprayed with machine gun fire.[2] Zimmitti was out of town that night, and his son was using Dad's car to drive his date to the prom. Thankfully, no one got hurt, owing to Gentile's lousy aim, but the Caddy was totaled.[3] In addition to Gentile's history of criminality, however, was the overarching contention that he was suspected of "continuously associating with members of organized crime from various families for over twenty-five years."[4]

Gentile had strong ties to Boston, and he'd been friends with Bobby Guarente since the 1970s, when they first met at a regional automobile auction near Hartford. In the 1990s, they went to work as bodyguards for Bobby Luisi, staying with him at his condo in the Boston suburb of Woburn, providing protection as he ran his multimillion-dollar cocaine trafficking operation. Back in the late '90s, Luisi felt that the Boston mob was unstable, so he began looking for backing out of state. Rebuffed by the Gambino family in New York, he reached out to Philly mobster Joseph "Skinny Joey" Merlino, who agreed to "make" Luisi and his crew.

And included in that crew of mobster debutantes was Bobby "the Cook" Gentile, of the Hartford Gentiles.

Gentile finally got his button.

Luisi became Merlino's contact in Boston, earning money through racketeering activities and kicking back $10,000 a month in "tribute" to the boys in Philly. At the time, Luisi was described by the FBI as a member of the La Cosa Nostra, or LCN, who "supervises a crew of gangsters which operate in Greater Boston and conduct criminal activities ranging from narcotics trafficking to illegal gambling and loansharking."[5]

Later in our investigation, we would hear from credible sources that Gentile had a knack for producing silencers, which he would test fire in the back lot of Gem Auto, plinking away at old tires and rusty oil drums. Apparently, our sources reported, they worked really well. This was an interesting hobby, given that after the aborted murder attempt on Jimmy Marks back in 1990, a silenced pistol was recovered from his would-be assassin's duffel bag.

And since we're back on the Marks homicide, Anthony and I solved it in 2010, when Elene admitted to us that her husband murdered Marks, known to her as "Irish Jim." It was during a subsequent interview, as Anthony and I were hoping to learn more about Guarente and Gentile, when Elene made this startling admission.

"My Bobby killed him," she said, referring to Marks. Although Guarente admitted to Elene that he murdered Marks, he had never provided her with a motive. She related to us that on the morning of the murder, Marks and Guarente had left Madison together, heading back to Boston. As they were leaving, Guarente told Elene that they were planning to go to the movies that night. As Anthony recalled, "She was very emotional when she talked about the fact that Marks had been killed by her late husband."[6]

Immediately after Elene's admission to us about Marks's homicide, we notified the Lynn Police, and Guarente became their leading—albeit deceased—suspect in the homicide. We also conducted a fruitless consent search of the attic space above Marks's former Broad Street apartment, the location where he once intimated to his girlfriend that the paintings had been stashed.

According to Marks's niece, Darlene Finnigan, shortly before his murder, her uncle told her that he "had something big coming up and he wasn't sure if he was going to do it." Finnigan assumed Marks was referring to a cocaine deal and scoffed at the suggestion that her uncle had any of the stolen Gardner pieces. "He was too much of a bragger," Finnigan said. "I think too many people would know."[7]

In the end, all it took was one.

Mark O'Toole was the Lynn detective who headed the investigation into Marks's homicide. He believes that the murder was related to the Gardner Museum robbery. "It's not a coincidence," O'Toole said. "Marks had connections to suspects involved in the heist [and] either had some knowledge or was somehow a participant in that crime that resulted in him being marked for assassination." According to O'Toole, "We don't know what, if any, role he had, but very likely it was related to his death."[8]

"At the time that Marks was killed, the chief suspect [was] someone that we believe had two of the Gardner paintings," Anthony points out. And with regard to the sighting of Guarente and Gentile at that Lynn diner shortly after Marks's homicide, Anthony notes, "and the person Guarente gave the paintings to was with him, traveling up from Connecticut."[9]

* * * *

As the investigation into Gentile intensified, we came to learn more and more about this enigmatic mason-cum-used-car-salesman-cum-mobster who lived in the unassuming ranch house outside Hartford. It turns out Bobby Donati and Jimmy Marks weren't the only ones who loved the ponies: On September 6, 1989, Double Daheen finished first at the Northampton Fair, edging out Blackie Norton by a nose, with Dream Nickle coming in third.

Double Daheen's owner and trainer was none other than Bobby Gentile.

* * * *

On April 30, 1999, Luisi sold two kilograms of cocaine to a Philadelphia mob associate named Michael O'Sullivan. O'Sullivan was gruff and taciturn, and what few words he did speak were filtered like baleen through a bushy mustache that barely fit under his nose and trickled out from the corners of his mouth. Luisi had been introduced to O'Sullivan through "Big Ron" Previte, a Philadelphia LCN member whose imprimatur allowed O'Sullivan and Luisi to freely discuss cocaine deals. Unfortunately for Luisi, Big Ron was cooperating with the FBI. And what was even more unfortunate for Luisi was the fact that O'Sullivan was actually Special Agent Michael McGowan, the same undercover who once dined with Corsican mobsters in South Beach whilst wearing those tube socks ensconced in a pair of Adidas slides.

McGowan had first met Gentile early on in the drug investigation, when Luisi brought him by McGowan's Boston office for a meeting. "You've got to remember when I did that case with Luisi and [Skinny Joey] Merlino, I was with those guys like nonstop for about six or eight months," McGowan recalled. "I spent a lot of time at Café Vittoria in the North End. I also had an office over on Milk Street where they would visit." McGowan advised that for many of these meets, the steadfast Gentile was right there by Luisi's side, quietly taking it all in.

Having spent his career working undercover, McGowan had perfected myriad techniques that allowed him to establish rapport with the criminals he befriended. "I would try to get these guys talking, and there were some of them I couldn't get to shut up," he recounted. Gentile, however, seemed the least amenable to developing a friendship with the burly mob associate from Boston.

"What I remember about Gentile is that he just never warmed up. The other guys would talk about him when he wasn't there, you know, telling me he's doing this and that type of thing, but I never developed a relationship with him. I never connected with him."

And like the rest of us, even the most seasoned undercover dislikes awkward silence. "I would be uncomfortable when Gentile showed up at the meetings because I knew they weren't going to be a gabfest. I remember if Gentile showed up at something I'd be pissed, because I knew it would be a wasted day."

Luisi was arrested by the FBI in June 1999 and charged in US District Court in Boston with cocaine trafficking. After his arrest, he admitted to the FBI that Gentile and Guarente were soldiers—that is, made members—of the Philadelphia LCN.[10] Much later, a federal prosecutor would describe Gentile's role to the court:

> It means that [Gentile] took an oath of allegiance to the Philadelphia crime family not to disclose the secrets of the family. He's on their books, as it were, as a soldier attending a Philadelphia family of La Cosa Nostra. He doesn't earn money for them; he's an actual member of the Mafia family.

The following June, Luisi and a number of his associates were convicted on federal racketeering and drug charges. Luisi took a plea agreement and offered to cooperate with the Feds in exchange for leniency. As a government witness, he confessed to a number of uncharged crimes, including the plotting of the April 1996 execution of Richard "Vinnie the Pig" DeVincent, a mob enforcer from Revere.

Absent from the defense table was Gentile. Although he was present for many of the incriminating conversations that led to his boss's arrest, "Gentile was very quiet," McGowan recalled. "The guy didn't drink, didn't smoke, no drugs; he stayed away from the women. He just stood in the corner, taking everything in."[11] It was because of his crafty reticence that the US Attorney's Office wasn't able to charge

Gentile in the drug conspiracy. Luisi, on the other hand, was sentenced to fifteen years in a federal prison in Pennsylvania.

"Luisi's arrest got a lot of publicity at the time because it tied into Joey Merlino down in Philadelphia," McGowan recalled. "I was getting calls from agents nonstop and Gentile's name would pop up, not just with you and the Gardner case," he said to me, "but it would pop up with all different kinds of things, especially mob activity in Connecticut and Philadelphia." McGowan continued, "And then for the next twenty years I'd constantly get calls from agents like you and other guys saying, 'Hey, I'm looking at this guy, Bobby Gentile; what do you know about him?'" Despite all the time they spent together, McGowan admitted that Gentile was a puzzle he was never really able to solve.

"I wish I could provide a better insight into him," he said, "but the insight is, I didn't have one."

* * * *

It's February 2010, and I'm westbound on the Mass Pike, accompanied by Anthony and Assistant United States Attorney Brian Kelly. We're heading to Manchester, a small town in the suburbs of a small city. Apparently, it was once home to the world's largest silk mill, although that's not the reason for today's visit. That would have to wait, because today we're planning to interview Bobby Gentile. Brian has brought with him a signed immunity letter, and Anthony has a giant novelty check balanced on his lap, already made out in Gentile's name. Okay, perhaps that last part is inaccurate, but Anthony does have the authority to offer the reward on behalf of the Gardner Museum, and that's kind of like a metaphorical big check.

It's been a week or two since we interviewed Elene, giving us sufficient time to cobble together all the information we have on Gentile, which isn't much. I have Gentile's phone number, a landline that has been subscribed to him for decades, although I've chosen not to call in advance. The more important the interview, the more loath I am to first make a phone call. And since we're investigating the world's largest art heist, this is one extremely important interview. Investigators basically get one shot to conduct a meaningful interview of a subject; it's the one opportunity to catch someone off guard and lock them into a story. If they have the luxury of time, then they have the opportunity to concoct an alibi, come up with a plausible lie, or call their attorney.

It is still morning when we pull up to a compact ranch on the bend of Frances Drive. An aging blue Buick and an even older brown one are parked in a driveway that's skewered by an inconveniently planted telephone pole. The house is clad in salmon-tinted shingles with red plastic shutters, and a recessed porch sits in the middle of the facade with an incongruous wall of dark brick to its right. Optimism is high for today's visit, and with good reason: Elene was specific about the events surrounding the handoff of the paintings, including the visit she and Guarente made to the Federal Probation Office in Bangor. A few days ago, I was able to confirm that on September 4, 2002, Guarente had, in fact, visited with his probation officer in Bangor. One of the very few benefits of a life of crime is the ability it gives law enforcement to estimate historical events by a felon's history of incarceration.

The shades are drawn and the porch light is still on. I ring the doorbell and we wait. And wait. Two cars in the driveway and no answer? I press my ear to the window and hear nothing, other than the distant sound of the doorbell. After a few minutes, we finally give up; maybe he took the bus or got a ride somewhere. We decide to wait it out.

And we waited a long time. Like a month. In fact, we made at least a dozen trips to Manchester and struck out every time. We tried early mornings, mid-afternoons, late nights; sitting in a coffee shop down the street from his house, giving it an hour. Or two. Knocking and knocking on his front door and ringing the bell, one ear always cocked to the window, listening for movement. We would then park at the end of his street, waiting for any sign of life. During one late-night surveillance, a neighbor called the cops on a suspicious Ford Taurus with Massachusetts plates and tinted windows, and as the cruiser rolled up behind us, I briefly flashed the rear blues concealed in the taillights before approaching the officer with my creds out.

On the twentieth anniversary of the heist, Anthony, Brian, and I participated in a panel discussion on the Gardner heist at the International Foundation for Art Research in New York City. It was during this event when Brian unequivocally stated to the gathered attendees that Whitey Bulger had not been involved in the heist. During the event, we were asked many questions about the status of the Gardner investigation, and I had to suppress the overwhelming urge to tell the gathered audience all about Guarente and Gentile.

This overnight trip to New York gave us two shots at the Cook—we stopped by his house on the way down and then lingered there for a few hours on the way back. We were becoming regulars at the Cosmic Omelet, a neighborhood breakfast spot chosen for its good coffee and proximity to Frances Drive. But these jaunts to Manchester were a time-suck, since a round-trip visit from the Boston FBI office to Gentile's front porch encompassed half a workday and nearly 250 miles in the Bucar. I appreciated the forbearance of my supervisor, Dave Donahue, the former "fucking gambling degenerate," who allowed me to make these drives rather than pawning off this crucial interview on a New Haven agent who knew nothing about the case.

Our last nocturnal visit culminated in the slightest movement of the living room curtain, a barely perceptible rustle that quickly stilled. It was at this point when we realized that not only was Gentile home, he'd probably been home all month, ducking our visits. I resigned myself to the dreaded phone call, knowing full well that I'd be leaving a message on his answering machine (and yes, as expected, it was an answering machine, not voicemail). The following day, I received a much-anticipated call from a Hartford attorney who claimed to represent Gentile. And while I was disappointed that we never had the opportunity to interview Gentile cold, I was hopeful that with the guidance of an attorney, Gentile would tell us everything he knew about the Gardner paintings.

I could not have been more wrong.

Stolen: Rembrandt's The Storm on the Sea of Galilee. Courtesy of the ISGM.

Stolen: Degas' Program for an Artistic Soiree, Part 1. Courtesy of the ISGM.

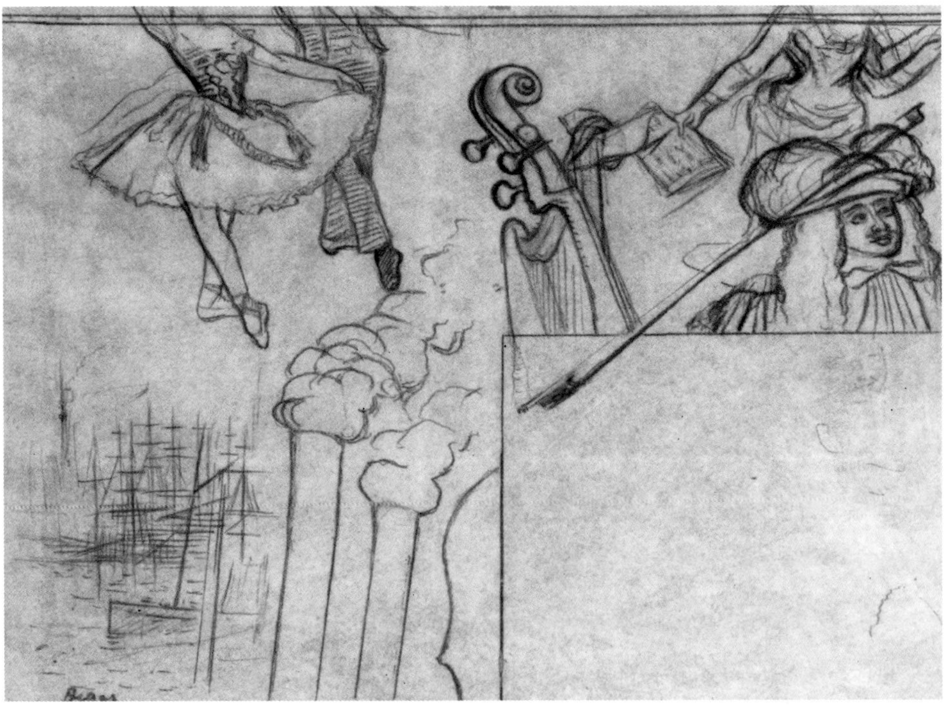

Stolen: Degas' Program for an Artistic Soiree, Part 2. Courtesy of the ISGM.

Stolen: Degas' Cortege Aux Environs de Florence. Courtesy of the ISGM.

Stolen: Degas' La Sortie de Pelage. Courtesy of the ISGM.

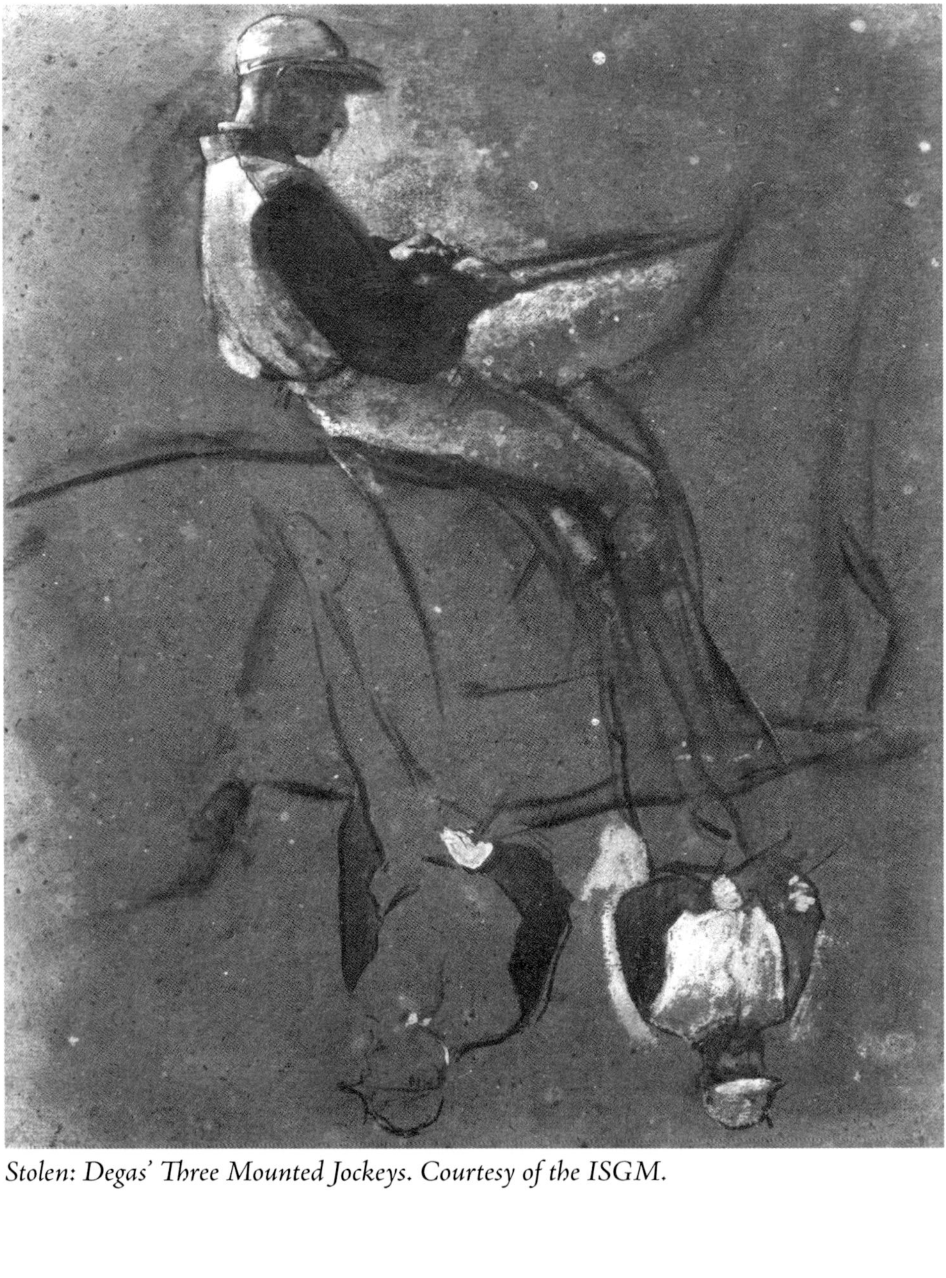

Stolen: Degas' Three Mounted Jockeys. Courtesy of the ISGM.

Stolen: Vermeer's The Concert. Courtesy of the ISGM.

Stolen: Manet's Chez Tortoni. Courtesy of the ISGM.

Stolen: Flinck's Landscape with an Obelisk. Courtesy of the ISGM.

Stolen: Rembrandt's self-portrait etching. Courtesy of the ISGM.

Stolen: Rembrandt's A Lady and Gentleman in Black. Courtesy of the ISGM.

Stolen: Napoleonic Finial. Courtesy of the ISGM.

Stolen: Chinese beaker (called a gu.) Courtesy of the ISGM.

CHAPTER 17

"Lies, Lies...all Lies"

That such remoteness from reality and such thoughtlessness can wreak more havoc than all the evil instincts taken together which, perhaps, are inherent in man.

—HANNAH ARENDT, *Eichmann in Jerusalem*

It can be difficult to manage an important case. The weight can be profound, and sometimes when a good lead looks like it may come to fruition, it's hard to keep your mind from going to those forbidden places you should never visit—imagining what it would feel like to finally see one of the stolen pieces in person. To snap a trophy shot, even though they're prohibited by Bureau policy, call Sonia ("*We got it!*"), and then announce the recovery to the world. I must admit there have been occasions on this case when I went to those forbidden places and imagined those forbidden trophy shots and exuberant spousal phone calls and triumphant press conferences. But when the lead ultimately fizzled out, as they always did, the crushing disappointment that followed was like a bad hangover after a night of revelry. And like the remorseful partyer who wakes with a crushing headache and vows "never again," I also committed to staying away from those forbidden places, places where *The Storm* once again hangs in its gilded frame and the finial finally alights in its Short Gallery aerie. But whether it's the bottle or a promising Gardner lead, temptation is a powerful thing, and so off I traipsed to another forbidden place.

And on March 23, 2010, that forbidden place is the Law Offices of Webber, Jacobs, Murphy & Horan in downtown Hartford.

* * * *

Anthony, Brian, and I were finally sitting across from Robert Vincent Gentile, a.k.a. Bobby the Cook. My first impression of Gentile was the startling resemblance he had to my grandfather, John Fiorito, the son of Italian immigrants. It may have been Gentile's bearing as much as any physical similarities, but in him I saw my grandfather's humility. Like Gentile, my grandfather was a car salesman, and when I used to visit my grandparents' apartment as a kid, there was always a stack of circa-1970s Dodge brochures waiting for me to peruse for hours on end. I saw my grandfather's qualities in Gentile, and it was probably for this reason I believed we could form a bond, an intangible but necessary characteristic of any successful interview.

This would prove difficult; actually, this would prove impossible. For while I may have seen my grandfather in Gentile's eyes, the feeling was certainly not reciprocated. With an unassuming bearing and a noticeable limp, Gentile didn't intimidate; he's the old man standing behind you in line at Petco. And if he spoke to you, it would be a mumbled whisper that would force you to lean in closer.

Attorney-managed meetings, regardless of the circumstances, are always conducted in the same manner. Attorneys act like boxing referees, droning on about proffer agreements and perjury charges like rabbit punches and low blows, while the client and I regard each other from across a well-polished conference table. Typically, I allowed the subject to come out swinging, allowed him to expend his energy on haymakers and uppercuts that didn't land. I would parry his jabs and look for an opportunity to strike. And when I did find an opening, my counters were usually lethal. It's a technique I learned from years of investigating telemarketing fraud, an arena populated by the heavyweight champions of bullshit. The efficacy of my strikes was not based on my debating skills or oratory prowess—far from it. The reason they were so effective was because they were the truth. I let my subjects tell their story, issue their strident denials, and spin yarn after yarn. They would tire themselves out in a prodigious flurry of lies.

And then it was my turn.

"I'm going to ask you some questions, and ninety percent of them I already know the answer to. The thing is, you don't know which ten percent I don't know." It's a common technique used by many effective investigators, and one I often used myself.

But this boxing match didn't go according to plan. When the bell rang, Gentile came out lying. And while Anthony and I countered with the truth, Gentile never went down. Not even a standing eight count. He never faltered, never staggered, never reeled. Anthony offered him the multimillion-dollar reward and Brian threw in an immunity letter, but Gentile bristled at the accusations and countered by denying any knowledge about the stolen paintings. He then landed a haymaker: he said he had never even heard of the Gardner Museum, and any suggestions to the contrary were "lies, lies…all lies."[1]

Gentile spoke softly, but there were flashes of anger that erupted suddenly, delivered with a staccato stomp of his cane. And while a rubber-tipped cane being struck against a carpeted floor by a septuagenarian with arthritis wasn't all that intimidating, it provided a window into an earlier, more menacing iteration of Gentile; a Gentile whose speech was crisper, who clipped off his words and spat them out with contempt. Then the burst of anger would subside, like a passing thunder cloud, and he would retreat back into his disguise, that of a tired old man standing behind you in line at the pet store.

Although Gentile spewed forth a litany of strident denials, for some inexplicable reason he confirmed that dinner with the Guarentes at a Holiday Inn in Portland back in 2002. And while he vigorously denied there had been any handoff of stolen artwork in the parking lot, Gentile shared details of the meal, describing the four of them tucked into a cozy booth. Why would he lie so outrageously about every important fact we presented to him but then admit to the meal? When we asked him why he made the three-hour drive to Maine, he claimed that Guarente wanted to show him a new Walmart that had recently opened in Bangor. While the grand opening of yet another big-box store would certainly be a boon for the residents of the Pine Street State, it made no sense for Gentile and Pat to make that drive all the way from Connecticut to experience it for themselves. And if that trip to Maine was really for a reason so pedestrian as to check out a Walmart and grab a bite to eat with the wives, why did he remember it so vividly, nearly eight years later?

It will take more than four years to finally get the answer.

When the final bell sounded, Gentile was still defiant and we were down on the canvas. Anthony, Brian, and I left the meeting confused and extremely disappointed. While the thought of returning victoriously to Boston with the Gardner artwork metaphorically strapped to the roof of the Bucar was the heady stuff of forbidden places, I had hoped that we would have at the very least obtained a solid lead on its whereabouts.

"We gave him a lot to think about," Anthony consoled. "Let him speak with his attorney." We were hopeful that as we were getting into my Bucar, Gentile and his attorney were upstairs, having a candid discussion about the artwork. Given the generous reward and the offer of immunity, I was hopeful that within a day or two I'd be getting a call from the lawyer.

Obviously, I didn't know Bobby Gentile very well.

* * * *

In the days following the meeting with Gentile, I waited for my phone to ring, hoping to get a call from his attorney. After nearly a week of silence, I finally called his lawyer, asking if his client had suddenly remembered anything about the Gardner artwork. I was advised that not only did Gentile not have any revelations to share, the attorney was no longer representing him.

Two weeks later, Gentile found a new lawyer. Austin J. McGuigan was a well-respected defense attorney who worked out of modest offices in downtown Hartford, ably assisted by his son, Ryan, heir apparent to the Law Firm of Rome McGuigan, P.C. Back in the 1980s, Austin was the chief state's attorney, and his investigation into the mob's influence on jai alai operations eventually inculpated Boston gangster Whitey Bulger, further bolstering the incomprehensible sport's notorious reputation for illegal betting.[2] Prior to his tenure as chief prosecutor, Austin headed a statewide organized crime task force that went after Connecticut's mob network. It was because of his position fighting organized crime that his son, Ryan, ended up on a first-name basis with many of these mobsters, since those were the names that were brought up around the McGuigan's kitchen table.[3]

Ryan McGuigan recalled the first time he ever spoke with Gentile. "A phone call came in on a Saturday from this old guy I'd never heard of," he recalled. The caller advised McGuigan that he had an issue with the FBI and they wanted his cooperation with an investigation. "It was a crazy call to get on the phone," McGuigan said, "so I told the guy, 'Sure, come in and we'll meet with you.'" Later that week, Bobby Gentile sat down with McGuigan and his father, but when Gentile "started talking to me about the Gardner Museum, and that the FBI wanted him to cooperate, I thought he was crazy."

"I'd heard about the Gardner, but as I'm looking at Bob Gentile, the last thing I'm thinking is that this guy has a billion dollars' worth of art," McGuigan said. "My conclusion of the guy was that the only thing he knew about art was a velvet Elvis painting."

As we talked, I asked McGuigan if he remembered that Gentile always referred to the stolen Gardner paintings as "the pictures."

"Right! 'The pictures, the pictures, the pictures,'" he said, doing an admirable impression of Gentile, who always pronounced the word like "pitchers" and often repeated himself for emphasis.

McGuigan told me that his father initially represented Gentile on a contingency fee basis, meaning that any payment for services depended upon the outcome of the case. "My father's original deal with [Gentile] was that we're going to go out and find the paintings, and when we do, we get forty percent of the reward," Ryan said. "That was an operating agreement that my old man had put together with him when they were out searching for the paintings."

Apparently, we weren't the only ones who believed that Gentile had the stolen artwork.

With McGuigan's prodding, Gentile agreed to cooperate with our investigation, which was using the term loosely, since he was continuing to deny any knowledge about the stolen paintings. Regardless, we hoped that amicable conversations with Gentile and his attorney might eventually lead to some candid revelations about the artwork.

During a meeting at McGuigan's offices on April 5, Gentile told us that over the previous weekend he had received three messages on his answering machine from Elene Guarente, who was imploring him to meet with her former neighbor and "soulmate," Earle Berghman, about a "very, very important" matter. Gentile and McGuigan were looking for guidance on what our next step should be.

"Call her back," I suggested.

* * * *

In the book *Master Thieves*, the author writes that Anthony and I were unaware that Earle Berghman, described as Guarente's best friend in Maine, was working with Elene in an attempt to recover the Gardner paintings. Accordingly, we were also unaware that in 2010, Elene summoned Gentile up to Maine to meet with Berghman "in a food court at a Portland mall" to discuss the stolen artwork. According to the book, when confronted by Berghman, Gentile vehemently denied any knowledge regarding them.[4]

What's not mentioned in the book is that this particular meeting between Gentile and Elene's "soulmate" occurred on May 12, 2010, at the Maine Mall in South Portland. What's also not mentioned is the fact that during the meeting, Gentile was wearing an FBI recording device.[5] And sitting on the far side of that Portland food court were two nondescript male shoppers, neither one saying a word. One of these shoppers was the FBI's lead investigator on the Gardner case, sipping his coffee, head resting casually in his hand. This was done not out of fatigue or boredom; it was done to hide the earpiece that was tucked discreetly in his ear, the one picking up the transmitter concealed in Gentile's shirt pocket. His eyes were shut as he strained to hear Gentile and Berghman discuss the stolen Gardner artwork.

Anthony and I knew all about Berghman, Bobby Guarente's one-time neighbor and full-time lover of his wife.[6] We were curious to know why Elene was reaching out to the Cook, prodding him into a meet with her late husband's friend. With the assent of McGuigan, Gentile agreed to wear a wire and meet with Berghman, and this is how I found myself in a food court in Maine, sitting across from my supervisor, straining to make out their garbled conversation. It was hard enough to understand Gentile when we were face-to-face; over an FBI transmitter, it was nearly impossible.

As soon as the meeting started, it became readily apparent that Elene and Berghman were conducting their own investigation, hoping to elicit some incriminating statements from Gentile about the stolen artwork. And just like in the book, Berghman did confront Gentile about the Gardner paintings, and Gentile, in turn, vehemently denied any knowledge of them. But of course, this made sense, considering the fact that Gentile was wearing an FBI recording device. It soon became apparent that Berghman didn't have the artwork either, and the meeting ended with Gentile's optimistic suggestion, "Let's get them and get a cut." And while the visit to the mall didn't damper our suspicions regarding Gentile—who was a pathological liar anyway—the meeting decisively closed the door on Berghman.

A few days after the meeting, we tracked down Berghman in Madison and interviewed him about Guarente and the Gardner artwork. He was certain that two of the Gardner paintings once hung on the wall of Guarente's farmhouse, and this belief, coupled with Elene's statements about the artwork going to Gentile, undoubtedly precipitated the meeting at the Maine Mall. Berghman told us that before Guarente died, they went to a local bookstore and Guarente showed him a recent issue of *Boston Magazine*, which featured an article about Carmello Merlino's crew and the Loomis depot robbery attempt. Guarente pointed out Turner in the magazine and told Berghman, "This kid here is my son, David."

We later interviewed Guarente's daughter, Jeanine, who also confirmed that the stolen artwork once hung in their living room in Madison. And while the information from both Berghman and Jeanine seemed credible—and ultimately may have been—our optimism was tempered by the fact that years earlier, they had tried to scam the Gardner Museum by providing paint chips that most likely had been peeled off a living room wall (at the time, I joked with Anthony that the Old Masters rarely painted in latex). During their second round of paint chip production, Jeanine offered up snippets of colored paper.

While these attempts to fool the museum with fake paint chips were juvenile at best, they demonstrated to us that there were a whole lot of people up in Maine who really believed that Gentile received the Gardner paintings from Guarente.

Join the club.

CHAPTER 18

Prime Time

There are more ways than one to skin a cat,
so are there more ways than one of digging for money.

—SEBA SMITH, *The Money Diggers*

As Gentile continued to deny any involvement with the stolen artwork, I reached out to Jamie Lawton, my old partner at Logan Airport in the months following 9/11. Jamie was a seasoned investigator who worked out of the FBI's New Haven field office, where he specialized in organized crime and cold-case homicides. Prior to the Bureau, Jamie worked as a street cop in Pittsburgh. When Annie Le, a doctoral student at Yale University's Animal Research Center, went missing on September 8, 2009, Jamie got the case.

"I left for work that morning and didn't come home for a week," Jamie recalled. He worked it as a potential kidnapping, managing a team that scoured the streets of New Haven, searching for the victim.

The investigation quickly focused on Raymond Clark, a lab technician whom Le had befriended at work. After he failed a polygraph, Clark fell asleep in the interview room. "That's when I knew he did it,"

Jamie said. "He'd been up for five days, pacing the floors. Now that he finally had some downtime, he took a nap." When a review of the security cameras confirmed that Le had never left the facility, they sent in the cadaver dogs, and one alerted in the vicinity of a locker room. On September 13, they recovered Le's body, upside down, stuffed inside a mechanical chase. And after a week of working the case straight, Jamie finally went home and got some sleep. In March 2011, Clark pled guilty to raping and murdering Annie Le and was sentenced to forty-four years in prison. His decision to plead was based on the insurmountable mountain of incriminating evidence that had been collected by Jamie and his team.[1]

I needed Jamie's help. We hadn't spoken since our stint at the airport concluded, but I gave him a call, and a day or two later I drove down to New Haven and we met for coffee (actually, I had coffee and Jamie had a Diet Coke). Jamie knew a little bit about Gentile; he'd heard rumors that a decade earlier, Gentile was tapped to be the lookout for a robbery crew that was planning to hit an armored car at the Mohegan Sun Casino in Uncasville, Connecticut.[2] At the time, Gentile was sixty-five years old, way too old to be plotting armored car robberies; he would've been better off with his contemporaries *inside* the casino, feeding quarters into the slots and waiting for the early-bird dinner.

But Jamie had two assets that would prove invaluable to this case. The first was John Durham, a prosecutor with the US Attorney's Office in Hartford. John was brilliant, one of those rare prosecutors who dedicated his entire career to public service. Along with Anthony and Brian Kelly up in Boston, we were assembling quite the formidable team to recover the Gardner artwork.

Jamie's second asset was Prime Time, the code name for a cooperating source who'd been working with the FBI for years, collecting information on organized crime activities in the Hartford area. The source knew Gentile, and knew him to be a Philadelphia and Boston organized crime associate. The source was first introduced to Gentile in 2007 at a used car lot owned by a loan sharking, labor racketeering, and truck hijacking mobster named Tony Volpe. Once described as "central Connecticut's top mobster,"[3] Volpe was an affiliate of a Springfield-based faction of New York's Genovese crime family. When they first met, Gentile told the source he was "with people in Boston," meaning, of course, that he was affiliated with organized crime figures. Gentile also claimed that his boss, Bobby Luisi, was "with," and supervised by, the Philadelphia LCN. With regard to the last, Gentile claimed that he had "a very good relationship with former Philadelphia crime family boss 'Skinny Joey' Merlino and had met him on multiple occasions."

Prime Time advised us that Gentile was friends with Andy Parente, a used car dealer who used to run a local strip club called Centerfolds. Parente owned Clean Country Cars, the used car lot on Franklin Avenue where Gentile wiled away his golden years.

The source agreed to meet with Gentile and record their conversations, and so in April 2010, we first wired him up, using a recording device known as an F-Bird, a clever acronym for an FBI Recording Device. Prime Time's instructions were straightforward—he was tasked with simply hanging around Gentile and engaging him in general conversation. While he was instructed to pay particular attention to anything Gentile had to say about the Gardner Museum, he was not to initiate any conversations on the topic. We were convinced that were Prime Time to bring up the robbery, the wily Gentile would immediately smell a rat.

In the end, it was Gentile who first brought up the subject of the Gardner, and as the tape recorder figuratively rolled (they're digital these days), he told Prime Time about how he was approached by the FBI and offered a $5 million reward in exchange for information regarding the stolen artwork. We noticed that whenever Gentile discussed the artwork, he referred to them collectively as "the pictures." He told the source that one of his old crew members, Bobby Guarente, had "masterminded the whole thing" and "flipped" before he died, which was apparently a reference to his recanted decision to cooperate with the DEA. During a subsequent meet, when Prime Time asked if he actually possessed the stolen paintings, Gentile "just smiled."

This was really good stuff. It wasn't nearly enough to charge him with possession of stolen property, of course, but it was more than sufficient to convince us that Gentile knew a lot more about the Gardner case than he was letting on. I would stir the pot by reaching out to Gentile's attorney and requesting another interview, hoping that my call would elicit more incriminating statements to Prime Time back at the car lot. And while the conversations that resulted from these pot stirrings confirmed his involvement with the Gardner paintings, I needed a bigger ladle with which to stir that pot. The Big Ladle wouldn't come for months.

* * * *

When source meetings conclude, the sources return to the staging area like homing pigeons returning to the coop, and FBI agents briefly become mimes. Since the sensitive recording devices are still active, any discussions will be memorialized for posterity and eventually turned over to defense attorneys through the discovery process. For this reason, nobody speaks until the devices have been turned off. And until that occurs, vaudevillian pantomimes ensue when the sources return and invariably and spontaneously begin revealing details about the meets. The case agents, meanwhile, gesticulate wildly for the device, shaking their heads and shushing with their fingers. In silence, the agents then remove the device from their hidden locations on the sources and fumble with the tiny little buttons on the tiny little devices that deactivate the tiny little recorders. They double-check it, and then triple-check it. Then they take the batteries out. Only then does the debrief commence. Every field office has its own cautionary tale of "that guy," the sacrificial agent who endured a withering cross-examination on the witness stand about inappropriate comments overheard on the tiny little recorder.

Seriously, don't be that guy.

* * * *

Throughout 2010, I met with Gentile on a number of occasions at McGuigan's law offices, hoping to gain any details about the Gardner artwork. It was frustrating to hear his continued denials about the paintings, especially because he was infinitely more candid in his conversations with Prime Time, conversations that were occurring during the same time period. Of course, I couldn't refute Gentile's bullshit by telling him about the information we'd learned from his surreptitious conversations with the source, and as much as I wanted to say, "That's not what you told Prime Time last week," that would've been counterproductive, to say the least.

The *Hartford Courant* reported that in late 2010, David Turner, Guarente's de facto son, wrote a letter to Gentile, asking him to meet with his associates to discuss returning the Gardner artwork.[4] When Gentile showed Austin McGuigan the letter, he immediately turned it over to John Durham, which prompted an immediate phone call to Jamie and me.

Ryan McGuigan recalled that in the letter, Turner referred to himself as Bobby Guarente's "son," and he reminded Gentile that he and Guarente once met with Turner's lawyer to discuss leveraging the stolen artwork in order to "chip a little" off his prison sentence.[5] Turner wanted Gentile to reach out to his girlfriend in Boston to arrange the details of the anticipated meet. The existence of this letter prompted another round of interviews with Gentile, yet when we challenged him about Turner's claim, Gentile denied that he and Guarente had ever met with the attorney.

"Bobby, that makes no sense," I said. "Why would Turner write to you about this meeting if it didn't happen?" My entreaties were met with a mumbling string of denials.

Why, indeed.

Gentile even denied to McGuigan that he and Guarente had once met with the lawyer. "He always maintained that he didn't do that," Ryan said. "I don't believe him," he added sharply.

During a court hearing for Gentile in 2016, John Durham advised the court that "prior to 2004, Gentile and Guarente attempted to trade two Gardner Museum paintings to help out a Guarente associate." Although Durham didn't name the associate in court, Ed Mahony, a reporter with the *Hartford Courant,* identified the person as Turner.[6] Mahony, who maintained an impressive network of sources who were dialed into the New England mob, interviewed Gentile on a number of occasions. The reporter once asked Gentile about this alleged meeting, and he confirmed that he and Guarente had, in fact, met with Turner's lawyer, although he minimized his own role greatly; he claimed that Guarente went inside to speak with the attorney while Gentile stayed outside with the car.

In Mahony's opinion, Gentile's feigned ignorance was utterly incredible.

"It was bullshit," he said succinctly.

A week after Mahony's article appeared in the *Courant, The Boston Globe* reported that "after a flurry of sealed documents were filed in Boston Federal Court in July 2011, Turner received a seven-year reduction on his 38-year prison sentence, fueling speculation he cooperated with the Government on the Gardner Museum investigation."[7] The FBI had no comment.

When Turner was finally released from federal prison in November 2019, a cluster of reporters was present to greet him when he exited the courthouse. One of them asked Turner how it felt to finally be free. "Wonderful," he said. "I'm going to Disneyland."[8]

* * * *

In December 2010, we were finally able to use the aforementioned Big Ladle to stir the pot, which arrived in the form of a federal grand jury subpoena. A federal grand jury is a panel of sixteen to twenty-three citizens who are selected to investigate potential crimes that occurred, or are still occurring, within their specific judicial district. Unlike jurors empaneled for a criminal trial, who must unanimously decide if proof exists beyond a reasonable doubt to convict, a grand jury only needs twelve votes to determine if a crime occurred. This is the basis for the old adage that "a grand jury would indict a ham sandwich." If the scales of justice tip ever so slightly in favor of the prosecutor, then the grand jurors vote to indict, a verdict known as a "true bill." If they can't reach a majority consensus, then they return a "no bill."

We served Gentile with a subpoena to appear before a federal grand jury in Boston that had been empaneled to hear evidence regarding the Gardner Museum investigation. Based on what we'd already gathered about Gentile and his penchant for prevarication, it seemed more than likely that he would lie to the grand jurors. And if he did, we were confident that we could refute those lies and potentially charge him with perjury. At the time, we reasoned that if the elderly Gentile was facing the prospect of jail time—even a short period of incarceration—it might be enough to finally gain his cooperation.

Hours after we served Gentile, Jamie wired up Prime Time and pointed him toward Clean Country Cars. The ensuing conversation was tense, with Gentile clearly agitated about the pending subpoena and the prospect of testifying under oath about the stolen artwork. During the meet, Gentile confided to the source that he couldn't testify about the Gardner case because he "would have to lie."

On the day prior to Gentile's appearance before the grand jury, we sent the source back to the car lot again, hoping to gain some insight into Gentile's state of mind. This is a type of meet that's referred to as "taking his temperature." Gentile was clearly still aggravated, and in a rare display of vulnerability and candor, he told Prime Time that he "never made a quarter" off the Gardner artwork.

The following day, Gentile drove up to Boston and testified that he knew nothing about the Gardner Museum artwork, which meant that

Brian Kelly had skillfully locked him into a story that we had already refuted.

Because these statements directly contradicted his sworn testimony before the grand jury, Durham would later tell a federal judge that Gentile had "perjured himself before the grand jury in Boston in December 2010." As a result of Gentile's prevarication under oath, Durham stated that by early 2011, the government had "terminated his 'cooperation' and were no longer attempting to gain his cooperation."

With Gentile locked into his testimony, we continued to gather evidence that would contradict those statements. We had already spoken with a number of credible witnesses, all of whom could refute his testimony, but at this point it was still basically Gentile's word against theirs. For all intents and purposes, we were dead in the water.

But then in September 2011, we were resurrected when I received a call from Jamie.

"You owe me," he said simply.

"Okay, and why's that?"

"Because the Cook just offered to sell drugs to Prime Time."

"You're right; I do owe you," I replied.

Durham granted the authority, and with the concurrence of the FBI's executive management and division counsel, the source began to engage in "otherwise illegal activity," which is defined as conduct that would be unlawful were it not under the direct supervision of the government.

And this was how Prime Time began making controlled drug purchases from Gentile and Parente. After searching the source and his vehicle, we would count out a stack of FBI funds that had been photocopied and has had its serial numbers recorded, known as buy money. Prime Time would then head out to Clean Country Cars to meet up with Gentile and Parente, and over casual conversation, the "hand-to-hand" would occur. During one particular buy, the source asked Gentile if he had a constant supply of OxyContin tablets, to which Gentile replied, "It hits every month."

We had already determined that Gentile had a prescription from a family medical practice in Manchester for 120 tablets of oxycodone and Percocet every thirty days, which Gentile paid for through Medicare. After he began selling to our source, at five dollars a pill, Gentile obtained another prescription from a Hartford neurosurgeon, which gave him another 160 tablets of Dilaudid each month.

This wasn't a case of two old men selling their much-needed meds for soup; they were running a profitable drug trafficking operation. In one recorded conversation, for example, Gentile and Parente were complaining to Prime Time about how Tony Volpe was muscling in on their OxyContin sales. Gentile freely discussed the thriving drug business with Prime Time as he doled out baggies of Dilaudid, Percocet, and OxyContin like it was Halloween:

"And what are you supposed to be?"

"I'm an FBI source."

"Well of course, you are! How adorable."

Forget about the perjury charge, we now had probable cause to arrest Gentile for conspiracy and intent to distribute a Schedule II controlled substance.

Almost all of the drug purchases occurred at Clean Country Cars...almost, because what happened during a twenty-two-minute period on October 17 was memorialized succinctly in Jamie's affidavit:

> On October 17, 2011 at approximately 1:00 pm, CW-1 [Prime Time] and Gentile walked out of Clean Country Cars and got into CW-1's vehicle and drove east on Franklin Avenue. Surveillance units placed the vehicle under continuous surveillance and followed the vehicle. At approximately 1:15 pm, CW-1's vehicle arrived at 69 Frances Drive in Manchester, CT, which was known to be Gentile's residence. Gentile exited CW-1's vehicle and walked inside his house. Shortly thereafter, Gentile exited

the residence and approached CW-1 vehicle. Gentile leaned into CW-1's vehicle and CW-1 counted out money which he provided to Gentile. Gentile then handed CW-1 a small package and entered his own vehicle. CW-1's vehicle was placed under continuous surveillance as CW-1 drove from the area at approximately 1:22 pm.

We now had probable cause to search Gentile's residence.

CHAPTER 19

"Peace and Quiet"

Robert Gentile is just a tired old man who was trying to live out his final years in peace and quiet

—RYAN MCGUIGAN, ESQ.

It's late morning on February 10, 2012. Gentile has just invoked his right to counsel, and Jamie and I have left him in the care of the US Marshals Service, where he will be photographed and fingerprinted. We're heading out to Manchester, and as we pull up to 69 Frances Drive, it's jarring to see Gentile's residence transformed into a crime scene. FBI vehicles, which hours earlier had filled a Dunks parking lot to capacity, have overtaken this quiet neighborhood. The driveway is filled with ERT trucks, and both sides of the street are stacked with a random assortment of Bucars. I double-park behind an evidence van and thread my way up the driveway, past a few FBI vehicles and Gentile's two Buicks. I walk inside, sign the search log, and peer into the life of Bobby Gentile.

Search warrants are almost surreal. I've participated in so many of them over the years that I've almost forgotten how bizarre they truly are. It's a court-authorized intrusion into the most intimate private spaces, laying bare for all to see the secrets and the betrayals, the fetishes and the ephemera, the sacred and the profane, all comingled in a sock drawer. The contraband will be seized, dryly labeled, cataloged, and entered into evidence as orderly columns of guilt. The rest of the stuff goes back with the socks.

* * * *

I once participated in a search of an Asian organized crime subject's home in Boston, looking for evidence of illegal gambling. As I scoured a desk drawer in the living room, my heart stopped. There it was; I'd been waiting my whole career for this moment. "Bingo!" I exclaimed, and as the gathered team of agents and detectives looked over to see the prize, I held up a pristine stack of shrink-wrapped bingo cards. Modest laugh; back to work.

* * * *

The search of Gentile's house reveals the cruel irony of mobster life: Since their outward lifestyle cannot betray the criminality that underpins their fortunes, they're forced to live a humble and even meager existence, forgoing the trappings of wealth which their legal counterparts can flaunt so easily. This seedy ranch spoke volumes about Gentile, and it said more than I'd ever learned from the many hours we had spent together and the many associates we'd interviewed.

The décor is eerily similar to my grandparents' old apartment, except my recollections were of a home that existed almost four decades earlier. Outside, on Frances Drive, it's 2012, but Gentile's interior is frozen in the 1970s, with virtually no intrusion from the ensuing decades. Dark furniture rests on acres of earth-toned carpeting. There's dusty trinkets and stacks of paperwork on the sideboard, a silent grandfather clock with a stationary pendulum, and a combination television set/heavy piece of furniture that for some reason is no longer popular. Gentile and his wife decorated their home once, then flipped on that monstrous TV and settled in to watch the latest episode of *The Rockford Files.*

When the FBI executes a search warrant, residents are not obligated to vacate the premises. Given the uncomfortable arrangement that often exists between the FBI and the homeowner during a search warrant, however, most normal people choose to leave.* Under an agent's supervision, they'll dress quickly, grab their phone and keys, and find somewhere else to be for the next few hours. But others choose to stay, planted in the middle of the well-orchestrated mayhem, scrupulously taking it all in.

And this was the decision of Gentile's wife, Pat, who was also circa 1970. She is an inscrutable woman with long hair, dyed jet black, which frames a hard face that betrays the toilsome career of a gangster's moll. She sits at the dining room table, blending seamlessly into the vintage décor, positioned in a location that gives her a clear vantage point of the front door. And from this roost she watches the comings and goings of the search team. I cheerfully introduce myself to Pat, who returns my greeting with a brusque nod before taking a pull from a lipstick-kissed cup of coffee. I apologize for the intrusion and thank her for her cooperation. That earns another brusque nod.

I've had worse. I'll take a brusque nod any day.

I find my supervisor, Dave Donahue, amidst the commotion. He gives me a brief update on the search and shows me the object that had prompted his earlier call when we were interviewing Gentile: The March 19, 1990, edition of the *Boston Herald* with the headline $200M OF ART STOLEN IN PICTURE-PERFECT HEIST. The newspaper is already sealed in a clear plastic evidence bag, as is that handwritten list of stolen items that had been tucked inside it like an advertising circular. I examine the list; the handwriting is distinctive, a looping amalgam of cursive and print. Next to each stolen item is a dollar figure:

* Personally, I find it awkward when the cable guy is in my house; I can't imagine an FBI search team.

Vermeer—*"The Concert"* (2 m)
Rembrandt—*"Storm Sea of Galilee"* (2 m)
Rembrandt—*"Lady + Gentleman"* (1.0 m)
Manet—*"Chez Tortoni"* (1.0 m)

...and so forth.

Neatly printed at the bottom of the list is the following declaration: "Total: $7,700,000."

We all agree that these dollar figures roughly represent the black-market value for each of the stolen pieces. I need a minute to process this find; this is a list of the artwork that had been stolen during the Isabella Stewart Gardner Museum heist, recovered inside a newspaper bearing a headline about the Isabella Stewart Gardner Museum heist, and recovered inside the home of an individual who claims to have never heard of the Isabella Stewart Gardner Museum heist. Okay, got it.

Each room is a hive of activity, with every piece of furniture being studied, emptied, and probed by agents, most of whom by now have doffed their raid jackets and body armor and work in shirt sleeves. I don a pair of latex gloves and descend two steps into the rumpus room; in reality, it's a family room, but in this atavistic house it seems only appropriate to use an atavistic term.

Being the case agent at a search location is stressful, and today is no exception. As usual, my phone is ringing and pinging constantly with calls, emails, and texts from executive management, our public affairs officers, other agents, and prosecutors in two judicial districts. Manipulating the phone while wearing latex gloves is nearly impossible, but it was still better than attempting to stretch a fresh set of gloves over sweaty hands.

Every few minutes I'm accosted by an agent, either holding up some random object and asking, "Do you want this?" or beckoning me to take a look at something in place. Over the course of the day, I will say "Yes, let's take that" or "No, we don't need that" at least a hundred times. There are a few occasions during the day, however, when an agent delivers a breathless, "You've *got* to see this!"

There's an old adage in law enforcement that goes, "It's not a search until you find the porn."* Gentile's residence is the exception, but what he lacks in obscenity, he makes up for in weaponry. They're everywhere. We find seven loaded handguns scattered about the house, in desk drawers, kitchen cabinets, even a bedside table, along with hundreds of rounds of ammunition of varied calibers. There's even a loaded pump-action shotgun hanging on a hook next to the front door, a place where a typical homeowner of Gentile's age might store his HurryCane.

I don't recall exactly when the dynamite was found, but its discovery definitely sends a ripple of agitation through the house. What septuagenarian doesn't keep a five-gallon bucket of high explosives in his house? The ERT team leader calls the bomb squad and orders the evacuation of all personnel—including Pat—from the residence. We're standing in the driveway when the bomb techs arrive in a pair of unmarked pickup trucks. Frances Drive is beginning to look like the parking lot of a very popular restaurant, minus the valet.

After the bomb techs remove the bucket o' dynamite, we resume the search. We find two six-foot-long elephant tusks leaning against a wall in the rumpus room. Since it's illegal to possess ivory, as well as the stuffed kestrel which is perched on a nearby shelf, their presence prompts a visit from a wildlife agent, whose forest-green pickup truck, clad in official US Fish and Wildlife livery, only adds to the traffic jam outside.

Around noontime the makeshift coffee bar we had assembled on the dining room table is restocked with wrapped sandwiches and bottled water. I continue to be summoned by agents each time items of contraband are found: hundreds of prescription pills, brass knuckles,

* The first instance was believed to have taken place in Milan, when authorities found a stack of Caravaggio nudes under a virginal. Actually, that's not true.

and $22,000 in cash, bundled in a thick wad, stuffed inside that taciturn grandfather clock.

I find a photo album tucked inside a sticking dresser drawer and begin to leaf through the images, square photographs crisply bordered in white, a roughly chronological timeline of the life of Bobby Gentile. Here he is posing awkwardly with a horse at the track; alongside Pat and some random couple next to a palm tree–draped swimming pool; and out in the driveway, wearing a golf shirt with impossibly wide lapels, leaning against a vintage car that was brand new when the picture was taken. While I was secretly hoping to find an image of the Gardner artwork, it was still fascinating to tour Gentile's life and the moments he felt were important enough to freeze, thirty-six images at a time. There were lots of "pitchers" of racehorses and mob associates, but not too many of his kids.

My reverie is interrupted by an agent bearing a "you've *got* to see this" item: a plastic Price Rite shopping bag containing four silencers. This latest find is noteworthy, since it corroborates the information we'd learned about the Cook's silencer-making hobby. It also causes me to think back on that silenced pistol that the Lynn Police recovered outside Jimmy Marks's apartment shortly before his murder.

A small pantry off the rumpus room yields a bonanza of contraband: Amidst the cartons of pasta and jars of marinara sauce we find baseball caps bearing insignias of the FBI, the Connecticut State Police, and the NYPD. It seems that Gentile's sartorial tastes lean toward the law enforcement variety, an unusual clothing choice for a mobster. There are police duty belts with the same type of drop holster I once wore as a cop (at least until my department transitioned from revolvers to Glocks), and while I understand Gentile's need for weapon retention—what with all those pistols—it would be impossible to conceal a firearm in these uniform holsters.

We also find handcuffs, a Taser, a set of walkie-talkies, police scanners, body armor (more commonly referred to as a bulletproof vest), and a leather case containing a police badge. All of this is interesting when taken in the context of the Gardner Museum robbery. In one drawer, we locate a stash of false identification documents in the name of Gentile's alias, Bob Gino.*

The most interesting room in the house is Gentile's basement, the location where my colleagues had found the old newspaper with the banner headline on the heist. I walk down a steep staircase and take in the surroundings. The room is filled with the detritus of a mobster's misspent career, arranged against a backdrop of imitation paneling. With faux seams inscribed into plywood, those four-by-eight sheets of knotty pine were a mainstay of so many childhood memories. A lopsided collection of adding machines and cash registers is stacked atop a slew of metal filing cabinets; they rest like tiny islands and archipelagos on a sea of wall-to-wall carpeting, its hue the muted dirty gray of a storm-tossed ocean, and it meets the paneling at an artificial horizon proscribed by a strip of cheap baseboard trim. And floating on that ocean like flotsam is a teetering tower of cardboard boxes filled with dozens and dozens of cans of bug spray; they literally must've fallen off the back of a truck. It's a lifetime supply of insect repellent for a lifetime poorly spent.

I stand there alone for quite some time, taking it all in. On the wall are framed photographs of racehorses, and standing next to the jockeys are younger, slightly leaner iterations of Bobby Gentile. There's a stack of old VHS tapes; I sort through them, unrealistically hoping that maybe there's a surveillance video labeled "ISGM 3-18-90." There is not. One tape, however, earns a wry chuckle; it's labeled in the Cook's inimitable scribble, and it seems to encompass the very essence of Bobby Gentile: *"Cooking Shows and Mob Hits."*

The search doesn't conclude until almost midnight. All the debris from our efforts is collected: the empty coffee cups and sandwich wrappers, inverted balls of damp latex gloves, and miles of coiled backing

* As previously detailed, when Guarente and Gentile were speaking with a Jimmy Marks associate shortly after his murder, they arrived in a vehicle registered to Bob Gino.

paper released from those finicky rolls of evidence tape. All the evidence has been bagged, the arsenal of weapons zip-tied into purpose-built cardboard containers that resemble pizza boxes. As required by the Federal Rules of Criminal Procedure, we leave Pat with a copy of the search warrant and a detailed inventory of every item we seized. Although the warrant was issued for "controlled substances, held in violation of 21 USC U.S. Code, § 841(a)(1)" and "controlled substance paraphernalia for packaging, processing, and distributing controlled substances," we are still authorized to seize any other contraband that we happen to come across during the search. For this reason, the inventory also contains the firearms, silencers, elephant tusks, police equipment, and fake identification. And of course, the *Boston Herald* and the handwritten list of the stolen Gardner Museum artwork.

And don't forget the dynamite.

As I sign the exit log, noting the time, I thank Pat for her cooperation. In return, I receive a final brusque nod.

Again, I've had worse.

CHAPTER 20

"It's Us Again"

'What is truth?' said jesting Pilate;
and would not stay for an answer.

—FRANCIS BACON, *Of Truth*

Gentile appeared before US Magistrate Judge Thomas Smith the following Tuesday in Hartford. Although we had walked Gentile into the cell block only a few days prior, today he was rolled into the courtroom in a taxpayer-funded wheelchair, a method of conveyance that would be repeated for every subsequent court appearance. Durham had already updated his criminal charges to include the possession of firearms and ammunition by a previously convicted felon, as well as the possession of the unregistered silencers. And as Jamie and I sat at the prosecution table, it took Durham nearly an hour to rattle off a description of the "twenty-five or so crates of drugs, cash, phony identification documents and weaponry that agents carried out of Gentile's home during a search."

Judge Smith seemed a little overwhelmed by the amount of evidence seized from the elderly man who sat before him in khaki prison garb.

Durham pushed for detention, and the judge seemed inclined to agree. "It seems to me that the search warrant in this case has produced a treasure trove of evidence against Mr. Gentile suggesting that he has a propensity to violence and to facilitate others who do."

Ryan McGuigan argued for home detention, describing the explosives as merely "large firecrackers," and claimed that "there was never any suggestion that…the guns or other items found in his house were there for anything other than either a collector's whim or for self-protection."

Whim or not, Judge Smith described the evidence as a "veritable arsenal" and ordered Gentile held without bail, despite his advanced age and the dearth of recent convictions. He was remanded to the custody of the Wyatt Detention Facility in Central Falls, Rhode Island.

* * * *

A few days later, Anthony identified the author of the list of stolen Gardner artwork. Over the years, Anthony had traded correspondence with Florian "Al" Monday, the notorious art thief who once robbed the Worcester Art Museum of a Rembrandt. Anthony had compared Monday's handwriting to the list's anonymous author and believed they were a match. I met up with Anthony at the museum, and he passed over a sheaf of letters penned by Monday. He was right—the handwriting was identical. All of the documents shared that distinctive looping amalgam of cursive and print. A day or so later, we tracked Monday down at the Faulkner Hospital in Boston and interviewed him in the cafeteria. Over cups of mediocre coffee, Monday admitted to us that he wrote the list.

He claimed that he wrote it shortly after the Gardner heist occurred, and did so at the request of an associate who knew both Gentile and Guarente. The associate was Paul Papasodero, a thief and forger from Milford, Massachusetts. According to Monday, Papasodero had lined up two prospective buyers for the stolen artwork and Gentile was going to be the middleman. According to Monday, "It was a list of the paintings and the prices that I was willing to pay for them."[1] In keeping with the day-late, dollar-short feel of the Gardner Museum investigation, Papasodero died on May 19, 2010, exactly one week after Gentile met with Earle Berghman in the food court of the Maine Mall. And although we didn't know it at the time, Gentile attended Papasodero's funeral.

We submitted the silencers to the Bureau of Alcohol, Tobacco, and Firearms for test-firing, and a few weeks later an agent informed us that not only did the silencers work, they worked really well. The ATF agent noted, however, that the silencers did not fit any of the firearms that were recovered from Gentile's house during the search. This information would soon prove useful.

Through court filings, the media learned of Gentile's arrest and the Gardner-related items seized from his residence, leading to a deluge of calls to our public affairs offices in Boston and New Haven, as well as to the National Press Office at FBIHQ. Based on the sudden interest in Bobby Gentile, I wasn't surprised to hear that an inmate at Wyatt Detention Facility claimed to have relevant information about the Cook. It's fairly common for inmates to come forward with information—often bogus—about their fellow cons, hoping they can leverage it for any kind of benefit. I was skeptical, but nevertheless, Jamie, John Durham, and I headed out to Wyatt and met with one of the corrections officers. We learned that the inmate shared a cell with Gentile, an arrangement that lent him a modicum of credibility, and one that brought to mind the old saying about strange bedfellows: Instead of his wife, the Cook was now bunking down with a young gangbanger.

When the inmate was finally brought in, he told us that Gentile had been bragging to him about having the Gardner Museum artwork. There was nothing proprietary about this information, since it was being widely reported in the news; however, the inmate claimed that Gentile had confided in him that the silencers didn't fit any of the guns that we seized from his house. This was a relevant piece of information, since the inmate could only have received that information directly from Gentile; in fact, we'd only received the ATF test results a few days earlier. According to the inmate, Gentile advised him that the FBI would never find what they're looking for because it's "buried underground." The inmate didn't know if Gentile meant this literally or figuratively, but based on this information, we applied for another search warrant.

* * * *

It's very early on May 10, and I'm soaking wet. We've reconvened at the same Dunks in Manchester, but today it's pouring rain. For this morning's search, the number of FBI vehicles has swelled beyond the confines of the parking lot and has spilled into the gas station across the street. In addition to New Haven search personnel, Boston's ERT has come down for the search, and they've brought with them thermal-imaging equipment and X-ray machines to scan inside the walls. And due to the ambiguity of Gentile's phrase "buried underground," we've brought a team up from Quantico to operate metal detectors and ground-penetrating radar, or GPR, which will detect any disturbances or anomalies in the soil.

Before I begin the briefing, I seek out a very wet and bedraggled Greg Comcowich, the agent who runs the Boston search team. In his dual role as Boston's public affairs officer and ERT team leader, Greg and I have become quite friendly. Over the years, his team has conducted a number of consent searches for the Gardner artwork, always handled professionally and without protest. Because of Greg's willingness to commit the team to the quest, he has earned my undying gratitude, since these searches would've been much more difficult—if not impossible—without ERT assistance. Whenever I reached out to Greg, sheepishly relating another wild-goose chase that required vetting, his response was invariably a cheerful, "Let's do it!" He was always more than willing to join me up in a musty attic or a dank basement, either holding the ladder or perspiring alongside me.

As I brief the morning's operation, the entire search team attempts—unsuccessfully—to huddle under the retractable awning of one of the search trucks. Although the search location is the same, I advise the team that this operation will be vastly different, since we aren't looking for illicit drugs. As I distribute copies of the Big Staple OPORD and agents flip through the pages and peruse the colorful images of the stolen artwork, I advise the team that today we are looking for the stolen Gardner Museum artwork.

When I finish the briefing, the team races to the sanctuary of their dry Bucars as the awning is furled. Jamie jumps in with me and we maneuver to the head of the line. When the clock on the dashboard hits 6:00, I take one last look at the long line of headlights in the rear-view mirror and we head out. One minute later, the caravan pulls up to Gentiles' house, and Jamie and I jog up to the front porch. Our expediency is not for any tactical considerations; it's due to the pouring rain. I jockey open the screen door, one of those metal ones that shuts with the velocity of a guillotine, and rap loudly on the front door. A minute later, Gentile's wife answers.

"Hi, Pat, it's us again," I say, almost apologetically, as I hold up my creds. "We have another search warrant for the house."

My bearing is sympathetic and sincere. Since the last search, Brian has coined a new nickname for Pat, *Ma Barker*, and it just describes her so well. But even a hard woman has a breaking point, and while Pat must've known that her husband operated outside the boundaries of the law, she wasn't a criminal herself. On this morning, however, I don't even get the brusque nod; she simply opens the door and steps aside. We perfunctorily clear the house and then assume our usual places. Including Pat, who nestles into a chair in the dining room and surveys the proceedings from over the same lipstick-smeared cup of coffee.

The rain begins to taper and by late morning the sun is peeking through the clouds. This is a good sign, since much of the activity is taking place outside. Unlike the previous search, when we toiled in obscurity, this time the media has been alerted to our presence, and by lunchtime there's a herd of reporters pressed against the police line that the Manchester Police have established at the intersection of Niles Drive, one block to the west. News helicopters roar overhead, a rhythmic rumble that keeps up all day, and I watch as the search teams operate. Agents are outside, sweeping with metal detectors and poking the ground with GPR probes, and inside, methodically running the X-ray machines up and down the walls. When necessary, they drill a small hole into the wall and insert a scope into the stud bay to probe a suspicious object or irregularity that's been captured by the X-ray machine.

The search yields more guns and drugs, including contraband that had been secreted in various hides scattered throughout the house. We even find more high explosives, which prompts another evacuation and another visit from the bomb techs, who were already on standby. How about a homemade pistol, known as a "zip gun"? Check. Perhaps a sword concealed in a cane? Again, check.

Just like the last search, I interrupt my phone calls and emails to answer agents who are asking, "Do you want this?" As before, there are a lot of "Yes, let's take that" and a few "No, we don't need that."

And just like last time, there is even a breathless "you've *got* to see this!"

I'm summoned to the backyard and, along with Jamie, Brian, and Anthony, escorted to the shed in Gentile's backyard. It's of the basic box-store variety, a smaller version of the house it sits behind. Although we searched it the first time around, today ERT has emptied out the entire contents on the lawn, including an area rug and a massive air compressor that was tucked into the corner. And it was underneath these objects that they've found a trapdoor that had been cleverly built into the floor. As I peer into the void below, I can clearly see the unmistakable blue top of a Rubbermaid container, concealed under a fine dusting of dirt. After an agent cuts through a couple of floor joists with a reciprocating saw, I exhume the container and carry it out into daylight. And as the search team looks on with great anticipation, I remove the lid.

It's empty. I can almost hear Geraldo Rivera singing about that toddling town.

But the presence of this container certainly begs the obvious question: For someone who keeps drugs, guns, and high explosives lying around his home, what's so valuable that he needs to bury it?

CHAPTER 21

INMATE 20823-014 (GENTILE, ROBERT V.)

'To my mind,' observed the Chairman of the bench of Magistrates cheerfully, 'the only difficulty that presents itself in this otherwise very clear case is, how we can possibly make it sufficiently hot for the incorrigible rogue and hardened ruffian whom we see cowering in the dock before us.'

—KENNETH GRAHAME, *The Wind in the Willows*

Now that we had gone overt with the much-publicized arrest of Gentile, the investigation really began to gather steam. We were conducting interviews on a number of his associates and neighbors. It would be hard to characterize any of these individual as "friends," since it was difficult to find anyone who hadn't been screwed over by Gentile at some point in their lives.

Jamie talks about that moment of synergy that seemed to infuse the case during that period. "The crucial turning point in the case was we started investigating it like an organized crime case instead of a theft case." I agreed with him. "I was working a historical case, and then all of a sudden we had the opportunity to be proactive, and not reactive," I reflected. "I think that was a big difference."

In late April 2012, McGuigan offered to have his client take a polygraph examination. He hoped that this would give Gentile the opportunity to prove that he knew nothing about the Gardner artwork. We jumped at the chance. It's been my experience that anyone who claims that polygraphs are inaccurate has, at one point, failed a polygraph. All truly gifted liars believe they can beat the test, but it's their physiological responses that ultimately betray them. A skillfully administered polygraph examination is an accurate measurement of a subject's candor, and Gentile's test was being administrated by Special Agent Ron Barndollar, considered one of the best polygraph examiners in the FBI.

During his polygraph examination, Gentile answered "no" to the following three questions:

1. Did you know about the Gardner Museum heist prior to its occurrence?
2. Did you ever have possession of the Gardner Museum paintings?
3. Do you know where the Gardner Museum paintings are currently located?

As Durham later advised the court:

> The results of the polygraph establish without question that the defendant was not being truthful in his answers to any of the relevant questions, a fact made known to the defendant and his counsel at the time the tests were run. Indeed, the probability of his answers being truthful was calculated at <0.1%, and, utilizing a second scoring system for comparison purposes, the probability of his answers being deceptive was calculated at >99 percent.

To put it in the simplest mathematical terms, Gentile failed the test with a 99 percent probability of deception.

McGuigan recently told me that he eventually came to believe Gentile really did have the stolen paintings after all, but by the time we started to investigate him, he no longer had access to them. I asked McGuigan if there was a specific moment when he realized that Gentile did, in fact, have the Gardner artwork. His answer was simple, and bolstered the credibility of Ron Barndollar's expertise:

"When he blew up the polygraph."

* * * *

In the book *Master Thieves*, the author writes that after failing the first polygraph, Gentile was given a second exam in which he admitted to receiving the Rembrandt self-portrait etching from Elene. According to the book, after this second test was over, the polygrapher "excused himself and retrieved the results from the other room: it showed that Gentile had answered honestly."

Actually, that never happened. Gentile was tested only once by the FBI, and he failed miserably. And as a general point of fact, the "polygraph machine" is not located in another room, dispensing its verdicts like a Magic 8 Ball. In reality, the examiner huddles over a laptop, studying the scrolling graphs and carefully making notations as each question is asked and answered. The expertise of polygraph examiners lies in their ability to interpret all of those squiggly lines as they move across the screen.

The Rembrandt etching did come up during our investigation, but not for quite some time, and the details surrounding it were obtained with the facility of a tooth extraction.

As evidence linking Gentile to the Gardner heist rapidly accumulated, our interviews continued apace. Austin McGuigan was eager to make some headway with the stolen artwork, so he made his client available to meet. Gentile would arrive in the back of a US Marshals van as Anthony and I would drive down from Boston and Jamie would head up I-91 from New Haven. We would all converge at Durham's Hartford conference room at roughly the same time (I say roughly, because Jamie was always a bit late). Once we were all present, Jamie and I would head downstairs to the Marshals lockup, and I'd sign for Gentile like some odious Amazon package. We'd then escort Gentile, clad in prison garb and sandals, into Durham's conference room.

When an investigator establishes rapport with a subject, it's like a spell has been cast. The conversations are earnest, with focused eye contact that isn't at all creepy. My subsequent interviews with Gentile seemed to follow a similar trajectory, and to an outsider, it would've seemed that we had a plethora of rapport. I would talk to Gentile and he would listen; he would nod at the appropriate times and respond readily with affirmations when asked innocuous questions about his past. Through my experience, Gentile was demonstrating the body language and affectations of a subject who was about to "go"; that is, finally confess. But then he wouldn't; he'd shake his head, utter a mild oath, and the spell would be broken.

Gentile would deny the undeniable, issuing formidable protestations against known facts, such as his status as a made man and the drug sales to Prime Time. He denied the possession of all the firearms in his possession, as well as the meeting with Guarente and Turner's lawyer.

During one interview, however, Austin asked for a few minutes alone with his client, so we vacated the conference room and waited outside. On the other side of the door we could hear Austin's raised voice. After a few minutes, he emerged and told us that Gentile had something tangible to share: He was prepared to admit to us that Elene once showed him the stolen Rembrandt etching, which she had secreted in her bra.

This was something. We rejoined the battle.

"Okay, Bobby, tell us about the etching," I said.

"What etching?"

Austin's temper flared and his exasperation was evident. "Bobby, you just told me two minutes ago that Guarente's wife showed you the etching!"

"I don't know what you're talking about" was the reply.

Another sidebar. And so it continued. After a few painful iterations, Gentile eventually took ownership of the claim and told us that Elene once withdrew the etching from her bra. Finally, we had one hard-fought admission linking him to the Gardner artwork, even if it seemed highly suspect. (Although he stood by the story, I always surmised that Gentile fabricated the Rembrandt-in-a-bra story in an effort to get back at Elene for ratting him out to the FBI.)

Anthony had stressed to Gentile on multiple occasions that even if he no longer had access to the artwork, if he could provide any information that led to a recovery, he would still be eligible for a sizeable portion of the reward. We reminded him that even if he had no interest in the reward money, it could be his son's birthright, and it was along these lines that Austin once suggested that perhaps Gentile's family could talk sense into him. As a result, we hosted a sort of intervention, and stood outside the closed conference room door while Gentile's son and daughter-in-law berated and harangued him about the artwork, imploring him to cooperate.

I recently sat down with Jamie to talk about the Cook.

"Why do you think he wouldn't cooperate?"

"This is a guy who was quasi-illiterate," Jamie said. "Gentile could barely write his own name, but he had a PhD in the street; it was ingrained in him." Having worked organized crime subjects for most of his career, Jamie understood the importance that was placed on being made by a crime family. "The only thing he'd ever really accomplished was the fact that he got his button," he said. "Being in the Mafia was so important to him that he didn't want to throw it away." We talked about the fact that Gentile once bragged to Prime Time that he was a soldier in the Philly mob. "I was skeptical, because those guys don't throw that around," he said. "But Gentile did because it was so important to him. He was low-key about a lot of stuff, but he wasn't low-key about that."

Despite the fact that we were threatening to put him in prison, Gentile was still moving chess pieces around the board, still maintaining total control.

"He's thinking that he has something everybody wants," Jamie said. "'I have what they want and I'm not giving it to anybody. It's mine; it belongs to me.' That's more important to him than the money." For Gentile it wasn't about the reward—you could really see how much he enjoyed being the center of attention.

"'They need me; I don't need them,'" Jamie mused. "It's interesting."

* * * *

It was about this time that I sat down at my desk and authored a Change Case Title communication to the file. In the "Justification" box, I typed the following:

"Title changed to reflect identification of captioned UNSUBS."

I then scrolled up to the case title, which had been carried as "UNSUBS" for more than two decades, and hit the delete key exactly six times. I then typed in an alphabetical list of names, actual names that had become so familiar to me over the past few years.

In a cold case, you take your victories wherever you can get them.

* * * *

In November 2012, Gentile pled guilty to a litany of federal drug and weapons charges and was sentenced to thirty months at the Federal Correctional Institution in Allenwood, a medium-security facility located smack dab in the bull's-eye of Pennsylvania.

It was behind these same prison walls where Jamie and I interviewed Bobby Luisi in April 2012,[1] one week after a federal grand jury in New Haven returned a three-count indictment charging Gentile with the illegal possession of multiple firearms, ammunition, and silencers. This had the potential to be a productive interview, since Luisi was quite close with Gentile and Guarente back in the late '90s, a critical Gardner-related time frame.

Jamie and I had deferred this key interview until after Gentile's arrest, concerned that if word got back to him that we were delving so deeply into his past, he may decide to lay low. But now that the cat was out of the bag—after having already been skinned—it was time to start delving deep. Which is why we found ourselves heading off into the hinterlands of central Pennsylvania, racking up even more miles on my Bucar.

By the time of our visit, Luisi had already been locked up for more than a decade, a decade in which his world of organized crime on the streets of Boston and Philly had faded into a distant memory. During his incarceration, Luisi had received a degree in theology and become an ordained pastor, quite the ecclesiastic reversal of fortune for the one-time mob boss. A year after our interview, he entered the federal witness protection program and changed his name to Alonso Esposito. But on the day of our interview, he was still just Bobby Luisi, the prodigal son of the well-perforated Bobby the Blade.

Our visit today, like every other jailhouse visit, was unannounced, as was the agenda. After we had a moment to get settled, a guard ushered in Luisi, clad in the federal penitentiary system's ubiquitous khaki scrubs that makes every inmate look a little bit like Steve "the Crocodile Hunter" Irwin. Luisi was cheerful, unassuming, and eager to speak with us about his past. He looked good for fifty-one, sturdy, with a slight paunch and just a shimmer of silver beginning to peek through a closely cropped helmet of black hair. With his gentle demeanor and wire-framed eyeglasses, it's difficult to fathom that by his own admission he'd been involved in at least half a dozen murders.[2] In fact, throw a whistle around his neck and he could've been my son's football coach. And while Luisi looks like he'd be right at home doing down-up drills with a bunch of high school linemen, it would've been a different situation altogether if I'd encountered him years earlier, outside the safety of these prison walls.

After we read him his Miranda warnings, standard protocol for anyone being interviewed while in custody, Luisi told us about his condo on Ryan Road in Woburn, the location where he ran his drug business back in the 1990s. He confirmed that Gentile and Guarente used to work for him as bodyguards. He related to us an insightful anecdote about Gentile, which occurred when Luisi was car shopping.

Luisi had brought Gentile, owner of Gem Auto, along with him to the dealership. Perhaps because he was drawn to the dignified concept of a motorcade, Luisi picked out four identical black Lincoln Continentals. Luisi recalled that Gentile was furious, admonishing him about his lack of discretion. Gentile said that a fleet of four matching Lincolns would put a target on them all. "You're gonna bring heat on us from the FBI," he hissed. "You need to drive old cars that don't stand out!" As Luisi recounted the story, I couldn't help but think about that pair of ancient Buicks in Gentile's driveway. Luisi's story of car shopping was an allegorical sketch of Gentile, equal parts wariness and parsimony.

We asked Luisi if either Gentile or Guarente ever mentioned the Gardner artwork, and he nodded enthusiastically. Luisi claimed that back in the 1990s, he and Guarente were watching television at the Woburn condo when a news story came on about the Gardner heist. Guarente turned to Luisi and admitted to him that he knew where the Gardner artwork was hidden. He asked if Luisi knew where he could sell it. Luisi told us that he knew "he couldn't move artwork that hot," and regardless, he had no interest in getting involved with stolen paintings.[3]

During our interview, Luisi mentioned a younger kid who used to work for him up in Woburn and knew about Guarente's artwork. As Jamie recounts the interview, "Luisi kept talking about that kid that worked for him, that 'fat kid Sammy.' He said he was a pain in the ass; Sammy, Sammy, Sammy."

Even though Luisi couldn't remember Sammy's surname, he'd given us a lead on another Gentile associate from the '90s. As we were diving back home through the rural countryside of central Pennsylvania, Jamie and I discussed the interview with Luisi. "So, you and I are driving up 76 or 80 or whatever it was," Jamie recalled, "and we're going over what he told us. And then the light bulb went off in my head."

Jamie was a seasoned investigator who knew every cop in Connecticut worth knowing. Two years earlier, when we first began looking into Gentile, a retired Hartford detective had told him that the Cook used to hang around with a career felon named Ronnie "Meatball" Bowes.[4] Jamie had managed to track down Meatball's older brother, who provided a wealth of historical information about Gentile. He also mentioned to Jamie that he and his brother had a cousin named Sammy. After Jamie got back to Connecticut, he made a phone call.

A week later, we interviewed Sebastian "Sammy" Mozzicato.[5] The son of Italian immigrants, Sammy had lived his whole life in Hartford, surrounded by a coterie of mobsters, wannabes, and a decent pastry shop. He was a bundle of energy, like tinfoil in a microwave, emitting sparks of enthusiasm as he talked about Gentile. Sammy confirmed that he used to work with Gentile and Guarente at Luisi's condo in Woburn, and he told us that back in the late 1990s, he'd been tasked with moving a package of what he suspected were paintings between two cars parked outside the condo. Sammy claimed that shortly after the paintings were loaded up, Gentile and Guarente drove them to Guarente's farmhouse in Maine.

As we interviewed Sammy, Jamie pulled out a folder and began leafing through photographs, showing him images of the stolen Gardner pieces. As Jamie flipped through the stack, Sammy stopped him on the finial. "Oh yeah, I remember that one," he said. "That used to be on a shelf at Gem Auto." A potential sighting of one of the lesser-known pieces, learned through yet another unscheduled interview, seemed promising.

Sammy agreed to cooperate with our investigation, and Jamie opened him as a source. The following day, Sammy called Jamie and advised that his cousin, Meatball, was willing to speak with us. It was already late afternoon, so I called Sonia to tell her I'd be home late once again and headed down to Connecticut. That night, in yet another nondescript motel room somewhere off I-91, Jamie and I interviewed Meatball.

The first thing that struck me about Meatball was his roundness. Short and balding, his nickname perfectly suited him. You could picture him doused in marinara sauce and bobbing in a tangle of spaghetti. Clad in black sweatpants, a baggy black T-shirt, and a black leather jacket, it was an ensemble we would come to know as his signature outfit. He was a diminutive black orb.

Meatball was also a triple murderer.

Back in the early 1980s, Meatball was living in South Florida and selling drugs. During a fifty-pound marijuana deal in the Florida Keys, Meatball's buyers attempted to rip him off, and in the ensuing gunfight, Meatball lost a thumb and three of his potential buyers were dead. Meatball was convicted on three counts of murder and sentenced to death, but an appeals court eventually overturned the conviction, agreeing with his defense of "excusable homicide."[6] After his release, Meatball moved back north. Since his return to the Nutmeg State, he'd been locked up a few times, although for nothing as serious as triple murder.

I liked Meatball immediately.

It was hard not to like him. Meatball was affable and expansive, and he neither acted nor looked like a three-time killer. Meatball's voice was uncharacteristically high-pitched, and he spoke in a garrulous manner that belied the dark context of the subject matter we discussed. When he related some ironic twist of circumstance which is so common in the world of crime, the story was punctuated with a disarming and slightly wheezy giggle. Like his cousin, Meatball also agreed to cooperate, and the next day it was my turn to author a source opening communication. (In the FBI, there's a tremendous amount of administrative burden and responsibility that accompanies source operations, so Jamie and I shared the load.)

It's an unusual relationship that exists between sources and their handlers. It's not a friendship, but it's not strictly a business arrangement either. You applaud their accidental successes, you mourn their losses (which occur all too often in their world), and you perpetually marvel at the fact that they're always broke. In order to successfully manage a source, it's imperative to form a bond, a mutuality that will establish rapport. If sufficiently cultivated, that rapport will eventually lead to trust. Establishing that bond can be difficult, since the lifestyle of many sources is diametrically opposed to that of their handlers. And while you probably differ on the major points ("no, I don't kill people"), the goal of a good agent is to find that elusive common ground ("I too love fusion jazz, Carl"). Finding common ground with Meatball was going to be tough. In the end, we found something over which to bond, maybe sports or dogs; it didn't really matter.

As we sat in that motel room off the interstate, Meatball recounted the story of how he and Gentile first met. This was many years ago, when Meatball was still just a cocky teenager teetering on the precipice of juvenile delinquency and staring into the abyss of full-blown criminality. He was looking to fence stolen diamonds, and someone introduced him to Gentile, a local mobster who claimed to know a jeweler who could fence hot stones. They drove to New York's jewelry district, and while Meatball waited in the car, Gentile took the diamonds and headed off to see his jeweler. He returned a few minutes later and told Meatball they weren't that valuable after all. As Gentile handed over the diamonds, Meatball realized that Gentile had swapped out his stones with inferior ones. He had the poor judgment to pull a gun on Gentile and demand his real diamonds back, and Gentile, conversely, had the good sense to turn them over. Meatball hopped out of the car and ran for his life. This could have gone badly for Meatball; although Gentile wasn't made yet, he was still a very serious player in the Connecticut underworld and he had some powerful connections. Fortunately, Gentile respected the kid's moxie, and word filtered down to Meatball that all was forgiven.

Meatball and Gentile became fast friends and partners in crime. Meatball told us that back in the 1980s, he and Gentile used to rob drug dealers by posing as cops and FBI agents. This was an interesting anecdote, given Gentile's closet full of police gear.

As we continued to debrief Meatball, I feverishly scribbled notes, trying to keep pace with his easy admissions about the criminal partnership with Gentile. But eventually he told us something that made me stop writing altogether: A dozen years earlier, Gentile attempted to move the stolen Gardner artwork through the Philly mob.

* * * *

The event occurred at Gem Auto. Gentile took Meatball into one of the garage bays and showed him a large cardboard box, laid flat on a workbench, from which he slid out a large oil painting depicting a ship on a stormy sea. According to Meatball, it was *The Storm*. Gentile laid the piece down on the bench and asked, "Do you know what this thing's worth?" Meatball shrugged, to which Gentile replied, "Nothing. This thing is worth nothing. Nobody wants it."

We asked Meatball if he knew what happened to the painting. He told us that a short time later, Gentile instructed him and a mob associate named John "The Jackrabbit" Jackmauh to drive a poultry truck down to the Philadelphia area. According to Meatball, they picked up the truck, which was parked near a barn in South Windsor, just a short distance from Gem Auto, and drove it down to a warehouse on the outskirts of Philadelphia. Meatball, a drug-dealing convicted murderer (three times, no less), told us he'd never been more nervous than he was during that long drive to Philly. When they arrived at the warehouse, Meatball and Jackmauh off-loaded three cardboard boxes, one of which he described as large and oblong. Meatball was certain this was the same box he'd seen previously at Gem Auto.

And while Meatball never opened any of the packages, at the time he assumed that he'd just delivered *The Storm* to Philadelphia.

* * * *

As the twenty-third anniversary of the heist approached, we had a meeting over at the US Attorney's Office to discuss whether we should go public with the recent information regarding the missing artwork. The meeting was attended by myself, Anthony, and executive management from both agencies, including SAC Rick DesLauriers and United States Attorney Carmen Ortiz. Based on the information we'd learned over the last four years, we were confident that we knew who pulled off the Gardner heist. We also had credible sightings of a few of the stolen pieces, sightings that occurred in Reissfelder's Quincy apartment, Guarente's farmhouse in Maine, the trunk of his Oldsmobile, and Gentile's used car lot in South Windsor. We also had credible source information indicating that at least one of the stolen pieces had traveled down to Philadelphia, where Gentile happened to be a made member of La Cosa Nostra.

During the meeting, I pointed out that publicity surrounding the heist had generally been limited to the Greater Boston area, and since we now had intelligence indicating that the missing artwork may have gone as far south as Pennsylvania, expanding the breadth of media coverage and publicity might benefit the investigation. We all agreed to move forward with a press conference, at which time Rick and Carmen would announce that the subjects responsible for the Gardner Museum heist had finally been identified. We would not, however, be providing names.

In a typical investigation, the FBI doesn't name subjects and instead lets the charging instrument, either a complaint or an indictment, speak on its behalf. But this wasn't a typical investigation; this was a recovery operation, and in my opinion, identifying the subjects might yield some fresh leads. We discussed the pros and cons of identifying the subjects who we believe pulled off the heist. Rick agreed with my proposal, but Carmen balked at the idea, concerned that if we were to identify people by name, it may jeopardize any future prosecutions.

And while I understood her desire to preserve the integrity of the investigation, I pointed out that the statute of limitations on the heist had expired nearly two decades earlier; none of these subjects could be prosecuted for the actual robbery. In the end, Rick ceded to Carmen's wishes and we agreed to withhold the identities of the subjects during the presser.

Back at the FBI office, I sat down with Greg Comcowich, this time in his role as the Boston FBI's public affairs officer. We both acknowledged that there would be some negative publicity if we officially announced a solution but didn't identify the subjects. But since the ultimate goal was to generate meaningful leads outside of Massachusetts, we reckoned that we could deal with some criticism. Greg had coordinated with our National Press Office at Headquarters, and they planned to run a targeted media campaign on the FBI's website that would coincide with the presser. He had also secured advertising space for a massive billboard campaign that would run from Boston to Philadelphia.

On March 18, 2013, the FBI, the Gardner Museum, and the US Attorney's Office held a joint press conference at the Boston field office. During his initial statement, SAC DesLauriers announced that the Gardner Museum heist had been solved, in that we'd identified the subjects responsible for the robbery and tracked the artwork's movement.

An excerpt from the SAC's statement:

> The FBI believes with a high degree of confidence that in the years after the theft, the art was transported to Connecticut and the Philadelphia region, and some of the art was taken to Philadelphia, where it was offered for sale by those responsible for the theft.
>
> With that same confidence, we have identified the thieves, who are members of a criminal organization with a base in the mid-Atlantic states and New England.

As I stood before the podium, alongside Anthony and Jamie, listening to Rick's speech and preparing for my own, I had a moment to reflect on the journey that had led us to this point. I'd always hoped that someday I'd be standing before the media, making an important announcement about the Gardner Museum robbery, but of course my hope was for a recovery.

Officially announcing the solution was a small victory, but there was still a much larger mystery to solve:

Where the hell were those damned paintings?

CHAPTER 22

Brotherly Love

We really have reached a point in the investigation where the whodunit part is over.

—FBI SPOKESMAN, March 20, 2013

Shortly after the press conference, I learned about Dave Schratwieser. A veteran Fox News reporter from Philadelphia who'd covered the mob for decades, Schratwieser was everything you'd expect from a hard-nosed organized crime reporter who'd spent his career working the streets of Philly. Although he certainly merits one of those *if you looked him up in the dictionary* literary devices, it's a moot point because you'd probably spell his name wrong. Let's just say that Dave Schratwieser is old school. Tall and solidly built, he has a shock of white hair and a matching goatee framing a mouth that emits the occasional profanity or two, delivered in an accent that immediately betrays his native New York heritage. Schratwieser's knowledge of organized crime in Philadelphia is encyclopedic, and he cohosts the *Mob Talk Sitdown* podcast with George Anastasia, a former *Philadelphia Inquirer* reporter who's been writing about the mob in his city for more than three decades. Suffice to say that when it comes to the Philly mob, Dave Schratwieser is a subject matter expert.

"I've taken FBI agents and US attorneys on what I call my South Philly mob loop of locations," Schratwieser told me. "They get out of the car stunned, because during one or two of those little trips we'd see several high-ranking people engaged in activities that they would pay their agents good money to record."[1] Schratwieser's prowess was built on the simple premise of tenacity: "We knew from years and years of sticking our heads down there in South Philly that this was where these guys might be. We knew the cars and we knew the players, and once you know the cars and you know the players, then you know what to look for. And all that's built up in muscle memory from years of covering the mob, and I've been doing it since the early eighties."

By March 2013, we'd been conducting investigation in Philadelphia for nearly a year, discreetly attempting to corroborate Meatball's claim that Gentile had once brought the artwork down to the City of Brotherly Love, looking for a buyer. After Schratwieser watched our press conference, he began backtracking, looking into the Gardner artwork's Philly angle, gleaning intelligence from the interwoven and competing community of mobsters and associates who trusted his discretion. The job descriptions of a crime reporter and an FBI agent are remarkably similar, and oftentimes the two avocations intersect during an investigation. And as Schratwieser polled his trusted network of informants, the seasoned reporter was learning some revealing details about the paintings—details that his sources would never divulge to the Feds.

Schratwieser had known about Bobby Luisi and his connection to the Philadelphia guys for years, including that doomed drug operation up in Boston that eventually sent Luisi to a federal prison. He knew of Guarente and Gentile and was aware that they were part of the Boston faction. He also knew about the Gardner Museum robbery. "The Gardner has always been this brass ring kind of story," Schratwieser mused. "I'm sure as an agent that's what it was for you," he told me. "It would be great to snatch that brass ring, or to crack that story, and we were hungry for it. Because we were like, there was this half-billion-dollar art heist in Boston and there's a Philly connection to it? And some of those paintings might've come down here? It's a sexy story, and an intriguing one, and a mysterious one, all combined."

As he began asking questions of his sources, Schratwieser heard that the paintings may have traveled down to Philadelphia between 1999 and 2001, about the same time as when Luisi and Joey Merlino had been arrested and were standing trial. "While they're on trial, Joe Ligambi, 'Uncle Joe,'" he clarified, "was believed to be the acting boss while Joey [Merlino] was locked up," Schratwieser said. "Ligambi was in charge during the time period we're talking about, and that's when we heard from various sources that the paintings came down through this area."

I asked Schratwieser if his sources ever specifically mentioned that it was Gentile who brought the paintings down. "Let me put it this way," Schratwieser answered. "I don't know that I can attach Gentile's name to it, but he was the likely person who would do that." Schratwieser continued: "Luisi was obviously locked up, and Guarente was either dead or locked up at the time. So if, in fact, they did come here—and I do believe they did—then Gentile was the guy people were most often talking about it."

Schratwieser's sources heard that two individuals transported the paintings down to a warehouse in Montgomery County, just over the city line. This information comported with Meatball's assertion that he and an associate, John Jackmauh, once drove a poultry truck laden with paintings down to a warehouse located just outside Philly, where they were dropped off.

Schratwieser's network of sources extended beyond the Italian mob; it infiltrated other organizations that existed in the Philadelphia area at the time, including Russian organized crime, the Kensington & Allegheny gang in northeast Philly, the Junior Black Mafia, and a number of loosely knit local street gangs. "I started just drifting out some questions to guys I knew in those different groups to see if they ever heard anything about the paintings coming down here," Schratwieser explained. "And two different sources—and I would say both of these individuals are reliable; people that I've used as sources before, not lightweights—indicated to me that they were told that three of the paintings came into Philadelphia."

I asked Schratwieser if his sources specifically identified which three Gardner paintings came down. "They were the smaller, less expensive ones," he said. "It might have been that one of them was the jockey, either a sketch or a painting." I asked Schratwieser if he was referring to the Degas sketch. "Yeah, that's it," he replied. "One of them might have been"—he paused for a moment—"what's the one that everyone always talks about?"

"*The Storm on the Sea of Galilee?*" I suggested.

"Yeah, I think that was also one of the other ones talked about," he replied.

Schratwieser's discrete network of discreet sources told him that the paintings ended up with an art dealer who lived in Rittenhouse Square, an elegant enclave of posh apartments that's arguably the wealthiest section of downtown Philadelphia. He heard that this art dealer, whom he was never able to identify, then moved the paintings up to New York.

"I was told that was the trail—they came from Boston into Philly, where they were discussed among organized crime figures, including this associate who had a relationship with a Rittenhouse Square art dealer, and that he used his connections to move the paintings up through New York." I asked if the art dealer was associated with the Philly mob. "No, no; he's a friend of an associate," Schratwieser advised. "I've described him as an associate because he was convicted once before on a federal tax case involving several of these people, but not an active member of the mob. He's an elderly individual; I'll describe it like that."

According to Schratwieser's sources, after the Gardner paintings reached the dealer's connection in the New York art world, the trail went cold. "Where they went from there, I don't know," Schratwieser said. "But I believe that the two individuals who told me about the Rittenhouse Square scenario knew what they were talking about. I can't prove where they went in New York or what art dealer ended up with them," although Schratwieser noted that "there were crazy rumors going around here that one of those paintings was literally hanging in the back room of a bar associated with an organized crime figure here in Philadelphia."

Schratwieser once spoke with Ryan McGuigan about his client and the paintings. McGuigan told him that "Gentile, till his dying breath, said he did not know where the paintings were. He didn't know anything about the paintings, and he claimed that till he took his last breath."

Schratwieser added, "I don't believe it, but that's what his lawyer said."

Every time Schratwieser reported on the Gardner paintings, "it drew quite a bit of attention" within the criminal underworld. "People would tell me, 'You know when you guys fucking talk about that all the time, people get nervous; they get upset. They don't like it.' And I'm like, okay, so what?" Schratwieser would counter; "I'd say, 'What people?' And nobody says who it is, but I know who they're talking about. There's three or four guys they're talking about."

Schratwieser also heard rumors that some of the paintings were sold and that a piece of the action—in the "half-million-dollar range"—was "carved off" down in Philadelphia, a story he once discussed on his *Mob Talk* podcast in November 2017. "That story was out and about. Some names were attached to it, but someone all of a sudden had access to a certain kind of funding years later when he got out of jail. And the question was, 'Was this a piece that got broken off that deal?'

"It doesn't take a rocket scientist to figure out when A, B, C, D, and E are there, then F, G, and H are right behind that, you know what I mean?" Schratwieser posed rhetorically. "Because that's the way it works, whether people like it or not. They can piss on it, complain about it, go on podcasts, and throw rocks at people about it, but that's the way it works.... All roads usually lead to something and in some cases—if you're smart—you can figure out where that road leads."

I asked Schratwieser if he had an opinion as to why none of the Philly mobsters came forward with the paintings, given the generous reward and the potential for immunity. "Unless, for example, you were to indict someone and include the receiving and interstate transportation of stolen property as part of a predicate act for racketeering," he hypothesized. "You could do that," he continued, "and you could also include the making ceremony recorded in 2015 where Joe Ligambi introduces everybody in the room and their rank and who people are with."*

He brings up a salient point, and it's one I had considered many times over the years. "That tape is still hanging over the heads of everyone who attended that meeting, including Ligambi," Schratwieser said. "And maybe those paintings are still hanging over somebody's head, as well. But that's just my opinion," he added. "Because if you believe the time period when Gentile brought the paintings down, and all the rumored things that were going on at that time, then it's on Ligambi's watch."

I asked Schratwieser if he believed that Gentile took the secret of the Gardner paintings with him to the grave.

"No doubt about it," he replied.

* * * *

One of the major hurdles to the investigation was the distinctly less-than-intimidating subject matter of beautiful artwork. As the Gentile lead gathered steam, we asked countless sources, inmates, and cooperating defendants if they'd ever seen any of it. We were surprised

---

* Schratwieser was referring to a 2015 ceremony to induct new members into the South Philly mob, which was presided over by LCN underboss Steven Mazzone. During the ceremony, which was picked up on an FBI wiretap, Mazzone warned, "Nobody break this chain . . . I know you were explained the rules already."

at how many of them readily provided positive information. When we asked why they had never divulged this information to anyone else prior to our interview, these individuals would invariably reply, "I didn't think anybody cared about artwork." I discussed this quandary with Schratwieser, and he readily agreed with me, adding, "I don't think anybody asked."

It's a logical assessment. If someone were planning to testify against the mob, for example, they would likely discuss homicides, drug deals, extortion, loan-sharking, and other high crimes and misdemeanors, the juicy stuff that typically underpins a good RICO case. They would be less inclined to mention the fact that years earlier, some old man with a limp showed off a piece of dusty artwork, even if it may have been stolen. To them, moving swag wasn't relevant; it was merely a trivial facet in the day-to-day operations of a criminal enterprise.

In the end, it simply came down to the fact that somebody was finally asking the right questions.

The Gardner's Philadelphia mob angle, which we first publicly reported during the March 2013 press conference, remained a viable line of investigation, right up until my retirement from the FBI. It was the reason why every few months I found myself sitting in a booth at Sonny's on Market Street, inhaling a cheesesteak and talking strategy with Jake Archer, my art crime team counterpart from the Philadelphia field office.

CHAPTER 23

"You mean 9/11?"

There's this dough, see? All this dough...
It's in this box buried under this big W.
You'll see it under this big W.
A big W; you can't miss it.

—*It's a Mad, Mad, Mad, Mad World*

With Gentile in jail, the investigation continued. This included a number of consent searches of locations where he may have hidden the artwork: neighbors' garages, vacant lots, vast tracts of woodlands amidst hunting lodges in northern Vermont, a decrepit barn in the Hartford suburbs, and the homes of some of his erstwhile mob associates. One of his associates even told us that Gentile had a hiding place for weapons and swag, possibly in upstate New York, but what do we do with that information? Even though we continued to strike out with regard to the Gardner artwork, we continued to stumble across criminals.

Back in April 2012, Jamie and I interviewed Dave Raymond, a somewhat forlorn antiques dealer from Glastonbury, Connecticut, who resembled an amalgam of Bono and a later iteration of Elvis. Diminutive in stature, even with generously heeled cowboy boots, his appearance was offset with a spiky mane of dyed-black hair and a Fu Manchu mustache that was forever racing itself to his chin. Jamie and I were following up on information from Sammy Mozzicato, who told us that Gentile had once met with Raymond about the stolen artwork.

According to Sammy, Raymond was introduced to Gentile because he claimed to be a connoisseur of fine art and antiques. When we sat down with Raymond, he told us basically the same story, confirming that in or about 2000 he was approached by Sammy, who had an associate looking to sell high-end paintings. The associate, of course, was Bobby Gentile. Raymond claimed that Gentile later showed up at his golf shop in Tolland, Connecticut, asking Raymond if he knew of anyone who might be interested in buying stolen artwork. Raymond was terrified of Gentile, so he claimed that he didn't know of any buyers. According to Raymond, Gentile was incensed; he turned to Sammy and hissed, "I thought you said this guy could find a buyer?"[1]

That initial interview of Raymond was conducted inside his house, a modest ranch that was cluttered in equal parts antiques and pet dogs. Raymond was cordial, and the interview was casual and nonconfrontational. He showed us some of his pricier antiques as we talked about Gentile. And he was a character—when we were trying to pin down dates relative to his meeting with Gentile, Raymond asked, "When did those planes fly into the buildings?"

"You mean 9/11?" I asked. Dave nodded.

"Let me see...that would have been September 11," I answered slowly, then added for good measure, "2001." Jamie and I exchanged a wide-eyed glance at that one, since that's usually a date that requires no additional calculation.

As we were chatting with Raymond in his living room, an attractive woman arrived in a tizzy. This was Andrea Dobrozensky, a self-professed friend of Raymond's and the office manager of a local medical practice. Her frantic visit came as soon as she heard that the FBI was talking to Raymond. To Jamie and me, she seemed just a little too concerned by our presence, especially after we explained to her that Raymond wasn't in any trouble.

At least, not yet.

Dobrozensky had good reason to be concerned about the FBI, since at the time she and Raymond were involved in an ongoing tax fraud scheme.[2] It was because of her overly suspicious demeanor that Jamie and I started to do a little digging, and it wasn't long before we uncovered some financial irregularities. Completely out of our league on the convoluted and esoteric world of tax law, we brought in the experts from New Haven's financial crimes squad, as well as a few agents from the IRS's Criminal Investigation Division.

It turns out that Dobrozensky, assisted by Raymond, had siphoned off nearly a quarter of a million dollars from her employer without paying the taxes. Her concern over the two FBI agents standing in her accomplice's living room was now completely understandable. Raymond, for his part, had been purchasing expensive rock and roll memorabilia on behalf of Dobrozensky's boss. As part of the scheme, she was paying Raymond with company checks, keeping them just below the $10,000 threshold that would cause the bank to generate a currency transaction report, known as a CTR.

Between August 2009 and the approximate date of our visit, Raymond received twenty checks totaling nearly $150,000 from the medical practice's bank accounts, which he then cashed at multiple bank branches. During one transaction at an Avon branch, bank employees stood by and watched with curiosity as Raymond directed Dobrozensky to write out checks that were, in his own words, "below ten thousand." Dobrozensky dutifully wrote out two checks, each one in the amount of $9,900.[3] As per the provisions of the Bank Secrecy Act of 1970, those bank employees diligently filed suspicious activity reports, or SARs, alerting the Feds to banking transactions that were intentionally kept under the CTR threshold, a money-laundering activity known as structuring.

"You mean 9/11?"

On December 19, 2013, the FBI and IRS-CID executed a search warrant at Dobrozensky's four-acre horse farm in New Hartford, Connecticut. As Jamie and I pulled into the estate and parked behind the two late-model BMWs in the driveway, I must say, we were impressed.

"Not bad for an office manager," I remarked.

"We're in the wrong line of work," Jamie retorted as we exited the Bucar and walked up the driveway.

The house's interior was equally majestic, with two-inch-thick granite countertops, custom cabinetry, and a closet full of Jimmy Choos (a notable fact related to me by a female agent). In October 2015, inside the same Hartford courthouse oft frequented by Gentile, Raymond and Dobrozensky both pled guilty to structuring currency transactions, with Dobrozensky also pleading to filing false tax returns.[4] This entire spin-off prosecution arose simply because Jamie and I were asking Raymond about Gentile and stolen artwork.

Everything that ensued was just a case of people not knowing when to shut up.

* * * *

Two weeks before the Dobrozensky search, Brian broke the news that he'd be leaving the US Attorney's Office and heading into private practice, joining Nixon Peabody, one of Boston's premier law firms. He was a brilliant attorney and I was sorry to see him go. We'd worked together on the Gardner case for years, and I considered him both a colleague and a friend.

"We'll always have the Cosmic Omelet," was all I could muster, referring to our old haunt in Manchester where we wiled away many a morning, waiting on the Cook.

"Yes, we will," he chuckled. "We'll always have the Cosmic Omelet."

CHAPTER 24

"They Didn't Get All of Them"

Art is not truth.
Art is a lie that makes us realize truth.

—PABLO PICASSO

On April 16, 2014, Gentile was released from FCI-Allenwood. He returned home to Connecticut on supervised release, meaning that for the next three years, his activities would be monitored by a federal probation officer. Under the terms of his release, Gentile was ordered to spend the first ninety days in home detention, the exception being medical appointments for himself or Pat, and only with prior approval from his probation officer.

Within days of his release, we wired up our brand-new sources, Meatball and Sammy, and sent them off to visit Gentile on Frances Drive. For months they'd been providing us with information about the Cook, and now we were eager to hear what insight Gentile might be willing to share with his friends. Technically, when they showed up at Gentile's front door, he was obligated to turn them away, since one of the boilerplate conditions of his release prohibited any contact with known felons. And since both Meatball and Sammy were convicted felons—a fact known to Gentile—their very presence would be enough to violate his probation and send him back to prison. Instead, Gentile invited them in. Strictly speaking, we gained leverage over Gentile the moment they crossed his threshold and traveled back with him to the 1970s, but realistically it would've been inappropriate to bust him for violating his probation for associating with known felons when we were the ones who'd orchestrated the association.

There was no need to resort to dirty pool, however, since Gentile began to consort with other convicted felons immediately after his release. Later in court, John Durham would tell the judge that in addition to our two sources, there were "at least six other persons that we know to be convicted felons with whom Mister Gentile has associated since his release."

During this first visit, our sources were instructed to act merely as a sounding board, listening to Gentile as he griped about his latest—and longest—stint in prison. They were not to bring up the Gardner artwork or any other type of criminal activity. When we wired them up for the meet, I also counted out a thousand dollars to Meatball, which he later passed on to Gentile as tribute—that is, a sign of respect for the sources' ongoing drug operation. Like the baggie of loose diamonds once provided to a Corsican mobster on an FBI yacht off Miami, the payment was designed to appeal to Gentile's pride and his innate sense of avarice. And since Gentile had to forfeit the $22,000 that was concealed in his grandfather clock, he was grateful for the cash. He added the crisp bills to his "broccoli wad," the thick stack of hundreds, folded once and secured with a fat, purple rubber band that is historically favored by mobsters.

Over the next few months, Meatball and Sammy met frequently with Gentile at his house. Ever the gracious host, Gentile would sometimes make them lunch, and the recorders were always rolling. As Jamie and I took notes during these painfully long conversations, we'd often put down our pens and take a breather when Gentile would prattle on tediously about the best way to pan-fry chicken cutlets or how to prepare a good gravy; his nickname was, after all, the Cook. Much to our frustration, Gentile loved talking about food, especially new and delicious ways to prepare traditional Italian dishes, a constant exercise in prandial one-upmanship with the sources, who also knew their way around a kitchen. And as anxious as we were to bring up the subject of the Gardner paintings, we didn't want to force the issue. There was a reason why Gentile had spent most of his life sleeping in his own bed: He was crafty, wary, and distrustful of everyone. He had just wrapped up the lengthiest prison sentence of his lengthy life, and it happened only because of the outright betrayal of a person he considered a friend. The treachery only served to reinforce Gentile's preternaturally suspicious nature, and so we needed to take it slow.

As we eavesdropped on their conversations, we learned a lot about Gentile, most of it bad. A few months before he was released from prison, his daughter, Donna Lynn, passed away unexpectedly. When Meatball and Sammy offered their sincere condolences on the passing of his only daughter, Gentile's frigid response was, "Yeah, and I had to pay for the funeral."

The source meets continued, as did the sporadic tribute payments. After Gentile's home confinement wrapped up that spring, he was eager to get out of the house, and while the subject of the Gardner paintings had yet to arise, Gentile was more than willing to discuss other criminal activity.

Over lunch at an Italian restaurant in East Hartford, Gentile told the sources about a potential score involving untaxed cigarettes that were being smuggled up from New Jersey. It was an illegal operation he'd learned about from a fellow inmate. Gentile wanted to participate in the score, and he asked the sources if they wanted to join him. Now, if our objective had been simply to ensnare Gentile in more illegal activity, this would've been the perfect opportunity. But that wasn't our goal; we wanted the Gardner paintings, and so we instructed the sources to pass.

During one recorded meet, Gentile told Sammy that he wanted Prime Time's last name. The fact that he wanted the identity of an FBI source whose cooperation had led to his ultimate conviction and imprisonment was a sobering revelation. At our direction, Sammy stalled for time, and eventually Gentile dropped the subject. During a recorded conversation that took place on June 3, he admitted to Meatball that "the FBI seized a lot of my guns, but they didn't get all of them." This was a disturbing disclosure, and one which tinged the occasionally humorous nature of these meets with an undercurrent of danger. Gentile may be old, but he was still dangerous.

As Durham would later tell a federal judge:

> In this particular investigation, he makes no bones about the fact that people are supposed to pay him respect because he's a made member of the Mafia, that he could have people killed if he chose to do so.

We had no illusions about Gentile. Were he to ever find out that his longtime friends were cooperating with the FBI, the consequences would be fatal.

* * * *

On May 20, 2014, I drove up to Maine with Jamie and Anthony. After so many trips to Connecticut, the change of scenery made for a nice break. We were headed to the Two Bridges Regional Jail in Wiscasset, a trip precipitated by our recent review of court documents relating to Bobby Guarente's federal drug case. We had found an old DEA report which advised that back in 1998, Guarente had once met with an individual named Joe Duchamp* because he needed help repairing an AK-47. A quick search of his name determined that a Boston FBI agent named Mike Kelly once interviewed Duchamp. I spoke with Mike, an outstanding street agent who had since retired, and he told

---

* Last name changed.

me that back in the 1990s, when he was investigating Guarente and Duchamp for cocaine trafficking, Duchamp claimed that his partner was also dealing in stolen artwork. Duchamp was someone worth interviewing, and when we finally tracked him down, we learned that he was back in jail, having been arrested the previous year for selling oxycodone. This was the reason for our trip to Wiscasset, and in keeping with the geriatric feel of the investigation, I did some quick math and calculated that Duchamp was nearly seventy at the time of this most recent drug arrest.

The guards were expecting us, but not Duchamp; he had not been forewarned of our visit. When we got there, he was just finishing up his work shift, doling out ladles of chow to his fellow inmates in the cafeteria. We set up shop in the pantry, pulling together four plastic chairs into a tight circle. The room had the cloying smell of the combined aromas of every industrial-grade meal that had ever been prepared on those stainless-steel countertops, intermingled with an abundance of disinfectant. The floor was a deep burgundy tile with matching grout, imperceptibly canted toward a center drain. It looked like any other commercial kitchen I'd ever visited. Other than the fact that there were no knives.

A guard escorted in Duchamp. He was tall, with a dark brown pompadour perched far back on his head. Over the years, that chestnut wave must have ebbed significantly, revealing an expanse of a forehead at low tide. He regarded us warily behind a pair of corrections-issued eyeglasses. After we introduced ourselves, I informed Duchamp that we were looking into the Gardner Museum heist and that Bobby Guarente's name had come up during our investigation.

"Did Guarente ever mention the stolen Gardner artwork?" I asked.

"Yeah, he had two of them."

Well, that was easy. Please continue, Joe.

Without fanfare, Duchamp told us that back in 1996, Guarente admitted to him that he had two of the stolen paintings, which were stored in his house up in Madison. Duchamp never actually saw the paintings firsthand; rather, he said that his knowledge was based on what Guarente had told him. Guarente advised Duchamp that he planned to make a lot of money when the paintings were sold, and he would use the proceeds to purchase more product; that is, cocaine.

"Do you know what happened to them?" I asked.

Duchamp told us that the paintings went down to Boston for a couple of days before they were moved to Connecticut. When questioned about the significance of Connecticut, Duchamp said that, at the time, Guarente was working with the Genovese crime family down in New Haven. I asked him if he knew the approximate date when the paintings left Maine, and Duchamp was able to provide a surprisingly accurate timeline: He initially stated that the paintings were moved prior to their arrest in 1997, but then he paused for a moment, ruminating as he stared up toward a bank of fluorescent ceiling lights.

"It was April of ninety-six," he finally announced with satisfaction.

"How can you be so sure of the date?" Jamie asked.

Because that was the month that Richie DeVincent, also known as Vinnie the Pig, was murdered, Duchamp stated. At the time, the police liked Guarente for the murder (and with good reason, since he most likely killed him), and they were starting to ask a lot of questions about his involvement. Duchamp advised us that because of the increased law enforcement scrutiny, Guarente moved the Gardner artwork out of Maine within a week of DeVincent's murder.*

Guarente never said how he came to acquire the pieces, but Duchamp recalled that Guarente had been close with Myles Connor, and he assumed the sale was being brokered through him. According to Duchamp, Guarente said that Bobby Donati was involved in the heist, although Duchamp didn't know if he actually committed the robbery or was merely involved in the planning.

In fact, Duchamp said, Guarente told him that Donati was killed because there was concern he might talk about the paintings, and

---

* Richard DeVincent was murdered on April 3, 1996.

Duchamp suspected that Guarente had been the one to order the murder. Guarente claimed that there were three subjects involved in the Gardner robbery—two went into the museum while one stayed outside.

Finally, Duchamp told us that Guarente once asked him if he knew of a fence for the stolen artwork.

"What did you tell him?" I asked.

"Not for that I don't."

You can't visit Wiscasset and not have a lobster roll from Red's Eats. The iconic restaurant has been a mainstay in the town since 1944. Nestled beneath the sweeping canopy of a Siberian elm, it sits at the intersection of Route 1 and the tidal Sheepscot River. We'd just left Duchamp and agreed it was worth driving three miles farther north to grab a late lunch. We discussed Duchamp's information and how much of it confirmed what we already knew about Guarente, especially the transfer of artwork to Connecticut. As cynical and jaded as we had become on this case, we had to acknowledge that it had been more than a decade since anyone had spoken with Duchamp about Guarente, and to my knowledge he'd never before been questioned about the Gardner paintings. Was it possible that Duchamp deposited a fabricated story in the bank, biding his time, just waiting to withdraw it in the event that he was ever interviewed about the Gardner case? It's possible, but unlikely.

Duchamp told us that Guarente moved the paintings down to Connecticut, which could only mean that they went to Bobby Gentile, but as we finished lunch, we had to ask ourselves, "So what?"

How much more information linking Gentile to the stolen artwork must we collect before he would tell us something meaningful?

Apparently, for Gentile there was no tipping point.

* * * *

During the source meets with Gentile, we'd been directing Meatball and Sammy to subtly sow the seeds of a scenario that hopefully might sprout into an undercover operation. For months now, they'd been talking with Gentile about Keith, a wealthy drug dealer from the Southwest who supplied them with their marijuana. The plan was pretty straightforward—if Gentile was amenable, Keith just might be willing to purchase Gentile's stolen artwork and return it to the museum for the reward. Keith knew a crooked lawyer who would middle the deal. We hoped Gentile would like the plan, since not only would he be able to monetize the stolen artwork, he'd get the last laugh when it was recovered a thousand miles from Manchester. In our scenario, Gentile could get rich and humiliate the FBI in one fell swoop.

For months now, I'd been meeting with Mike McGowan, at the time the undercover coordinator for the Boston FBI field office. Relying heavily on Mike's expertise, we had already crafted the story that the sources had been parsing out to Gentile. But since there really was a Keith, and he really was a weed dealer, and he really did live in the Southwest, it would be impossible to find a Bureau undercover who was tailor-made for the role. Instead, we decided that Keith would be leaving the heavy lifting to his underling, a mobster from New Jersey named Tony who would negotiate for the paintings on Keith's behalf.

And although we didn't have a Keith, we did have a Tony.*

Mike submitted the proposal to FBIHQ, and we got the green light to move forward with the undercover operation. Mike came up with the case title, Operation Gardner Grab.

On July 17, 2014, it was finally time to initiate the plan. Over lunch at Champions Pizzeria in Manchester, the sources told Gentile that Keith had offered to purchase the stolen artwork for $500,000 a piece. Gentile was receptive to the idea and vigorously huffed out a few enthusiastic "yeah, yeah" interjections as they related their plan. He especially liked the part about how the artwork would be recovered far away from Connecticut, leaving the FBI with egg on its collective face.

* UCE name changed for security reasons.

Meatball and Sammy asked for a ten percent finder's fee for the deal, but Gentile scoffed at the offer. "I'm not a pig," he said. "We'll chop it three ways."

And in a silver Chevy Impala idling a block away, the one with a Diet Coke in the left cup holder and a large Dunks in the right, Jamie and I listened to it all:

> CHS 1 [MEATBALL]: *Tomorrow when I see Keith, he's going to want some kind of answer. Are we doing anything with these paintings or what?*
>
> GENTILE: *Tell him I gotta go to Boston to get 'em. Tell him I can't get out of town yet. They're [FBI] still watching me.*
>
> CHS 1: *Well if they're watching you…*
>
> GENTILE: *I don't wanna bring heat to you guys.*
>
> CHS 1: *So tomorrow with Keith?*
>
> GENTILE: *We haven't gone to Boston yet. We will.*

In between mouthfuls of pizza, Gentile told the sources that he'd received many offers for the "pictures," but no one was "serious." We later asked Meatball and Sammy what he meant by this statement, and they interpreted it to mean that no one had the half million in cash. The sources suggested that Gentile meet with Tony, Keith's underling from Jersey.

And Tony was very serious.

There was an important takeaway from this lunchtime meet, and it finally answered a question that had been lingering for years. It was about Gentile's dinner in Portland with Guarente and their wives. We could never understand why Gentile, who lied so provocatively about every aspect of the Gardner case during our first interview, inexplicably confirmed that the dinner actually took place. As Gentile and the sources discussed the Gardner "pictures," Gentile brought up that dinner in Portland and told them how Guarente gave him the artwork in the hotel parking lot. Gentile admitted that he "screwed up" and used his credit card to pay the check. It seems that Gentile believed that we'd learned about that fateful meal by examining his old credit card receipts and not from our interview of Elene. Stingy to a fault, Gentile even complained to the sources that Elene had ordered the expensive twin-lobster dinner, and more than a decade after picking up the tab, he was still whining about it.

Over lunch at La Casa Bella in South Windsor the following week, Gentile told Meatball and Sammy that back in the late '90s, he and Guarente had heated discussions about giving one of the stolen paintings to the mobsters in Philly. Guarente had brought up the idea, arguing that it would be an appropriate tribute to the mob for inducting Luisi's crew into the fold, but Gentile was dead set against it, pointing out that the paintings were far too valuable to simply give away, even to the mobsters who'd straightened them out.

During the meet, Gentile agreed to meet with Keith's henchman, Tony. He told the cousins that they would test the plan with one painting. "Bobby starts going, 'If that goes over good, we could probably do others,'" Sammy recalled. "My cousin and I are thinking, 'Bobby's dead in the water. This is all on tape.'" Yes, it was, Sammy; yes, it was.

Meatball suggested that they leave the restaurant and grab one of the paintings, but Gentile said that it was located a five-hour's drive away. Gentile agreed to sell the first painting to Tony for half a million, and he instructed the cousins to "Set it up. I need a week."

Meatball asked if they could tell Keith's underling that Gentile was prepared to sell him the first painting.

Gentile replied, "Yes, I'll do it."

It was time for Gentile to meet Tony.

CHAPTER 25

Operation Gardner Grab

But Grandmother, what big teeth you have!

—THE BROTHERS GRIMM, *Little Red Riding Hood*

Special Agent Steve M.* and I both joined the FBI about the same time. After graduating from Quantico, Steve was assigned to the Newark field office. He did his perfunctory stint on the applicant squad, conducting background investigations on prospective candidates for special agent positions and White House appointees, before being assigned to work Italian organized crime. It was his expertise investigating the wise guys of New Jersey that eventually led him to become a Jersey wise guy himself: Steve became an undercover and changed his name to Tony.

If Gentile was right out of central casting, then Tony was sitting in the chair next to him with a script in his lap, practicing his lines: "*And may their first child be a masculine child.*" With a slicked-back head of hair, a few strategically placed tattoos, and an authentic Jersey accent, he was the embodiment of a wise guy.

* Last name redacted.

We'd fully briefed Steve on his quarry, the enigmatic Bobby Gentile, also known as the Cook. "After you told me about Gentile and the type of guy he was, I went in with that preparation in my head." Steve drew on his many years of working undercover against old-school mobsters. "I refreshed myself about how they acted, and it turns out that Gentile was exactly what I'd envisioned from that older generation."

As Steve tells it:

> Over the course of my time in Jersey, the demeanor of the wise guys changed. When I first started as a driver and a bodyguard, the old-school guys were more measured, like Gentile. They were measured in the way they lived, they were measured in the way they acted, and they were measured in their temperament. I studied the older wise guys and emulated the way they acted. So when I met Bobby Gentile, I was mentally prepared.[1]

A week before the meet, we introduced Steve to Meatball and Sammy, since their impressions of Gentile would be more instructive than the intelligence that Jamie and I could provide. Around a cluster of parked cars in a town park in South Windsor, we sipped coffee and listened to Meatball and Sammy as they provided their insight into the Cook. First and foremost, they warned Steve to be vigilant, since they both feared for their safety when they were around him. "They wouldn't go into the kitchen with him alone," Steve recalled. "They would sit on the porch and try not to go inside the house, because even they were concerned about him." Meatball was more fearful of Gentile than his cousin, which surprised all of us, considering Meatball was a three-time convicted murderer who'd known Gentile for decades.

"I remember Meatball saying that he would try never to be alone with him in the house because he didn't trust him," Steve said, "and they'd known each other for years and years and years." Meatball's warning resonated with Steve. "I had that in the back of my mind that if this guy knew him his whole life and wouldn't go in the kitchen with him, then that's the kind of guy I was dealing with," he reflected.

"And I'd have to figure out how to deal with that."

* * * *

On August 17, 2014, Tony and Gentile finally met. Tony had driven up from New Jersey to begin negotiations for the stolen paintings, and to demonstrate to Gentile that he was "serious," he had a half million in cash stuffed in the trunk of his UC car. In anticipation of the meet, the previous day I'd signed out $500,000 in cash from the Federal Reserve Bank in Boston. This was "flash money," meaning that it doesn't walk; it's used merely to show the bad guy that we're serious. And the FBI wanted it back at the conclusion of the meet. Every single dollar. Although I'd signed for the cash, because I was running the operation, I had to delegate its caretaking to another agent, arguably one of the scarier moments of my career.

"Please don't lose this," I entreated a squadmate as I handed over a bulging hockey bag stuffed with fifty packets of banded hundreds.

Steve and Gentile met over lunch at the Olive Garden in Manchester, a location chosen by Gentile. For someone who prided himself on his discerning palate, we were surprised he'd chosen a chain restaurant. It was also surprising since we knew that Gentile would undoubtedly leave the check for Tony.

As Gentile slid into the booth, Steve heard the unmistakable sound of the butt of a gun, discreetly sandwiched between Gentile's waistband and his ample girth, striking the hard back of his seat. As a veteran undercover, it was a sound Steve had heard on many occasions. "One of the things that I do is to give somebody a hug to check them for a gun. But the *clunk* always gives it away," Steve recalled. "And so I heard that *clunk* and I knew exactly what the fuck was going on." Successful undercovers live by a combination of wits and collective senses, and Steve was no exception. "I could tell it had a wooden grip, because the rubber ones would've sounded different. With a rubber grip, you would've heard a *clung*." As he spoke, Steve did a remarkable impression of gun butts of differing materials striking hard objects.

"Yeah, I know exactly what it sounds like," he said.

I asked Steve about his first impressions of Gentile.

"He acted a little bit more feeble; I remember him portraying a little bit of feebleness."

I asked him if he thought it was an act.

"Oh, a hundred percent," he quickly replied. "One hundred percent an act."

After the introductions were over, Steve's first move was to question Gentile's choice of restaurant. "I said to him that even Italian dogs don't eat at Olive Garden." Steve laughed as he recounted the story. "I remember saying that, and I thought of you when I said it. I'm thinking, Geoff's gonna giggle when I say this."

Outside in the parking lot, I giggled.*

Steve explained the rationale behind that statement. "You know when two male dogs are playing and then they start fighting? They're trying to establish dominance, and it's the same with the old-school Italians; they're trying to exert dominance in a subtle way."

He continued: "I realized immediately that Gentile was that older personality, and that's why I inserted that thing about Italian dogs." Steve needed to exert his own form of dominance over Gentile, and he relied on his vast experience as an undercover mobster to achieve that goal. "I'll try to get in your head first, because I don't know what makes you tick. Until I do, I don't know how to assert dominance."

For better or for worse, that Italian dog comment really struck a nerve with Gentile.

"He got visibly upset with me," Steve recalled.

The mood was tense as the two sized each other up, separated by nothing more than a basket of never-ending breadsticks. "So, the minute I started doing it and he started doing it, it was already like this." Steve demonstrated by punching his fists together. "I knew right away that if I tried to be friends with him, he would sense that as

---

* And for the record, I like the Olive Garden.

weakness, and I wouldn't be the legitimate person that I claimed to be. I was mirroring him. Some people want to be your buddy, but he was absolutely cold as ice. Cold as ice," he reiterated.

"He was never going to come out and be braggadocios or anything like that," Steve said. "He exuded what he needed to exude, and that's one of the techniques that I had adopted years earlier."

As Steve began to learn more about Gentile, he believed that he was dealing with a sociopath. "He fit perfectly my expectation of a guy who'd been in jail, and had been in the mob for that long," Steve said. "He was deceptively dumpy and scary at the same time. And because of his age and his physical condition, you'd think you could blow him over with a feather." Steve, however, knew better than to underestimate his dumpy and scary lunch date.

"But you could sense right away he was a bad motherfucker. That's what I remember from our first meeting, it was me going backwards emotionally."

During their meet, Gentile mentioned to Steve that he had been "straightened out." For Steve, this came as an unusual boast, since mobsters—especially those as self-effacing and humble as Gentile—typically don't acknowledge the fact that they're made men. "That's not something we admit to," Steve said. "We kind of intimate it instead."

Steve and I spoke about the subtle manner in which mobsters discuss their LCN affiliation. "So, if I were to bring you to dinner, I would say either 'he's a friend of *mine*' or 'he's a friend of *ours*.'" In this hypothetical scenario, the choice of possessive pronoun would depend upon whether or not I was made. Since I am not, I would be a friend of *his*.

For Operation Gardner Grab, Tony was not a made man, since Gentile would be able verify the claim through his mob contacts. "I would never present myself as a made guy unless I had a source, maybe in New York or Chicago, who would vouch for me," Steve advised.

After they ordered, Gentile and Tony talked. "We spoke about Keith, and about life in general. He asked me where I was from and I gave him the story that we'd discussed." Steve steered the conversation toward the Gardner paintings, and as Gentile tucked into a plate of farfalle pasta smothered in alfredo sauce, he claimed that while he may have trouble getting the artwork, Tony was "first in line."

The statement resonated with Steve "because it made me realize that now I've got to figure out who's second in line." The statement was also an acknowledgment from Gentile that he knew about the stolen paintings.

"But why was there a line, and how do I get in that line?" Steve wondered.

When lunch concluded, Tony offered to let Gentile take a peek at the cash in the trunk of his car, but Gentile demurred. "No, no, we're good," he said. Apparently, Gentile trusted his seriousness—a good sign. I was so busy running the investigation and the undercover operation that I forgot all about the hockey bag for a day or two, right up until I got a call from the division's financial manager telling me the cash was due back at the Federal Reserve.

"Hey, Russ, do you still have that half mil?" I asked my squadmate.

Fortunately, he did.

* * * *

Every single summer since Jack was a toddler and his younger brother, Will, was an infant, we'd spend a family weekend at the Jersey Shore. It was a trip that I looked forward to all year, and it represented the continuation of an annual pilgrimage that started when I was Jack's age, when we'd load up the Pinto wagon like the Clampetts and head off to the boardwalk of Ocean City.

At strategic times over the past summer, on those rare occasions when I wasn't in Connecticut, Sonia had been asking if she should make hotel reservations, and each time I requested that she hold off.

"No worries, we'll skip it this year," she'd offer cheerfully. "I know you're busy."

"No, we're going; definitely, we're going," would be my boilerplate reply.

Now, with summer winding down and school about to start, it became painfully clear that there would be no family vacation this year. Making tape with two sources and running an undercover operation in another state simply left no time for a holiday, not even one lousy weekend at the shore.

As I reflected back on the past three months, it was pretty pitiful to realize that I hadn't even had two days off from the Gardner case.

CHAPTER 26

Bobby Makes a Friend

I will destroy the strength of the Gentile kingdom.

—HAGGAI 2:22

Operation Gardner Grab was off to a good start and we were up and running. Generally, we alternated undercover meets with source meets, which gained some hard-fought perspective into how Gentile regarded our little crew of deceivers. Although we'd dissuaded him from the untaxed cigarette scheme, Gentile was still itching to engage in other criminal activity. It wasn't just the stolen paintings—Gentile now wanted a piece of the sources' marijuana operation with Keith and Tony.

As John Durham would later relate in court papers:

> Gentile also provided a small, sample size quantity of marijuana to the CWs and in return, wanted a sample of the marijuana "TONY" (the undercover FBI Agent) had available for distribution.

We were like kitten wranglers, attempting to steer the playful Gentile away from career felons and other assorted vices like they were dangling balls of twine. Tony and the sources kept delaying the prospect of a marijuana deal with Gentile, continually shifting the focus to the stolen artwork deal with Keith. Gentile and Tony met regularly to discuss the artwork, and it was always the same: little nuggets of evidentiary gold prospected from a stream of idle chatter. "He talked a lot about food," Steve recalled. "A lot." I knew that well. I'd listened in on all of their lunchtime conversations, my stomach growling as Gentile talked about the Italian delicacies that he loved to prepare.

"He was a cook, obviously, and we talked about food constantly, constant recipes," Steve recounted. "We talked a lot about frying meatballs versus baking them."

"What was his preference?" I asked.

"He used to bake them. And then you go in the oven and turn them so they don't get that hard spot." As exasperating as these conversations may have been, I did pick up a few decent cooking recipes that I was able to pass along to Sonia. I came home from Connecticut one night to a dinner of fettuccini and meatballs. The meatballs were baked; Sonia had turned them in the oven so they didn't get that hard spot.

While the conversations about food were entertaining for Steve, and perhaps even a bit informative for me, it was Gentile's curious manner of conversation that rattled my undercover. "I never got into a rhythm with him," Steve recalled, "and that was his defense mechanism. He kept me on the head of a pin."

Steve was getting a crash course in Gentile's unique personality, a style we'd known for years. "He didn't speak fluidly when we would have a topic of conversation," Steve said. "He was always jumping around, and I always felt that he was testing me for consistency, to make sure I was who I said I was. He would bring things up at an inappropriate time that had nothing to do with the conversation, and make me repeat something I'd said before, especially about my kids." Despite his relaxed persona of bonhomie around Gentile, Steve was constantly rattled by this crafty old man.

"I always remember feeling that I was never comfortable with him."

* * * *

Steve and I spoke about Gentile's deceased daughter, and how her name came up during one of their meets. Steve recalled the conversation vividly: "Gentile said to me, 'that cancer cost me all this fucking money.' I went to you and said, 'you're not gonna believe this fucking guy!'" Steve continued: "I'm telling him I feel bad about his daughter and oh my God, he says to me on tape that he had to pay for a fucking funeral and that cancer cost him all this fucking money."

Gentile's comments were so outrageous that they remained with Steve, well after the meet concluded. "I actually went home and told my wife—and I never tell her anything—but I told my wife, I said, 'you know, I met a guy whose daughter passed, and he told me how much it cost him that she died.'" He shook his head ruefully. "That's all I told her, because I didn't want to worry her. And she was like, 'oh my God.'"

Considering the amount of time they were spending together, I asked Steve if he thought that Tony and Gentile ever established a friendship.

"Yes, the first time I realized that we were friends was during that car ride," he recalled. "You and your guy kept telling me not to be alone with him, that he's a dangerous guy. But I got in the car."

Ah, yes, the car ride.

* * * *

That car ride occurred in October 2014, on a day when Steve and Gentile had scheduled a lunchtime meet in Hartford. When I pulled into our briefing location, a McDonald's parking lot off I-84, I noticed that Jamie was on the phone, wearing an exasperated look. *This can't be good,* I thought as I got out of my Bucar. When the call ended, Jamie told me that we'd just lost our air support for the day. Since ground-surveillance assets were thin, I knew we'd quickly lose Gentile and our undercover when they went mobile. Jamie and I discussed the alternatives and agreed that we had to postpone the meet; it simply wasn't safe for Steve to meet Gentile without backup. And when a black Tahoe with New Jersey plates pulled into the parking lot a few minutes later, we met Steve at the driver's door and gave him the bad news.

He still wanted to do it. Of course he did. Steve was an undercover, and he'd spent days preparing for today's meet with Gentile, memorizing his lines and establishing a game plan. During his drive up to Hartford, he had been undergoing the transformation from an FBI agent to a Jersey mobster, changing the rhythm and cadence of his speech and affecting wise guy mannerisms. By the time he parked his Tahoe, Steve was, for all intents and purposes, Tony. And Tony wanted to have lunch with the Cook.

As the case agent, I didn't have the same excuse. Steve's safety was my ultimate responsibility, and I knew that Gentile was dangerous. I'd heard the stories and inventoried the arsenal from Frances Drive. But I wanted this meet to occur as much as Steve did, probably more. I wanted to hear Gentile talk more about the Gardner paintings.

Steve and I recently talked about that decision.

"As the case agent, I said we should just cancel the meet," I recalled. "I told you that you didn't have to do this, but you were insistent."

"That sounds like me," Steve laughed. "Going against my better judgment."

And so against my better judgment, I relented, and we moved forward with the meet.

It was a decision that I quickly regretted.

In the FBI, whenever a particularly dangerous undercover meet takes place, a SWAT team will be staged nearby, poised to rescue the undercover, or UCE, on command. When I was on the team, we regularly practiced for this type of contingency, known as a hostage rescue mission. Unlike a typical building entry, where rooms are cleared deliberately as the team moves through the interior (think of warm honey flowing through a gently tilted labyrinth, slowly swallowing up danger areas and hidden voids), this action is fast and extremely violent. Time is crucial, and the primary focus is to fight to the *X*; the *X* being the exact location of the undercover. The team moves quickly through a hostile environment, conducting what's known as "dirty clears," that is, quick sweeps of each room to address only overt threats, continuing to drive to the metaphorical *X*. It goes without saying that a hostage rescue mission is dangerous for everyone and is used only as a last resort. It rests slightly below *begging for your life* on the undercover agent's threat continuum.

During these UCE SWAT missions, there was always an undercover embedded with the team. Steve explained that he wanted the decision regarding whether to execute a hostage rescue mission to rest with fellow undercover agents. He wanted UCEs who knew him and would appreciate the current situation. A former operator himself, Steve pointed out that "SWAT guys are bad judges of danger; everything's dangerous. If they see a subject with a gun, then they'll make the decision to execute a hostage rescue." I chuckled as he told me this, because he was right.

"Of course there's gonna be a gun, it's a fucking bad guy! That's why I'm here," Steve emphasized. "Just because there's a gun doesn't make it dangerous."

For today's meet, not only did we lack a SWAT team, we didn't even have adequate surveillance assets. Yet we launched Steve anyway.

Jamie and I followed Steve as he drove to the meet location, a deserted industrial park situated on the outskirts of Hartford. We peeled off as he entered the lot. Gentile was waiting for him, standing next to his old blue Buick.

We watched from our vantage point across the lot as Gentile greeted Tony.

Steve suggested that Gentile follow him to the restaurant, but Gentile waved him off. "He was like, 'no, no, no, get in,'" Steve recalled. I felt the first pangs of unease as we watched Steve exit the Tahoe, leaving behind a cell phone in the cup holder and a firearm tucked under the seat. The doors of the Tahoe locked with a flash of parking lights and a chirp we were too far away to hear. We watched helplessly as Steve climbed into that ancient Buick.

Gentile lumbered into the driver's seat, slamming the door with a squeaky thud heard only by Steve. As Steve settled in, Gentile pulled a piece of bungee cord across his ample belly, casually remarking that his seat belt was broken but this jury-rigged solution kept him from getting pulled over. Steve couldn't help but appreciate the absurdity of this aging mobster binding himself into the faded velour seat with a knotted length of elastic bungee. Steve noticed a pair of dainty hand towels laid out on the center transmission hump and the seat between them, and he was concerned that Gentile may have stashed a handgun under one of those towels. He watched Gentile's right hand carefully as it dropped the transmission into drive, then assumed a position on the wheel with the left hand, six and nine.

They headed off, leaving behind Steve's Tahoe, his cell phone, and his gun.

Gentile quickly accelerated across the wide expanse of pavement and threaded the Buick between two abandoned warehouses. The vehicle pulled onto an obscure access road that ran behind the rear of the complex and merged into the outskirts of Hartford. As Steve regarded his chauffeur, Gentile expertly navigated through the buildings, casually flicking his eyes up toward the rearview mirror, looking for a tail.

There wasn't one. We'd already lost him.

We strained to hear their conversation on Steve's transmitter, which had an effective range of only a mile or two. It grew fainter and fainter, jousting with static until eventually the static won. With no other options available, Jamie and I returned to the McDonald's parking lot and waited. And waited. And waited.

Meanwhile, Gentile was giving Tony a tour of Hartford, pointing out landmarks where he "grew up into the life," as Steve recalled. "He was basically showing me the places that came to define him." As

Gentile drove Steve past the car lot on Franklin Avenue, Steve's head was reeling. "Every time he showed me something new, I'm trying to speak, listen, and think at the same time," he said. "Why is he showing me this? Why is he showing me that?"

They finally made it to an Italian restaurant off Franklin Avenue, and as they had their lunch, talk turned to Keith and the Gardner paintings. "He called him the 'pictures,'" Steve recalled, pronouncing the word as *pitchers*. "In fact, my partner used to say to me, 'did you get the pictures yet?'" When Tony asked Gentile if there had been any progress, he stated that he wanted the deal to move forward, but he was being harassed by his probation officer. He claimed that he was routinely being tailed by the FBI, which explained his tactical drive through the deserted industrial park.

Gentile told Tony that before he could sell Keith the pictures, he had to meet with someone in New York. Gentile instructed him to be ready to complete the deal and to make sure the money was available when Gentile was ready to move. In response, Tony stated that the money for the paintings was already in Connecticut.

"That's the only time that I knew he believed me," Steve said. "He never gave me confirmation that he believed my story. He always left me wondering."

"Whether he believed the story about Keith or whether he believed you weren't a cop?" I asked.

"Oh, he never thought I was a cop," Steve scoffed. "He would've walked out of the Olive Garden in the middle of the meal if he thought I was a cop." It was the story regarding Keith's offer that Gentile questioned.

"He was uncomfortable with that, and I don't know why."

I asked Steve if he believed that Gentile still had the paintings.

"He believed it," he said simply. "And he tried convincing me that he did."

After lunch, they drove to Gentile's favorite bakery. As Gentile waited for his number to be called, he pulled out his broccoli wad and asked an older female customer if she could break a hundred dollar bill. Gentile nudged Tony and whispered, "You always show them the big bills." The woman couldn't change a bill that large, and Gentile laughed at her for not having sufficient cash. "I remember laughing, forcing myself to mirror his enjoyment in her discomfort," Steve recalled. "I remember how uncomfortable I was, but I did it anyway." The interaction with the customer stayed with Steve "because of how boldly rude he was to this innocent and vulnerable woman."

"Gentile enjoyed stepping on her," Steve said. "He relished that. You could see it in his eyes how much he loved humiliating her."

Eventually they headed back toward the deserted industrial park where Steve's Tahoe was parked. "I wasn't as worried when we were out on the main roads," he said, "but when we went into the industrial park, I started getting a little more anxious on the inside, like, what if this fucking guy comes at me or whatever?" Steve began assessing his options. "I'm just gonna fucking punch him in the face and try to jump out of the car, you know, that kind of thing."

Steve's concerns were unfounded. Ultimately, Gentile dropped him off at his Tahoe and they exchanged warm goodbyes.

"That feeling I had in his car that day was that it's obviously dangerous," Steve said. "I was watching his hands and all of those things, but that's the day that I got him."

Bobby and Tony were friends.

* * * *

Meanwhile, back at the McDonald's, panic was beginning to settle in. It started as a taut pull in my stomach and it just kept pulling. We hadn't heard from Steve in hours, much longer than even a leisurely lunch should take. Did Gentile figure out that Tony was an FBI agent? We'd been careful, but the fact remained that Steve's life was literally in the hands of the two convicted felons we'd signed up as sources. Anything could've tipped off the cagey Gentile: an inappropriate slip, a drunken revelation, or even an outright betrayal. Jamie and I started discussing next steps, and we considered calling the Ops Center to have them broadcast a be-on-the-lookout, known as a BOLO, for Gentile's blue Buick.

Three hours after we launched Steve, my cell phone rang. I grabbed it immediately and saw that Steve was calling.

"You good?" I asked.

"We're good" was the casual reply.

Jamie and I let out a collective wide-eyed sigh and treated ourselves to a rueful fist bump as we waited for Steve's arrival in the McDonald's lot. After we shut off his recorder, I gave Steve an earnest handshake that morphed into a big hug.

"Let's not do that again," I said simply.

* * * *

As the operation dragged on, I was haunted by a nagging question: Why didn't Gentile simply cooperate with us and collect the reward? I needed closure to this maddening riddle, so during a recorded meet on October 27, I directed the sources to ask him why he didn't just turn in the stolen artwork himself and make millions. Gentile's reply spoke volumes:

> Yeah, the FBI are motherfuckers. You give them one or two and they don't know where the rest of them are, they put the heat on you and they still put you in jail. They're motherfuckers.

Up until that day, we'd been operating under the premise that Gentile's obstinacy may have been based on omertà, the notorious code of silence sworn to by members of the Italian mob. The code dictated that these "men of honor" were prohibited from cooperating with law enforcement, under any circumstances. We'd assumed that Gentile, a mobster who deeply revered his status as a made man in Philly, was adhering to the precepts of the LCN; he was refusing to cooperate with the FBI simply because it was his obligation to refuse.

But his admission to the sources provided new insight into Gentile's reasoning. Perhaps it wasn't omertà after all. Gentile simply didn't trust us to follow through on our promise of immunity and the hefty reward, regardless of what his lawyer was telling him. He still believed that we would arrest him if he were only able to produce a painting or two.

We're motherfuckers.

Jamie, perhaps, but me?

There was another aspect of his statement that was telling—it was the fact that he specifically mentioned just "one or two" paintings in his hypothetical scenario. This was a consistent thread running through our investigation. It was consistent with the information from Guarente's niece, who told me that only a few paintings were stored in her uncle's farmhouse; it was consistent with Elene's statement that Gentile received a few paintings from her husband; and it was consistent with the jailhouse information we learned from Duchamp.

CHAPTER 27

Unraveled

If you're going through hell, keep going.

—WINSTON CHURCHILL

By September, Jamie and I began noticing that Meatball was losing weight. At first it was subtle, and for a brief period he looked really good, shedding those excess pounds that formed the basis for his spherical nickname. But as the months progressed, the weight loss became more pronounced, and as Meatball began to flounder in that ubiquitous black ensemble, it became too obvious to ignore. We finally asked him about it, and Meatball admitted to us that he had terminal cancer. He was deteriorating rapidly, and by the time Steve had been introduced to Gentile, Meatball was in pretty bad shape.

As Meatball's condition worsened, Steve met with Gentile at an Italian deli in Hartford. Gentile told him about Meatball's terminal cancer, and Tony feigned surprise. Gentile said that he wanted to cut Meatball out of his share of proceeds from the sale of the "pictures." He confided in Tony that even though he'd promised to give Meatball's share to his sister, he had no intention of following through on his pledge.

And it wasn't just the proceeds from the stolen artwork—Gentile wanted to excise Meatball from any future marijuana deals as well. To that end, Gentile wanted Tony to get from Meatball the phone number of his weed customer. This would allow Gentile to cut Meatball out of future transactions. Gentile rationalized his perfidy by telling Steve that "it was a waste to give Meatball money because he was going to die anyway."

Tony wasn't as ruthless, and he refused Gentile's request to get Keith's number. He hoped that by doing so it would show Gentile that he valued allegiance. Steve believed that perhaps Gentile was merely testing Tony's loyalty, and if he remained loyal to Meatball, Steve reasoned, then he would remain loyal to the Cook.

"I distanced myself to that betrayal," Steve told me. "I wasn't going to participate in that betrayal with him, but he gave me the 'Bob growl.'"

"The Bob growl?" I asked.

"I called it the Bob growl." Steve explained: "He would be rational and lucid, and then something would aggravate him and he'd have this type of a growl. He liked to get his own way." I knew that growl well, although I'd never given it a name.

But Gentile's anger with Tony was genuine. This wasn't some kind of a test; he really wanted to steal Meatball's share of the proceeds and cut him out of any additional drug deals. And Tony's unwillingness to betray their mutual friend was hampering his plans.

"That was part of his coldness," Steve reflected. "This was a guy he'd known his whole life, and he was gonna screw him out of his end."

* * * *

On October 30, 2014, Gentile and Tony had lunch together at an upscale Italian restaurant in South Windsor. This would be their last meeting, and after the frightening car ride from a few weeks earlier, we were leaving nothing to chance. There would be no more road trips;

Steve was meeting Gentile at the restaurant. In addition to the mobile surveillance teams that took Gentile from his house to the restaurant, four of the patrons inside that restaurant were FBI agents, miming casual conversation as they carefully watched Gentile from the corners of their collective eyes.

The purpose of this meeting was for Tony to deliver an ultimatum: Enough was enough. The operation had been dragging on for months, and while there had been some scintillating statements from Gentile about the artwork—and some pretty good pasta recipes—we'd gotten nothing substantive. Gentile enjoyed playing with the elasticity of his timeline, promising an impending development and then suddenly putting on the brakes.

"This was one of those 'speed it up, slow it down' type of things," Steve recalled.

Now it was time for us to speed it up. Over lunch, Tony informed Gentile that Keith's group would not be selling any more marijuana to Meatball and Sammy until the Cook sold him the paintings. Discussions were over—Keith wanted the artwork.

Gentile began making excuses. He told Tony that the deal was delayed because he had to meet with people in Boston, but he couldn't leave Connecticut because he was still on probation. Gentile added that if he was caught out of state, he'd go back to prison for three more years.

He then claimed that $500,000 a painting was too low and suggested that Tony should speak with Keith about increasing the sale price. Tony was expansive and willing to negotiate, but when he asked for a specific price, Gentile claimed not to know the exact amount his partners wanted for the artwork.

"He told me that he didn't have them in his garage," Steve said. "Gentile said he was the conduit to them, and not the possessor of them."

Gentile claimed that he had three of the most valuable pieces available for Keith: A small sketch, *The Storm*, and "a gold eagle that sat at the top of a flag or a statue."

"He told me multiple times during this meet that I just can't do it now," Steve recalled. "He kept saying that Keith's got to give me more time."

There were too many excuses. We were all growing tired of these fruitless meetings with Gentile, so Tony told him that they were out of time.

This did not sit well with Gentile.

"He became extremely violent, even though he was sitting down." Steve chuckled. "I never saw someone act that violent sitting down."

Steve became concerned that Gentile was going to come at him from over the table. "There were only two times that I felt physically threatened by him," he said. "It was this time, and that time in the car. Those were the times that I was physically ready."

At first, Steve thought that it was an act, part of Gentile's "acceleration/deceleration thing" where he suddenly uncoiled in rage and then quickly reeled himself back in. But the rage didn't subside, and Steve realized that Gentile's anger was sincere.

"I'm always apprehensive and always careful. Very rarely have I been scared, but that day was close. I knew he could be carrying a gun, and if he became irrational..." Steve trailed off. He took a moment to form his words carefully: "Like, it was an irrational, unnecessary outburst, you know what I'm saying?"

Gentile was furious, and warned Tony that he was a made member of La Cosa Nostra. "Do you know who I am?" Gentile hissed. "I could have people killed and make them disappear."

As Gentile ranted, four other diners casually put down their utensils and slid toward the edge of their booths, hooking their legs around the corners, ready to move. "It was like totally out of place," Steve said. "I was like, 'holy fuck, if it's gonna happen, it's gonna be here.'"

But despite Gentile's remonstrations, Tony held firm. He told Gentile that until he produced artwork, his business with Keith was done.

"I think it was a camouflage screen because he no longer had the paintings," Steve opined.

Gentile stood up from the table and stormed through the dining room, skirting the FBI agents who formed our inner surveillance team. As Gentile exited the restaurant, those four diners picked up their forks and knives and resumed eating. Outside, I watched Gentile's halting gait as ambled across the parking lot toward his car. He swung open the driver's door and threw his cane across the seat before following it into that old blue Buick.

"He was just good," Steve said simply of Gentile. He struggled to put his thoughts into words. "Like, his whole life; everything he did was just by design. He was not an accident. You see what I'm saying? He was not an accident."

* * * *

A few days later I received from the New Haven division an interoffice envelope, known as a cheesy. It contained the lunch check from the four agents who surveilled the meet between Gentile and Steve. They were submitted to me for reimbursement out of case funds. I called Jamie.

"Hey, who the hell ordered the steak?"

Jamie chuckled. He told me that it was an agent known for his largesse when the Bureau was picking up the check.

"Jesus, what is he, Elene?" I asked. "Why didn't he order the twin lobster?"

CHAPTER 28

When Meatball Finally Enters the House Alone

They can do what they wanna do, when they wanna do it.
They suck you in.

—ROBERT GENTILE, describing the FBI (July 26, 2010)

By the new year, Operation Gardner Grab was drawing to a close. We'd given Gentile some time to cool down and reconsider, hoping he'd reach back out to Tony. Eventually, Steve grew weary of me pestering him with the litany of "anything yet?" phone calls, and with discussions about the stolen artwork at a standstill, it was time to discuss the next logical steps in the investigation. Our conversations kept circling back to the sobering fact that Gentile, a convicted felon on federal parole, bragged to our sources that "the FBI seized a lot of my guns, but they didn't get all of them." This statement, coupled with the clunk (not a *clung*, but a *clunk*) that Steve heard during the Olive Garden meet, made it clear that we couldn't just walk away from Bobby Gentile.

We devised a straightforward plan to address the outstanding firearms issue: Meatball would attempt to purchase a gun from Gentile. And while none of us harbored any illusions that Gentile would talk if he were arrested once again, given his astronomical track record of obstinacy, we would afford him one last opportunity to cooperate. We planned to interview him before placing him under arrest; perhaps, given the recent decline in his wife's health and the prospect of a second term in federal prison, he might reconsider. In all likelihood, however, we assumed he'd continue to plead ignorance.

Jamie and I sat down with Meatball and told him the plan. He was amenable and agreed to meet with Gentile once again.

* * * *

In early February, I got a call from Jamie:

"Hey, Meatball's in the hospital. It's not looking good."

I drove down from Boston that night, and Jamie and I visited Meatball in the hospital. He looked frail and vulnerable, clad in a patterned hospital johnny and tethered to a network of chirruping medical equipment. We represented perhaps the most ironical trio ever to assemble at Hartford Hospital: two veteran FBI agents visiting a convicted triple murderer. It wasn't friendship by any means, but it was mutual respect. Meatball's body was wracked with cancer, and there was little the medical staff could do other than dull the pain.

For more than two years, Meatball had provided us with actionable intelligence on Gentile. He wore a wire—the ultimate betrayal of the criminal code—and helped introduce an FBI undercover to his friend. In return, we paid him well for his services, money that would help out his family after he passed.

Meatball was done.

Actually, he wasn't. "I'm still gonna do this for you guys," he said in that high-pitched voice that no longer seemed so incongruous, now emanating from a withered shell that was distinctly un-Meatball. He still wanted to go through with the plan to buy a gun from Gentile.

There was no more money in it for Meatball—not that it really mattered to him at this point—but he felt that he owed it to us.

He was doing it out of loyalty.

* * * *

Meatball was released from the hospital a few days later. It wasn't an "all better" release, it was a "get your affairs in order quickly" release. Time was running out, but still he wanted to make the deal happen for us. He called Gentile.

On February 22, 2015, we wired up Meatball and followed him to Frances Drive. Using a scenario which we'd crafted for him, he told Gentile that he was owed money from a drug deal and the buyer was refusing to pay up. Meatball needed a firearm. Gentile advised him that he should always carry a gun, and added that he should probably be carrying one, as well. Gentile knew someone who could get Meatball a Luger for a thousand bucks and said that it would take a couple of days to acquire.[1] As Jamie and I listened to the conversation, we had to hand it to Gentile—he was insulating himself from what amounted to a patently illegal transaction by claiming that the firearm was coming from a third party. We assumed he already had the gun, and it turns out, we were right.

Five days later, Meatball and Gentile again discussed the proposed firearm sale. Gentile told Meatball that the seller, who was most likely a figment of Gentile's warped imagination, wasn't comfortable traveling with the weapon during the week, so Gentile would meet with him over the upcoming weekend. Gentile advised Meatball that he would give him a call, either on Saturday or Sunday, and if he asked, "Have you spoken with your cousin?" then this would be a code phrase indicating that he had obtained the firearm. Gentile informed Meatball that if this were the case, the deal would occur the next day, Monday, March 2.

In Hartford that Sunday, it began snowing around noon, and by evening it was approaching blizzard-like conditions. As the snow began to accumulate outside, Meatball finally received a call from Gentile. As discussed, Gentile asked Meatball if he'd heard from his cousin, and then he cryptically instructed him to come over to his house immediately and get the gun. Gentile was impatient and told Meatball that he wanted it out of his house.

As soon as he hung up the phone, Meatball called Jamie with the news, but due to the inclement weather, it would've been impossible to assemble a surveillance team to cover a nighttime gun buy inside the Cook's house. Jamie instructed Meatball to call Gentile back and tell him that due to the poor weather and his health issues, the transaction would have to wait until the next day. A few minutes later, Meatball dutifully reported back to Jamie that although Gentile was furious, he agreed to do the deal Monday morning.

The weather on Monday, March 2, was beautiful. It's known as "weather whiplash," yet another example of the stark climate extremes that are so common in the Northeast. As the sun began to break through the cloud cover, two agents searched Meatball and his vehicle for contraband while Jamie counted out $1,000 in government funds. The recording device was activated, and after final instructions were theatrically mimed, Meatball headed out. A surveillance team tailed Meatball to Frances Drive and watched carefully as he walked through the front door, finally alone with Bobby Gentile in the one place where he never wanted to be alone with Bobby Gentile. And to purchase a gun, no less.

As recorded on the pinhole camera secreted in Meatball's jacket, we later watched as Gentile brought him into a small room off the foyer and unzipped a couch cushion. Gentile reached inside the cushion and produced a zippered blue bag and, like Russian nesting dolls, unzipped this bag and finally withdrew the firearm. After Meatball counted out the thousand dollars, Gentile handed over the weapon. Meatball, obviously uncomfortable with the entire scenario, stuffed the bag into his leather jacket and quickly exited Gentile's house. The surveillance team watched as, for the last time, Meatball backed out of

Gentile's driveway and turned onto Frances Drive, a wet black stripe bracketed by twin blankets of fresh snow.

Back at the New Haven office, Jamie and I examined the firearm. While Gentile had promised to sell Meatball a Luger, a valuable pistol manufactured in Germany, Gentile had stiffed his buddy yet again and instead sold him a Colt Cobra revolver, a much cheaper alternative.

In order to charge Gentile federally with possession of a firearm that had traveled in interstate commerce, we needed to demonstrate that the weapon had indeed crossed state lines. The easiest way to prove this essential element is based on the manufacturer—if the company is located outside of Connecticut, then obviously at some point the firearm must have traveled interstate. And of the thousands of licensed gun manufacturers around the world—like Luger, for example—luck would have it that Gentile sold Meatball a gun that was manufactured in the good old state of Connecticut. Of course it was. I opened the cylinder and dumped out the six rounds of .38-caliber ammunition that were nestled snugly in their chambers. The ammunition was Smith & Wesson, manufactured just over the state line in the Commonwealth of Massachusetts. Jamie and I breathed a collective sigh of relief; although we couldn't charge Gentile federally with the firearm sale, we still had him for the ammo.

When the firearm was traced by the ATF, we found out something really interesting: Back on October 27, 1970, it had been purchased by Gentile's wife at a gun shop in Manchester. Since none of us actually believed that Pat was packing heat, she had obviously been a straw purchaser for her mobster husband.

I sat down and drafted yet another arrest affidavit for Gentile:

> Based on the foregoing, there is probable cause to believe, and I do believe that on March 2, 2015, Robert Gentile, a previously convicted felon, did possess .38 caliber Smith & Wesson ammunition which had traveled in interstate commerce (and which was contained inside the .38 caliber Colt Cobra) in violation of Title

> 18, U.S. Code, § 922 (g)(1). Further, there is probable cause to believe, and I do believe that on March 2, 2015, Robert Gentile sold a firearm and ammunition, namely the above-referenced .38 caliber Colt Cobra which was loaded with .38 caliber Smith & Wesson ammunition, to a known felon, in violation of Title 18, U.S. Code, § 922(d)(1).

It was time to arrest Bobby Gentile again.

* * * *

The FBI uses a matrix to determine if a subject should be arrested by the SWAT team. There are a number of factors that trigger a tactical solution, things like the subject's previous criminal history, especially any crimes of violence, and access to firearms. Despite the fact that Gentile ticked virtually every box, a SWAT arrest was out of the question. The first time I arrested Gentile, I'd casually sauntered up to his vehicle while traffic roared below us on I-384. This was, of course, before we discovered the arsenal of weapons stashed in his house. We would not be so cavalier again. We had to find middle ground, a scenario that ensured everyone was safe—including Gentile.

On April 17, 2015, Gentile's probation officer called him in for a routine interview, a fairly common request and one that wouldn't arouse suspicion. The Federal Probation Office happens to be located inside the Hartford courthouse, just down the hall from the US Attorney's Office. All visitors to the courthouse—especially ex-cons on supervised release—are required to pass through a phalanx of armed security personnel and an array of magnetometers, a security regulation that ensured Gentile would be unarmed when he met with his probation officer.

The meeting that morning was a ruse, of course, scheduled at our request. During his pretext meeting with his PO, Gentile answered some perfunctory questions about his lifestyle and made assurances that he was staying out of trouble. When the meeting concluded,

Gentile exited the office and was met in the hallway by two FBI agents, who politely asked that he accompany them to the US Attorney's Office. Gentile was accommodating, limping alongside the agents, assisted by his trusty cane.

Jamie, John, and I were sitting in Durham's conference room, just down the hallway, when Jamie received a text alerting us to the imminent arrival of Gentile and his escorts (imminent being a relative word, since his glacial pace of travel kept us waiting a bit). We overheard their murmured conversation as they plodded along on their journey. When Gentile was finally ushered inside the conference room, his amiable conversation with the agents stopped abruptly and his eyes narrowed, flicking back and forth, settling briefly on each member of a hunting party that he hadn't seen in years.

"Have a seat, Mr. Gentile," Durham said.

He was sanguine, but there was a wariness as he took his seat, resting his hands on the cane before him. He regarded us quietly. I told Gentile about Meatball and Sammy, and how they'd been working with us for more than a year, recording those lunchtime conversations and deflecting his entreaties to engage in drug deals and untaxed cigarette schemes. I told him about the firearm he sold to Meatball, a Colt .38 that was purchased in his wife's name. To punctuate the allegation, I slid an 8 x 10 photo across the table toward him; it was a "pitcher" of his firearm, with a blank evidence sticker already affixed to the corner, ready to be admitted as a court exhibit. Although his emotions betrayed little, I could only imagine how he must have seethed at the abject betrayal by Meatball and Sammy, who until moments before he counted amongst his inner circle of friends. I told Gentile about the recorded conversations he had with them about the stolen Gardner paintings, and how he admitted to his involvement.

"I didn't talk about no pitchers," he countered.

"Bobby, we have you on tape talking about it!" His reply was a dismissive shrug.

I'd been preparing for this interview for weeks, anticipating this moment, and I'd crafted a script, or at least one half of a script, for today's performance. The amount of time that goes into the script varies greatly depending on the situation. Interrogating a newly arrested robbery suspect, for example, may be more of the improv variety, while the interview of the main subject in a case like the Gardner is the culmination of months, or even years, of investigation. Interviews are crafted carefully, using information gleaned from the case file, court transcripts, and, as in this case, even our Behavioral Analysis Unit. The script is memorized and rehearsed, until it's ready for opening night. But remember: It's a one-night stand, so you better get it right the first time.

As I spoke with Gentile, I was reciting lines from a mental script I'd been working on for weeks, a soliloquy that had been crafted and refined. The culmination of years of investigation. And like any great play, it needed a great line, one that would have the critics talking. I'd been honing that line for weeks now, perfecting the wording and the delivery, even rehearsing it in front of the mirror like De Niro. (*"You talkin' to me?"*)

It was time for my line.

"Bobby, we got you once, and maybe we just got lucky," I said. "But we just got you again, which means we're just smarter than you."

I was hoping for a '70s sitcom moment, one of those situations when Sammy Davis Jr. or Shirley MacLaine makes a surprise appearance and the audience roars with delight. The applause continues and the actors freeze, waiting for the din to subside so they can move on with the show. I did not get that.

"I guess you are," was all he said.

Gentile denied everything. Weed deals, gun sales, the Gardner paintings. Everything.

"Tell us about the paintings, and you'll get to go home tonight," Durham offered. Gentile feigned ignorance, denying that he ever mentioned the stolen artwork. He claimed that Meatball and Sammy were lying.

To continue the theatrical metaphor, it was time for the climax, the moment that would signal the curtain and the house lights. It was time to rattle Gentile. I sent a discreet text from my phone, and a few seconds later that moment arrived, just as we scripted it:

Enter Tony, Stage Right.

The slicked-back hair, the smattering of tattoos, the Jersey attitude. Except it wasn't Tony. It was Special Agent Steve M. He was wearing an FBI polo shirt, with a gold badge clipped to his belt, nestled snugly against a holstered Glock 22.

"How ya doin', Bobby?" Steve asked casually.

"You could see the fucking blood just leave his body," Steve recalled. "He just melted. He was like a snowman Florida. He became just like a big fat snowman in Florida."

All those lunchtime meets, the conversations about mob life, the poignant tour of the old neighborhood and the shared enjoyment in the humiliation of that poor old lady in the bakery. Recipes and cooking tips, discussions about deal drugs and offers to sell stolen paintings—all of it had occurred with an undercover FBI agent. That one had to sting.

Gentile quickly composed himself, and he mustered a reserve that was, quite frankly, impressive. After taking a moment, he casually replied back to Steve: "Oh, hey Tony, how ya doin'?"

Steve took a seat and we continued the interview. To thoroughly beat the metaphor to death, there was no denouement. Gentile never confessed to anything of value. When Steve looked him in the eye and told him that they discussed the stolen paintings on tape, Gentile replied, "I don't know what you're talking about." Over and over and over again.

Sometimes an interview goes on so long you're secretly wishing that the subject will lawyer up, since investigators hate to admit defeat. This was one of those situations; Gentile would've stayed there all day, denying every incontrovertible fact we put to him. Finally, there was a tacit agreement amongst us that this interview was unproductive and not likely to change. I stood up and walked around the table to Gentile.

"All right, Bobby, stand up for me. You're under arrest." The command wasn't designed to be authoritative or intimidating; it was one of resignation and frustration. With my assistance, Gentile rose unsteadily from his chair and proffered hands that still grasped his cane. And for the second time, I clasped my handcuffs on those aging and arthritic wrists. The arrival of Steve had to have crushed Gentile, since it completed the circle of treachery; in the end, it turned out that his universe of friends was comprised of two FBI sources and an undercover agent.

Despite the torturously slow gait, Jamie and I walked Gentile the short distance down the hall to the US Marshals Service for booking. The key verb in that sentence is *walked*. For two hours later, when Gentile appeared before Judge Robert Chatigny, the same judge he appeared before years earlier, he was rolled up to the defense table by a deputy. The wheelchair would be a courtroom prop that Durham would bring to the judge's attention during Gentile's detention hearing three days later:

> THE COURT: I can see the risk of flight grounds and I can see the dangerousness grounds, and I can see why you would classify selling a weapon to a known convicted murderer would present an element of danger, but the man is in a wheelchair now, so how do you envision that he would be absconding and not showing up? I mean obviously, he's not going to run away, not going to walk away. What do you think—I mean how would it happen that he would fail to show to answer these charges?
>
> MR. DURHAM: Well, I would indicate, as we indicated on the record when Mr. Gentile came to the courthouse last Friday, he was not in a wheelchair. He walked in on his own, went to Probation walking on his own, eventually came down to the third-floor

> walking on his own. It was only after we had arrested him in connection with a gun that he found the need for a wheelchair, and the wheelchair that he was in on Friday and I'm presuming the same one he's in today actually belongs to the US Marshals Service. So he's more ambulatory than it might appear.

During Gentile's initial appearance, Judge Chatigny told Gentile that "every boxer knows when it's time to hang up the gloves." Apparently, the judge mused, Gentile still didn't know that it was time. He was ordered held once again. Outside the courtroom, Ryan McGuigan told a group of reporters that "if this isn't about the Gardner heist, I'll eat my hat."[2]

Bon appétit, Ryan.

After Gentile's initial appearance, both he and McGuigan met with us back in Durham's office. For all the courtroom theatrics and bluster, McGuigan was hardly an adversary; he was attempting to help his client to the greatest extent possible, and that meant getting him to cooperate with the government. Gentile had already defied his attorney's advice once before and ended up serving thirty months at FCI-Allenwood. Now we had him again, dead to rights, and Ryan was still advocating in Gentile's best interests, even if Gentile was sabotaging his counselor's earnest efforts.

"We're professionals," Ryan later said of the arrangement. "When we go to court it looks like we're fighting like rabid dogs but when we're done, everybody respects one another." Even with his attorney present, Gentile continued his illogical denials. Steve had joined us and tried unsuccessfully to engage Gentile in the recorded conversations they'd shared about the Gardner artwork, prodded on by McGuigan.

Gentile had refused his lunch back at the cell block, so as the meeting dragged on, I offered to get him something to eat. He asked for a chicken parmigiana sandwich, so I left the federal building and found a Subway a few blocks away. (Who doesn't like Subway?) I bought him a chicken parm sandwich and headed back to the office. My mom's right—I am a good person. I handed Gentile the sandwich.

"What's this?" he asked as he studied the wrapper.

"It's a chicken parm, Bobby."

"That's not a chicken parm," he lectured. "You gotta go to Franklin Avenue to get a real chicken parm," he continued, directing me to one of the authentic delis in Hartford's Italian district. With a contemptuous flourish, he tossed the still-wrapped sandwich into the waste basket, where it landed with a hollow echo. That really pissed me off, especially since I hadn't eaten all day.

"Remember that chicken parm when you're eating your bologna sandwich back at the jail tonight, Bobby," I seethed.

His response was a noncommittal shrug of those sloping shoulders.

Steve remembers the event clearly. "He wouldn't eat the sandwich. Remember he wouldn't eat the sandwich?" he posed rhetorically and chuckled. "I'll never forget that."

CHAPTER 29

The Case of the Mysterious Visitor

They denied that the Moon was Stilton;
they denied she was even Dutch.

—RUDYARD KIPLING,
The Gods of the Copybook Headings

Two weeks after Gentile sold Meatball the gun, Anthony, Rob Fisher, and I once again interviewed Rick Abath at the US Attorney's Office in Boston. At the time, I was in the midst of preparing an affidavit to arrest Gentile for the gun sale, and Rick represented one of those awkward idiosyncrasies of the Gardner case, rapidly traveling back to March 1990 in order to investigate a historical museum robbery, then seamlessly returning to the present day in order to trace the current whereabouts of the stolen artwork.

The reason for the latest interview of Rick hinged on his puzzling decision to open the Palace Road service door twenty minutes prior to the arrival of the subjects. Over the years, Rick had steadfastly maintained that checking that exterior door was part of the guards' nightly security protocol, despite the abundance of evidence to the contrary. Based on the security data recovered from the computer hard drive, we were aware that he had also opened the service door the previous night, Friday, March 17.

Rob reasoned that since the exterior door was situated at the far end of the mantrap, he wanted to see how Rick could have opened that door without getting locked inside. Rob offered to take a look at the accompanying surveillance video, so I had our Electronic Surveillance Room, known as ELSUR, burn a copy of the March 17 surveillance video. A day after I dropped the disk off with Rob, he gave me a call.

"Hey, you guys need to come over here and take a look at something."

A few hours later, Anthony and I sat down with Rob in his office and huddled around a computer, watching fuzzy black-and-white surveillance images play out from the night prior to the world's largest art heist. At 12:48 a.m., the exterior footage showed a car pull up and park directly in front of the Palace Road service door. We watched as a lone figure emerged from the driver's side of the vehicle and approached the door. We then turned our attention to the interior camera, which depicted the back of Rick's head, a blurry tangle of curls seeping out from under that ludicrous cowboy hat. The visitor, now discernible as a white male, cleared the mantrap and approached the watch desk. He appeared to chat briefly with Rick as he leaned casually on the counter, before he disappeared off-screen for a minute or two. After reappearing on-screen, he and Rick exchanged a few final words before he exited out to Palace Road. By 12:53 a.m., he was gone.

We sat down with Rick on March 20 and played the surveillance footage for him. "I remember the day that you, Anthony, and I showed Rick the video and just how much time he spent looking at it," Rob recalled. "I was thinking that he was finally going to come around and say something more than he'd said over the years, but still nothing."[1]

The Case of the Mysterious Visitor* would be solved a few months later, and the solution would uncharacteristically absolve Rick from blame—at least for letting that unidentified individual into the museum on the night prior to the robbery. But there were still concerns about that surveillance video, specifically the poor quality of the images, and they called into question Rick's observations of the subjects when they showed up at the service door the following evening.

"If you look at his original statements when he said, 'I could see the police pull up and I watched two policemen get out of the car,'" Rob pointed out, "from the previous night's video, however, you can see shadows but you would never know those are policemen."

It was a valid point. That exterior video was horrible—it showed a darkened street, with a tightly proscribed halo of gray emanating from a streetlight positioned above the screen. The Mysterious Visitor's car was no more than an angular black box with two white blotches for taillights. And when he exited his car, cloaked in darkness and abysmal video quality, he was no more than a dark gray blob silhouetted against the slightly lighter gray of the sidewalk.

And since the video images from March 17 would be the same as those from the following night, we had to conclude that there was simply no way that Rick, from his perch at the watch desk, could have discerned that the subjects were wearing police uniforms. Not surprisingly, Rick had no explanation, other than to suggest that perhaps the video images on the watch desk monitor were sharper than the images that were recorded on the videotape.

"Wherever you look," Rob reflected, "every part of Rick's story was extremely questionable."

* * * *

On May 28, 2015, Ronald "Meatball" Bowes died. I sat at my computer and opened his informant file so I could submit the source closing

---

* Not a Nancy Drew title, but should be.

communication. Under "reason for closure," I scrolled through the drop-down options and dispassionately settled on "deceased."

Jamie is reflective when he talks about Meatball:

> He was an enforcer. He was drug dealer. He was a weed dealer and he sold coke. He beat the shit out of people. He killed people. He shot people, and he put guns in people's mouths.
>
> But that guy never told us a lie. Never.

* * * *

On July 21, 2015, McGuigan filed a motion to dismiss the gun and ammunition charges, an argument premised on the claim that the government targeted Gentile for criminal investigation, and through our outrageous conduct, we caused him to engage in criminal conduct "in order to force him into cooperating in its investigation into the largest art theft in history."

According to McGuigan's motion:

> The Government has engineered the instant prosecution, solely for the purpose of pressuring the Defendant into cooperating with a wholly unrelated investigation...by means of placing into his life a confidential informant wired for sound and bearing government-issued money in order to induce the defendant to commit crimes.

Ironically, McGuigan's motion was based on a pleading filed in US District Court in Massachusetts nearly two decades earlier by none other than David Turner, who made a similar argument; that is, that the FBI had coerced his participation in illegal activity in order to force him to cooperate with the Gardner investigation. As detailed earlier, Turner's motion was ultimately dismissed by both the district court and the First Circuit upon appeal.

We fully expected McGuigan's motion, as well as his posturing during the subsequent court hearing on the matter. While prosecutors typically have the luxury of declining to prosecute cases that have a dubious chance of success, defense attorneys are forced to play the hand they're dealt. As a result, they're often at a distinct disadvantage, especially when their clients are just plain guilty. When the facts are unassailable, then defense attorneys must assail everything else, often by going after the conduct of the government, as was the case with Gentile's latest charges. McGuigan advocated valiantly on behalf of his client, despite the mountain of evidence stacked against him.

Durham responded to the defense motion, arguing that there was nothing to suggest that Gentile was anything other than "a predisposed, eager, ready-to-make-a-buck purveyor of the firearm." He noted that "this was a relationship between what Gentile believed to be a fellow criminal engaging in criminal commerce to make some money" and concluded just because "law enforcement agents took advantage of the defendant's avarice hardly constitutes 'outrageous government conduct.'"

As with the previous motions heard before Judge Chatigny back in 2012, this latest motion was soundly dismissed.

* * * *

By the summer of 2015, the Case of the Mysterious Visitor had not gone away; in fact, it was only gathering momentum. In mid-July, Rob told me that his boss, US Attorney Carmen Ortiz, was planning to hold a press conference and make a public appeal for assistance in an effort to identify the Mysterious Visitor. I surmised cynically that the timing was not coincidental, since Deirdre Daly, who was Carmen's counterpart at the US Attorney's Office in Connecticut, had just made international headlines yet again with news of the latest arrest and prosecution of Gentile.

I felt it was a mistake to overplay the importance of the Mysterious Visitor, since I was confident that he had absolutely nothing to do with the robbery. I knew from my review of the case file that all of the surveillance video had been meticulously reviewed within days of the robbery, and presumably, this individual had been identified and cleared of suspicion. I headed over to the US Attorney's Office and pleaded my case before Carmen, Rob, and Fred Wyshak, a veteran prosecutor who a few years earlier had successfully prosecuted Whitey Bulger.

"This was a dry run for the robbery," Wyshak pronounced, stabbing the grainy surveillance image for emphasis.

"Fred," I argued, "that makes no sense." I pointed out that this individual parked his car right in front of the service door, directly underneath a surveillance camera. Once he entered the museum, I reasoned, he made no effort to conceal his identity as he stood before the watch desk, casually conversing with Rick. It seemed obvious to me that if this visitor were, in fact, one of the subjects who had come back the following night to rob the museum, then he would've taken Friday's VHS tape along with the one from the night of the robbery, since it clearly depicted his face.

Wyshak shook his head. "This was a dry run," he reiterated. Fred was unmoved.

I later vented my frustration to Rob and Anthony, and while Rob agreed with my assessment, he conceded that the decision was out of his control. Back at the FBI office, I sat down with Rick DesLauriers's successor, Vincent Lisi, and we discussed the US attorney's intended publicity. Two years earlier, Rick and I had stood alongside Carmen at the podium when our respective agencies announced to the world that the Gardner case had been solved. Vince shared my concern that Carmen's anticipated press conference might infer that the case was anything but solved and cause some in the media to interpret our March 2013 press conference as a mere publicity stunt. This proved to be a prescient observation, since a number of media outlets would report just that.

"Boss," I said, using the colloquial form of address for Bureau executives, "the answer is in the case file. We can find it, but it's going to take time." This was an accurate statement. In March 1990, the

FBI was still using paper files, so there were no simple keywords to type into a database. A search would require a manual review of the paper files, and I was in the midst of yet another federal prosecution of Gentile down in Hartford. It would take weeks to get through the thousands of documents that comprised those first few weeks of the Gardner case file, searching for a needle in a filing cabinet–size haystack. I reached out to Dan Falzon, since retired from the Bureau, to tell me what I already knew about that surveillance video. He confirmed that the initial video review had been comprehensive and had left no lingering questions or outstanding leads. Simply put, the Mysterious Visitor was a nonissue.

Vince spoke with Carmen and was able to negotiate something of a compromise. While she refused to delay her appeal to the public, which would've allowed us time to pore over the case file, Carmen did agree to issue a press release instead of a full-blown press conference.

On August 6, 2015, the Boston US Attorney's Office released an excerpt of the March 17 surveillance video, along with the following language:

> Today we are releasing video images from the night before the theft—images which have not previously been seen by the public—with the hope of identifying an unauthorized visitor to the museum. With the public's help, we may be able to develop new information that could lead to the recovery of these invaluable works of art.
>
> The video footage released today, captured by Museum security cameras 24 hours before the Gardner heist, shows an automobile pull up next to a rear entrance of the Museum. The car matches the general description of a vehicle that was reported to have been parked outside the Museum moments prior to the theft on March 18, 1990.[2]

I was concerned with much of the language, to say the least, since I believed it vastly overstated the relevance of the Mysterious Visitor.

Actually, I was furious. I thought it was misleading and disingenuous to suggest that the visitor's car "matches the general description" of a 1988 Dodge Daytona, other than it appeared to have four wheels and a roof.

My concerns were well-founded, since it turned out that the car wasn't a Dodge Daytona. Furthermore, it turned out that the Mysterious Visitor had absolutely nothing to do with the Gardner Museum heist.

Shortly after Carmen's statement was released to the media, I got a call from Anthony, advising that the museum had already received four calls from former employees, all of whom identified the Mysterious Visitor as Larry O'Brien. Back in March 1990, O'Brien was the Gardner Museum's deputy director of security and Rick Abath's immediate supervisor.[3] Now that I had a name, I quickly found the 302 memorializing O'Brien's interview, which had been conducted four days after the heist. During his interview, O'Brien volunteered to the interviewing agents that just after midnight on Saturday, March 17, he was in the vicinity of the museum when he experienced car problems. In the days before cell phones, O'Brien stopped by the museum so he could call a mechanic.

The interview had been conducted contemporaneous to the video review that was ongoing in the squad area, and presumably the Mysterious Visitor's identity would have been reconciled immediately after it was paired with O'Brien's interview, thus underpinning Falzon's assertion that there had been no unanswered questions left after the video review was completed.

* * * *

Later that day, I received a call from Pete Kowenhoven, one of the assistant special agents in charge of the Boston division. Pete was a great ASAC, a former Navy fighter pilot who'd worked his way up through the ranks of the FBI. He was an unflappable leader with a great sense of humor and a genuine concern for the welfare of his agents.

"Hey, we've officially stated that both subjects are dead, right?" he asked.

"Uh, no Pete, we've never publicly released that info."

"Oops," he chuckled. "I just told the AP."

"Oh well," I managed as I returned the laugh.

"Man," Pete interjected, "I thought we'd released that." He was still amused.

"I guess we just did."

The following morning, news outlets around the world picked up the story from the Associated Press, printing variations of the same headline: 2 SUSPECTS IN BOSTON ART THEFT WORTH $500 MILLION ARE DEAD, FBI SAYS.[4] To be honest, I was relieved to see that the information about the erstwhile UNSUBS had finally been released, even if the disclosure had been made inadvertently. In my opinion, the more information we could provide to the public regarding the robbery, the better the chances of capturing our thirteen fugitives.

Despite the fact that the Mysterious Visitor lead was vetted conclusively, that video clip has been scrutinized and dissected endlessly, becoming the Gardner Museum's own version of the Zapruder film. And the legacy remains—since the date of the press release, both the FBI and the museum continued to receive an unyielding influx of leads from tipsters who believed that someone, either a loved one or an enemy, resembled the Mysterious Visitor.

CHAPTER 30

Boxing Clever

Remember it! I could walk it blindfold.

—CHARLES DICKENS, *A Christmas Carol*

On March 1, 2016, Bobby Gentile sat down with a pen and paper and authored a sworn affidavit in which he described his interactions with Tony, Sammy, and Meatball. Gentile wrote the admission to demonstrate his acceptance of responsibility, one of the twelve steps in the government's program to treat crime addicts.

In his inimitable and barely legible handwriting, Gentile wrote:

> Sammy said that the guy they're selling the grass to read my name in the paper and knew about the paintings from the Gardner Museum. Sammy said that the guy wanted to buy the paintings so he could sell them to a guy out of the country for a couple of a million apiece. Sammy and Ronnie [Meatball] kept asking me about the paintings and telling me that the boss that sold them the grass wanted the paintings...We met with [Tony] about three more times. The last time was at a restaurant. We were having lunch. Tony told me that the guy told [him] not to buy any more

> grass from Ronnie if I didn't sell him the paintings. I don't have any painting [*sic*], so I told the guy that he's stupid. I told him your boss is an asshole.

While most of the affidavit either vastly misrepresented or minimized his actions, and was contradicted by his own statements obtained from the surreptitious recordings, the last two sentences about Tony and Keith were actually quite accurate. And as we continued to eke out information about the stolen paintings from Gentile, we were reeling in another line of investigation, one that would bring us back yet again to Frances Drive.

In April 2016, we received credible information from an inmate at the Wyatt Detention Facility that Gentile may have concealed the stolen artwork in a defunct oil tank buried on his property. According to the inmate, Gentile claimed to have switched over to natural gas in 2010, and since the tank had been devoid of oil ever since, Gentile was using it as a hide. This latest tip certainly comported with the earlier jailhouse information, when Gentile claimed that the artwork was buried underground. It was further bolstered by the Rubbermaid container that he had buried underneath his shed. We checked with the local utility company and confirmed that, sure enough, in 2010 Gentile had closed out his account with a local oil company and opened a new account with Connecticut Natural Gas.

On May 2, 2016, we executed our third search warrant at Gentile's Manchester home. After the obligatory coffee- and Munchkin-fueled briefing at the Dunks on Hartford Road, we made our way back to 69 Frances Drive. Now that his undercover persona had been compromised, Steve came along with us this morning, and instead of his undercover Tahoe, he was driving a distinctly overt Dodge Charger. We pulled into Gentile's driveway, a ritual that over the years had become almost routine. With clear skies and Gentile's continued incarceration, there was no need to race to the front door, so Jamie and I strode, and despite Bureau regulations, we opted to leave our body armor in the trunk. Once again, I jockeyed open that potentially lethal screen door and rapped loudly. It took Pat a few minutes to answer, and when she finally opened the door, her resentment was palpable.

"Hi, Pat," I said regrettably as I held up the warrant. "We're back."

As with our last visit, there was no brusque nod; she simply stepped aside. And after yet another perfunctory clearing of the house and snapping of entry photos, Jamie and I headed down to the basement. We were looking for any pipes coming through the concrete wall that would help determine the exact location of the exterior oil tank. We traced a steel pipe from the furnace, along the floor, and to its termination point in the southwest corner of the basement. On the other side of the wall, at eye level, the Evidence Response Team began to methodically sow the ground with metal detectors.

With the presence of so many FBI vehicles, a portable tent in the driveway, and scores of agents scrambling over the Gentile residence, the arrival of the media was inevitable. As with the last search, the onslaught was overwhelming, and once again, the Manchester Police did an admirable job of keeping them contained behind a flapping strip of crime scene tape. McGuigan showed up, giving me a smirk and a shake of his head that seemed to say, "You gotta be kidding me," just before he said, "You gotta be kidding me." I returned the head shake and then we shook hands. I respected McGuigan; he had a hard job, trying to corral his wily client and keep him out of jail. It was an unenviable and ultimately futile task.

It wasn't long before ERT located a large metallic anomaly underground, and they began to dig. Eventually they unearthed the concave roof of a rusty 500-gallon oil tank, exactly as Gentile had described it to the inmate. The tank was sealed, so we called for a local welding company. As we all looked on in anticipation, and as the press snapped pictures with telephoto lenses, the welder fired up his torch and cut a U-shaped hole in the roof of the tank. An agent peeled back the steel flap, assisted with a few well-placed strikes from a mallet, and we took turns peering inside. As we feared, the excavation yielded little more than some water-tainted heating oil sloshing around in the bottom of the tank.

I returned to the basement and surveyed Gentile's workshop. There was a rusted coffee can on his workbench. I peered inside and saw that it was filled with more than 160 rounds of ammunition. "What's the point of ammunition if you don't have firearms?" the case agent thought to himself wryly.

Obviously, there was no point, a contention bolstered by the subsequent recovery of three more firearms secreted in Gentile's basement. Tucked up on a floor joist, Steve found the Luger that Gentile had once promised to Meatball. On the workbench, behind the coffee can o' bullets, I found a holstered .22, a weapon historically favored by the mob for executions, since the lightweight, lower-velocity round tends to ricochet around inside the skull cavity after its initial entry. And rounding out the collection was a lethal MAC-11 machine pistol, a compact weapon known as a "bullet hose" for its rapid-firing capability—about 1,300 rounds per minute. The MAC-11 was an interesting find, considering the fact that back in the 1980s, Gentile once sprayed Frank Zimmitti's Cadillac with a machine gun, narrowly missing Zimmitti Jr. and his horrified prom date.[1] I took a swing by the backyard shed and lifted the trapdoor. Another silencer lay in the dirt.

Besides demonstrating Gentile's penchant for contraband, these latest finds were telling in one major way: During two federal search warrants in 2012, Gentile's house had been swept clean of all weapons and contraband by FBI search teams using the most sophisticated search equipment available. We were confident that after the second search was completed, his house was pristine. Yet between Gentile's release in April 2014 and his arrest eleven months later, he'd managed to replenish his arsenal, including the .38 Colt Cobra that he sold to Meatball. Gentile purchased that weapon back in 1970, which means that he hadn't acquired it subsequent to his release. He already owned it, and had stored it somewhere other than at 69 Frances Drive.

This fact begs two salient questions:

1. Where was Gentile's weapons cache?
2. And what else was hidden there?

* * * *

During a status hearing on August 2, 2016, McGuigan expressed concerns to the Court that Gentile may have been suffering from a mental disease or defect that would've rendered him mentally incompetent to the extent that he couldn't understand the nature and consequences of the proceedings against him or assist properly in his defense.

Simply put, McGuigan argued that Gentile was not mentally competent to stand trial. Over Durham's objections, Judge Chatigny agreed to McGuigan's request to have his client undergo a thirty-day psychological examination, and in the interim, he ordered that "no statement made by the defendant during the course of the examination will be admissible against the defendant on the issue of guilt in any criminal proceeding."

Gentile's health began to deteriorate rapidly, and he was transferred to FMC-Butner in North Carolina. On September 28, 2016, his family received a call from the US Marshals Service, advising them that Gentile was in critical condition. The Marshals recommended that they prepare end-of-life arrangements for Gentile. Ryan promptly flew down to meet with his client in person. He called Pat and Bobby Jr. from Gentile's bedside and then handed over the phone. According to McGuigan, Gentile wept as he said his final goodbyes to his wife and son and told them how much he loved them.[2]

McGuigan told me that during that visit, he entreated Gentile to finally share his secrets about the Gardner. "I said to him, 'if you tell me where the paintings are or even just give me any clue that you haven't told me before, John Durham told me he would medivac you out of here and you could die next to your wife in your own bed.'" McGuigan delivered this message with conviction, and with good reason. "I trust John Durham," reflected McGuigan. "He was one of the guys in my kitchen when I was a kid growing up and he was on the statewide organized crime task force with my dad, so I trust John; my father trusted John. And I still trust John to this day." As he sat next to Gentile in the prison hospital bed, McGuigan implored him to confess. "I told Gentile that 'I guarantee you that you'll die next to your wife this evening,' and he just started crying 'but there ain't no paintings, there ain't no paintings,'" recalled McGuigan, doing his best Bobby Gentile impression.

"And I'm like, that's it."

* * * *

We heard the news about Gentile's failing health at the same time as when we heard the news that McGuigan was heading down to speak with him. While it was enticing to think that Gentile might provide some kind of deathbed confession, none of us placed any stock in the prospect of him finding religion, either figuratively or literally. The fact is, Gentile's health began deteriorating shortly after his release from prison back in April 2014. After we arrested him the following year, medical staff at Wyatt determined that Gentile had a severely infected ulcer on his leg, which they immediately began to treat with antibiotics. The Marshals advised us that according to the prison's medical personnel, had we not arrested Gentile when we did, he would most likely have died from the infection.

So, it came as no surprise when we learned from McGuigan that Gentile still claimed ignorance, nor was it a surprise when he pulled out of critical condition and recovered.

Just as a federal judge once remarked in court, Gentile didn't know when it was time to hang up the gloves.

CHAPTER 31

"The One and Only"

In the Land of the Blind the one-eyed man is king.

—DESIDERIUS ERASMUS

One of the enduring criticisms that I encountered throughout my tenure on the investigation was my apparent inability to consider any theories that didn't align with my trenchant beliefs. It's a criticism that I maintain is without merit, and usually originates from one of the many "theorists" who believe that since The Solution has yet to yield the stolen paintings, it can only mean that I've perfunctorily dismissed it, either through my incompetence or hubris. And while the case had been focused squarely on Gentile for years, I continued to receive tips that were wholly unrelated to our investigation down in Connecticut. Despite the fact that they posited theories that contradicted what we firmly knew about Gentile and the paintings, we still thoroughly investigated them. And by January 2017, one of those tips would result in a spinoff investigation and yet another federal prosecution.

That was the month when both the Gardner Museum and the FBI received a number of tips advising that an anonymous seller, going by the nefarious pseudonym Mordokwon, was offering for sale two of the stolen paintings, *The Storm* and *The Concert*, for $5 million and $50 million, respectively. Mordokwon was selling the pieces through the online marketplace Craigslist Global and was seeking buyers in Venice, Egypt, and London. In the listing, Mordokwon wrote, "I do not have to sell. I could easily keep and enjoy it. Do not ask for additional photos, especially of the edges for obvious reasons." In an effort to bolster the illicit nature of this deal, this mysterious seller would only communicate with potential buyers through an encrypted email account.

While it was obviously a scam—and a feeble one at that—it was also a crime, and I felt we needed to do something more than the typical *knock it off* interview. Rob was leaving the US Attorney's Office to join Brian at Nixon Peabody, so I reached out to his replacement, First AUSA John McNeil. I briefed him up on the scam, and he agreed with my assessment that Mordokwon had invested more than minimal planning in his attempt to pull off this fraud. McNeil advised that his office would be willing to prosecute, assuming that we could make the case.

Anthony created an encrypted email account, paintings@protonmail, and on January 19, he contacted Mordokwon, offering to purchase *The Storm* for $5 million.

"*Let's make a deal. I'm in a position to make this work and I'm ready to get down to business,*" Anthony wrote. "*Get back to me asap.*"

"*Sounds good,*" replied Mordokwon. He instructed paintings@protonmail to mail a $5 million cashier's check, made out to 10tothe7th, LLC, to an address in Beckley, West Virginia. Incidentally, Beckley is a locale that would rarely, if ever, be characterized as the hub of international art theft.

But just to firm up those pesky but critical elements of the fraud statutes, Anthony wrote:

"Just to be clear, you're not going to send me some photograph of The Storm on the Sea of Galilee for $5m. My associates and I are expecting the painting taken from the Gardner Museum in 1990." The "associates" part was all Anthony, and I loved it. It reeked of Russian oligarchs and Colombian drug cartels.

Mordokwon's response was concise and unequivocal: *"Painting is real."*

"Real from the Gardner Museum?"

"The one and only."

Now that we'd satisfied the necessary elements of the crime, it was time to untangle the intricate web of deception that obfuscated this criminal mastermind's nest of subterfuge. *To the Bat Cave!* Actually, no; I only needed a computer with internet access. I searched the address in Beckley and learned that it was a UPS Store. With a quick call to the store manager, I determined that the mailbox had been rented earlier that month by an individual named Todd Desper. I opened another tab on my computer, searched West Virginia's Secretary of State records, and found that the intended payee, 10tothe7th, LLC, had only one registered officer, namely Todd Desper. And finally, I determined that the IP address for Mordokwon's Craigslist account resolved to the Beckley home of, yes, you guessed it, Todd Desper.

If only every case were that simple. I swore out a brief affidavit charging Desper with four counts of mail fraud and attempted mail fraud, and on May 22, 2017, he was arrested by FBI agents down in West Virginia. The following February he pled guilty in Boston Federal Court and was sentenced to time served, which ended up being about a year.[1]

In a surprise twist that no one saw coming, it turns out that Desper never had the Gardner paintings, after all. In the end, we probably did him a favor. While it's highly unlikely that anyone with $5 million in disposable income would be gullible enough to fall for such a facile scheme (reality stars and social media influencers notwithstanding), it was still probably safer for Desper that we arrested him before some Russian oligarch or a Colombian drug czar got to him first.

With Desper out of the picture, I turned my attention back to Gentile. With regard to his mental health, US Magistrate Judge Donna Martinez subsequently ruled that he was mentally competent to stand trial, and in a hearing on April 6, 2017, McGuigan advised the court that his client would plead guilty. With Gentile's mental acuity confirmed, his attorney next raised questions regarding his physical infirmity, suggesting that due to his advanced age and poor health, prison would be, well, unhealthy. In response to the motion, that September Judge Chatigny ordered the Bureau of Prisons to conduct a medical examination to determine if Gentile was physically fit to endure another round of incarceration. On November 20, a medical doctor at the Metropolitan Detention Center in Brooklyn, New York, examined Gentile and determined that his medical condition was "stable," other than having what was referred to in the examination report as "nasopharyngitis; otherwise known as a common cold."

Based on the medical report, Durham argued that there were no changes in Gentile's circumstances that would warrant a change in his current detention status. The following day, Gentile was flown by the US Marshals Service back to FMC-Butner, the federal medical center in North Carolina that has held such notable ailing prisoners as Bernie Madoff and Ted Kaczynski.

* * * *

In September 2018, WBUR, Boston's NPR news station, teamed up with *The Boston Globe* to produce a five-part podcast on the heist entitled *Last Seen*. According to the podcast episode, "The Big Dig," Guarente told Bobby Luisi back in the 1990s that the artwork was buried under the concrete floor of a lakefront home he once rented in Orlando, a house that had been razed a decade earlier.[2] This wasn't new information; in fact, when we interviewed Luisi back in 2012, he told us a similar story. The podcast's producers began researching this lead and found an old DEA report that placed Guarente at an address in Florida back in the early '90s, so in December 2017, an engineering firm hired by the *Globe* and WBUR surveyed the property and their geologists located an "anomaly" buried "about 4 to 7 feet below existing grade."*

Buried four to seven feet underground. In a lakefront rental. In Florida.

After locating this anomaly, the producers promptly punted the tip over to me. In my opinion, it seemed obvious that they were waiting to see what the FBI would do with the information. I sat down with my supervisor, Kevin White, and we discussed this lead that had been dropped so unceremoniously in the Bureau's collective lap.

Like myself, Kevin was a former cop who spent the majority of his career working violent crime, most recently out of the Key West Resident Agency. In addition to being affable and approachable, Kevin possessed the single most important quality in a great boss: He didn't want to be a boss. He took the promotion, leaving behind the idyllic shores of Florida's southernmost tip, simply to be closer to home.

"Kevin, seriously, who buries stolen artwork under the garage floor of a rental?" I posed rhetorically.

Actually, no one. This was absurd. Once Guarente moved out—and all renters inevitably move out—he would lose access to the property and thus would have no way to recover the artwork at a later date. Even if the new tenants were sound sleepers, I'm quite certain they'd hear a jackhammer breaking through concrete. If Guarente really wanted to bury the artwork, his home in Madison abutted literally thousands of acres of pristine forest—he could tramp through fifty yards of brush, mark the nearest pine tree, and start digging. And when I say digging, I don't mean four to seven feet, since that's a tremendous amount of soil to move. In contrast, when Gentile buried

* The engineering report, provided by the *Globe*, reported the depth as "4 to 7 feet below existing grade." The podcast incorrectly reported the depth as "four to six feet underground."

that Rubbermaid container under his shed, the lid was covered with no more than a half inch of topsoil.

Finally, I pointed out to Kevin that the property in question sits on a lake in Florida, our swampiest state.

"Kevin," I said, "it has to be a septic tank."

He agreed with me, of course, but our hands were tied. In conversations with executive management, they concurred with my assessment that the *Globe* basically had us over a barrel—if we did nothing on this tip, our inaction would be their lede, underpinning spurious allegations that the FBI wasn't really serious about recovering the Gardner artwork. For this reason, I grudgingly set a lead to Tampa, the division that covers Orlando, requesting that they dig up the anomaly, buried underneath a now-vacant lot. Before they could excavate, however, we had to first obtain consent from the property owner, secure the necessary approvals, and rent the heavy equipment. Which meant that I also needed to secure funding from FBIHQ.

My request to Tampa was remorseful, and I apologized in advance for sending them out on what amounted to a costly snipe hunt. In my lead, I wrote that the anomaly detected underground was "most likely a discarded septic tank or cistern," but due to the anticipated media coverage, the search had to be conducted nonetheless.

On January 31, 2018, Tampa's Evidence Response Team began excavating the site. It seemed that reporters had already staked out the area, for as soon as the excavator swallowed its first big bucketful of wet, swampy earth, the news cameras were rolling. Or so I heard. For while I've traveled around the globe running down leads with even mediocre potential, both Anthony and I were so certain that this excavation was a waste of time that we opted to stay back in Boston. Neither of us wanted to be onsite to watch the breathtaking excavation of an abandoned septic tank.

A few hours later I received a call from the Tampa ERT team leader.

I answered the phone with a question. "Is it a septic tank?"

"Yes, it is" was the curt reply. As we spoke, she texted me a photo of a concrete cylinder, half exhumed from the mud, which once contained a substance not dissimilar to the composition of the *Globe*'s latest tip.

When the podcast's episode dropped that November, the producers reported that they "were in Florida to track down a lead—one that was probable enough that the FBI was the one ordering the excavation." I guess that's one way to describe it. The podcast's website included an action photo from the dig, and despite the fact that Anthony and I were noticeably absent from the shot, they blithely asserted that "this was essentially the federal government agreeing that there is a possibility of a recovery here."

A possibility of a recovery so very promising that we stayed home.

CHAPTER 32

At a Full Boil, not a Simmer

Well, I must endure the presence of a few caterpillars
if I wish to become acquainted with the butterflies.

—ANTOINE DE SAINT-EXUPÉRY, *The Little Prince*

Bobby "the Cook" Gentile was released from prison on the eve of the twenty-ninth anniversary of the heist. There was little fanfare when he finally returned to his home in Manchester. During his last stint in prison, Pat had passed away, leaving him to rattle about that modest ranch house alone, without even the company of his firearms or dynamite.

Over the years that we investigated Gentile, he would assume rational mannerisms, then flip a switch and briefly flare with anger, only to return to normal. It was an idiosyncrasy not lost on Steve, who coined the "Bob growl" term. "It was this little undercurrent of rage, when he'd show a little bit of what's bubbling beneath the surface," Steve reflected. "I adopted that technique myself, and I still use it as an undercover. It's a self-preservation technique, because if I don't show you that, then you're never going to be wary about me."

Steve was an experienced undercover, and it was humbling to think that perhaps his interactions with Gentile might help him with future cases, possibly even keep him safer. Now that would be a meaningful legacy for Bobby Gentile.

"He was very, very good at what he did," Steve offered. "Even though he went to jail or whatever, he was old-school consistent, exactly what you would expect." Steve was right; there was a consistency to Gentile in every aspect of his life. I had to admire him for his convictions, regardless of how misguided they might have been.

"He's who I try to be now," Steve said, referring to his own undercover persona.

"You use traits that you learned from Gentile?" I asked.

"Absolutely, I use what I learned from him."

Steve continued: "He taught me a lot. When I met him, I'm like holy fuck, this is exactly what I'd been seeing from the older guys years ago." He pointed out that it was because of this old-school mentality that Meatball was more frightened of Gentile than his younger cousin. "Sammy didn't understand him as well as Meatball did," Steve said.

"Because that's what it was," he mused. "It was that old-school fucking real-deal quiet. He was a very humble and real scary guy. I try to be that kind of guy."

I asked Steve if he got the sense that Gentile had access to the paintings during their discussions. "I think somebody else had them and he was going to get them, okay?" he mused. "And I think during the negotiations money wise, I always felt that he had to take care of somebody else to be able to get them."

Throughout the course of Steve's undercover career, he'd befriended serials killers, terrorists, and a motley collection of criminals whom he described as "really, really, really bad fucking human beings." He uttered the phrase slowly and with repetition, to provide full import to their depravity.

"He made me feel the most uneasy of anybody I ever met, ever," Steve explained. "He was excellent at keeping me off my game, and I think he did it by jumping from topic to topic and then being hot and cold within a matter of minutes. I can always tell if I've got a guy, but I never felt that I had him." I was surprised to learn that Steve had been more uncomfortable dealing with Bobby Gentile than with any other subject with whom he had interacted throughout his lengthy undercover career.

Steve was metaphorical when he explained the varied responsibilities that comprise an undercover operation. "You run the show," he said, referring to my role as the case agent. "You write and produce the movie, and I'm just the actor that comes in and does it." Steve was correct—undercover operations were highly choreographed productions that were staged, rehearsed, and minutely critiqued. Each scene had to be flawless and utterly believable, and unlike a Broadway production, a flop could have consequences more serious than just a theater critic's bad review.

"But the problem is," Steve continued, "when I leave, it's still in me somewhere, and as a UC, I've got to put it somewhere, because I experienced it versus observed it. And so, one of the things I always tried to do was make sure that I had room to put it." He sat back in his chair and took a deep breath. "And sometimes I'd say no to a case because I didn't have any room to put it at that time. And in here," he pointed to his chest, "that constant feeling of unsteadiness around Bobby was fucking exhausting. I would be with him for two or three hours and have lunch with him or whatever. I would leave feeling like I ran a fucking marathon."

Steve described the complicated mental dynamics that underpin every undercover meet. "I've got to be here talking to you rationally, absorbing and understanding the current conversation." He looked me carefully in the eyes, to underscore the effect. "But I'm also ten minutes ahead so I know where to lead the conversation, and then I'm an hour ahead of that because I've got to get home safe. So, I have to be in three realities at once, and to do that with someone like Bobby was just fucking exhausting. I would leave him just drained; drained from the unsteadiness and the uncertainty that he would bring."

I'd known firsthand the difficulties of interacting with Gentile, but only from one single reality—the reality of an FBI agent investigating one very stubborn subject. As a result, I only dealt with him on the periphery of his mania, and that was exhausting enough. Although Steve, Jamie, and I had spent a number of evenings together in Hartford bars, chuckling about the Cook over beers, I never realized the mental toll that the operation had taken on Steve.

I wanted to give him a big hug.

"And then I would have to drive back home, you know," Steve said, "and I would literally just stand in the shower and let the hot water hit the back of my head because I was always at a fucking full boil. With Bobby, it was like a pot of water at a full boil, not a simmer."

We talked some more about the case, and about this enigmatic gangster who had the ability to mind-fuck just about everyone with whom he interacted, like some demented puppet master who was always pulling the strings, and sometimes wrapping those strings firmly around your neck.

"I loved working with you and Jamie, and obviously, the case—forget about it," Steve said, casually lapsing into the persona of Tony without even realizing it. "I'd do anything for this case to make it successful, but it was terrible. It was awful and it was zero enjoyable." Steve took a moment to compose his thoughts before continuing. "Like I usually enjoyed what I did, and I enjoyed the intellectual jousting with people. I liked to sit there and get into people's heads and bounce around and see what made them tick. I found that I got energy from that, from figuring people out. People don't realize how much of a psychological game this is between me and the bad guy." Steve lowered his voice. "But I had zero joy with Gentile," he said softly.

"I dreaded it. I actually dreaded it."

"So, I guess I'm paying for lunch?" I asked.

* * * *

I sat down with Ed Mahony, the *Hartford Courant* reporter who reported on Gentile throughout the pendency of two federal prosecutions with an insight and level of granularity that was frankly more intuitive than anything the Boston papers had ever mustered. I asked him about Gentile. "He's uneducated, he's semiliterate, he can hardly speak," Mahony said carefully. "But I think intuitively he's a smart, smart fucking guy. I think he's ruthless and he's got no conscience."

As a veteran mob reporter, Mahony had covered organized crime in Connecticut for decades, and he'd heard a little bit about Gentile over the years. "I remember that Gentile always had a reputation as a violent guy, a guy who could've potentially been a tough guy if he wasn't so small."

As Gentile's name began to circulate around Hartford after his first arrest in 2012, Mahony began his own investigation, attempting to find out more about this crazy story involving the Cook and the Gardner Museum paintings. He reached out to one of his reliable contacts, Jack Farrell, a mob associate who lived two houses down from Gentile. Back in the day, Farrell ran high-stakes poker games throughout New England. Farrell was a card mechanic, or a *sharp*, using his superior card dexterity to substantially increase his odds of winning. According to Mahony, Farrell was the "Fort Knox of information on Bobby Gentile." They'd known each other for decades, and Farrell once recounted to Mahony the story of how he learned that Gentile had been straightened out in Philly.

Farrell was doing yard work when Gentile's car pulled up to his house, with Sammy behind the wheel. Sammy said that Gentile wanted to speak with him, and Farrell replied, "So tell him to get out of the fucking car and drag his fat ass over here if he wants to talk." Sammy was insistent, so Farrell relented and approached the passenger side of Gentile's Buick. With a smug grin, Gentile said to Farrell, "Hey, I just wanted to tell you that I got made." Farrell replied, "You stupid son of a bitch, what are you, out of your fucking mind? You take a pinch now, it's like another ten years."[1]

Farrell claimed that Gentile kept his wife a virtual prisoner in her own house. Farrell stressed that while it wasn't criminal, Pat didn't have the normal social interactions with friends that other wives enjoyed. "Farrell told me it was almost like she adopted Gentile's speech patterns with the 'dems' and 'dose' and you know, 'those motherfuckers,' and 'this, that, and the other thing,'" Mahony advised. "Farrell really felt sorry for the old lady."

Mahony attempted to interview Gentile, and because of his reputation with local mobsters as a no-bullshit reporter, Gentile agreed to sit down with him. The two spoke frequently, and Mahony forged a relationship with Gentile that continued throughout his two stints in federal prison.

"Bobby was a big cement guy. He was the Michelangelo of cement, honest to God, really. He used to brag about it," Mahony said. "It was the most productive thing he ever did in his life. He would say, 'I did that parking lot over here,' and 'I did this Stop & Shop there.' All those round pillars in the parking garages that hold up the next floor? Gentile did that."

Mahony pressed Gentile on his organized crime connections, but Gentile denied all of it. "'All I did was cook,'" Mahony recalled Gentile saying, using his own dynamic Gentile impression; an impression that I must say was pretty good. "He said that he used to make dinner for some guys he knew who played cards. That's all he did."

When Mahony heard from Sammy that Gentile had once driven down to Philly looking to move the stolen paintings, he questioned Gentile about it. "I asked him if he went to Pennsylvania," Mahony told me, "and he admitted that he did." But when Mahony asked for details, Gentile claimed that he and Pat drove the five hundred miles for dinner.

"You drove your wife to Pennsylvania for dinner?" Mahony asked incredulously.

Gentile replied, "Yeah, we wanted to try some of that Amish food."

Mahony was skeptical. "Amish food, Bobby?"

"Yeah, Amish food," was Gentile's reply. "Take my advice," he added. "Don't try it. It fucking stinks."

Gentile admitted to the dinner at the Portland Holiday Inn with the Guarentes, and even Mahony had to listen to him complain about Elene's extravagant dinner order. "'She ordered the most expensive thing on the fucking menu,'" Mahony recalled Gentile saying. And once again, Mahony gave me his best Gentile impression: "'If she's not paying, then she's supposed to order something cheap.'"

Dear God, how expensive were those lobsters?

I asked Mahony for his opinion regarding Gentile and the stolen Gardner paintings. He sat back in his chair for a moment as he pondered the question. "I think he had knowledge of them, participation with them, and likely had possession of a limited number of them for some undetermined period at a time," Mahony said carefully. He took a long pull from a bottle of Budweiser and then leaned forward. "I mean, how more much do you need to put Gentile right in the middle of it?"

CHAPTER 33

"More Weight"

Every man has two deaths, when he is buried
in the ground and the last time someone says his name.

—ERNEST HEMINGWAY

Robert Vincent Gentile died in his sleep on September 17, 2021. He was eighty-five. A few days later, McGuigan told a *Globe* reporter, "They say he was a bad guy, but he became a friend. He was the last of his kind."[1]

The last of his kind. For everyone's sake, Ryan, I hope you're right.

After Gentile died, I spoke with McGuigan about that purported trip to Philadelphia, when Gentile and Guarente attempted to move the stolen paintings. I was surprised when McGuigan confirmed to me that they did, in fact, travel down to Philly to meet with the mob and discuss the Gardner paintings.[2]

"Yeah, it was Gentile and Guarente who did that," McGuigan said. "And Gentile was the one saying, 'Don't give them the paintings, let's take them back. You don't want to give them the paintings because if you give them the paintings, then all of a sudden, we don't have anything anymore.'"

"Gentile told you that?" I asked.

"That's what Gentile told me, yeah."

Despite the fact that McGuigan represented Gentile, he admits that Gentile lied to him about a number of substantive facts related to the case. "I know he maintained a lot of stuff that was just not true," McGuigan said. "Finally, you know, at the end he would always just have a smirk on his face, and that's how you knew he was just full of shit the whole time."

Said Gentile's attorney.

* * * *

A month after Gentile died, his son graciously allowed us the opportunity to take one final look through his father's house. On a cold morning in November, I pulled up to Frances Drive for the last time. Those two effete jalopies were still parked in the driveway, inexorably sinking into the asphalt as their tires gradually lost air. I walked up to the front door, accompanied by Jamie and Anthony, and gave the bell one last ring. This time, Bobby Jr. answered, the soft-spoken and law-abiding son of a gangster. There was no brusque nod from Bobby Jr.; he was polite and welcoming.

When Bobby Jr. was fourteen or fifteen, he and his friends broke into the neighborhood grammar school. Nothing serious, just kids being kids. It was a minor indiscretion that back in the day might have earned him a smack from his dad, but Gentile beat him so badly that he missed two weeks of school.[3]

As Bobby Jr. sat at the dining room table sorting through papers, we wandered through the house, looking like a trio of indifferent shoppers at a flea market: picking up objects, perusing a picture, shaking open a sticky drawer. But I was drawn to the basement once again. It was the nucleus of Gentile's world, where the manifestations of the many facets of his life accumulated: mason's tools, a rolodex from Gem Auto, assorted swag.

In the end, the search was unproductive: no more firearms, explosives, or police badges. Of course, there were no paintings, or else this book would've been titled *Ten Perfect Fugitives* or *Eleven Perfect Fugitives*, or whatever. We thanked Bobby Jr. for his forbearance and apologized for the intrusion into his family, the collateral damage wrought by his father's lifetime of poor judgment.

I returned to my Bucar and watched Gentile's house recede in the windshield as I backed out of the driveway, only to disappear completely as I swung out onto Frances Drive.

Bobby Jr. later told me that he filled four thirty-yard dumpsters with the contents of his parents' house. "He was a hoarder, for sure," Bobby said, and added, "No paintings, though."

* * * *

I sat down with John Durham recently to talk about Gentile and the case. There had been some notable developments since we last worked together: A year after Gentile's last conviction, John was appointed to serve as the US attorney for the District of Connecticut. Of course, John never wanted the job, which made him the perfect choice. And then in May 2019, Attorney General William Barr appointed Durham as special counsel to look into claims of Russian interference in the 2016 presidential election, a counterintelligence investigation that was code-named Crossfire Hurricane. Throughout the investigation, I was irritated whenever I heard partisan criticism in the media about John, since he is one of the most principled public servants with whom I'd ever worked. John retired from his position as US attorney in February 2021, and his role as special counsel concluded two years later.

After the first round of beers arrived, I started with a loaded question, one that I've asked John many time before, and one that was intentionally designed to underscore his scruples.

"Still driving that Volvo?" I asked.

"Of course," he replied in the same matter-of-fact demeanor I'd heard so many times in the courtroom. He added with a defensive chuckle, "Why not, it's a great car."[4]

The Volvo in question is a 2004 V70 station wagon with more than three hundred thousand miles on the odometer. John opted for the more economical two-wheel-drive model, and when I last saw him behind the wheel, it was riding on four mismatched tires. Although he's far too modest to admit to it, I know that since he retired from public service, John has turned down a number of lucrative partnership offers from the big firms. Instead, he provides pro bono legal assistance to military veterans. And so John continues to serve, without fear or favor, and he's more than content to drive that old Volvo wagon with the mismatched tires. And why not? It is, after all, a great car.

"The truth of the matter is that the work you and Jamie did here in Connecticut was remarkably illuminating about Gentile," John said to me. "We produced a mountain of evidence showing that not only was he a made member of the LCN, he was directly involved with the stolen Gardner artwork."

John scoffed at Gentile's argument that he knew nothing about the stolen paintings. "Despite all the incriminating evidence hidden inside his residence and blowing up the polygraph," he said, "he just refused to cooperate." Gentile always had choices. Throughout the pendency of two federal prosecutions, he had ample opportunity to tell us the truth about the stolen artwork and apply the brakes to the fearsome apparatus of the Department of Justice.

"In the end," John said with a shrug, "Gentile opted for prison."

* * * *

Gentile always reminded me of a guiltier version of Giles Corey, the Salem, Massachusetts, farmer who was accused of witchcraft back in 1692 and sentenced to death by pressing, a punishment known as *peine forte et dure*, French for a "hard and forceful punishment" (the French think of everything). Over a three-day ordeal, Corey was sandwiched between a board and the bare floor, while "as great a weight as he could bear" was placed on top of him (and they say the Italians invented the panini). As more and more stones were placed on top of the obstinate Corey, he still refused to confess; his only response was "more weight."

While I admired Gentile's adherence to his values, however illicit they may have been, any comparisons to the Salem Witch Trials stop there. Because Corey refused to confess, his estate was not subject to forfeiture by the government and instead was passed down to his children.

For Bobby Gentile, it was just the opposite. All he left for his family were four dumpsters full of junk.

* * * *

As Ed Mahony said, Gentile was a mason, and by all accounts a good one, as evidenced by all those multilevel parking garages in Connecticut with the smooth, round pillars that have yet to collapse. He could have lived a much better lifestyle as a law-abiding tradesman, proud of his accomplishments, building things up instead of tearing things down. Instead, he chose to be a gangster; he chose to live like a miserable pauper in a miserable old house, a time capsule exhumed from an earlier generation which was better left buried.

What was the point of it all?

* * * *

I always considered the Gardner Museum case to be two discrete yet interrelated investigations. The first part was the *whodunit* regarding the events that transpired on that cold March evening back in 1990. When we announced in March 2013 that the case had been solved, it meant that we knew who robbed the museum. This wasn't done as some kind of collective pat on the back; we made the announcement because we believed that it was time to focus on the other—and in my opinion, primary—investigation: finding the stolen artwork. In the FBI, the absence of a recovery has no bearing on whether the investigation is considered solved; a case is solved when the subjects responsible for the crime are identified and the case title changes from UNSUBS. I've often used the example of the terror attacks of 9/11, which were solved almost a decade before Osama bin Laden was finally located and killed by a SEAL team in Abbottabad, Pakistan.

Even though decades passed since the date of the heist, both the FBI and the museum continued to receive new theories regarding who pulled off the robbery. I would politely take the tipsters information, but to be frank, I no longer wanted to hear speculation about dead grandfathers or neighbors' cousins—we had moved well past the point of entertaining fresh and novel what-ifs about a decades-old crime. And it's not because of some collective myopia about the robbery (our confidence that the case was solved notwithstanding); it was simply because we were not going to start from scratch, armed with nothing but a brand-new list of all-dead suspects, all of whom were culled from mere conjecture. After so many years of investigation, the tips we sought were related to actionable intelligence regarding the current whereabouts of the lost artwork. I simply had no inclination to review any more theoretical string charts and radar maps. But if it was a tip about a possible location of the artwork, on the other hand, it was vetted out thoroughly, whether or not it comported with established theories about the heist.

I was perpetually amused and equally bemused by armchair detectives who conducted their own investigations, searching for the missing artwork while simultaneously castigating and excoriating the FBI—and me personally—for not making a recovery. The FBI did not then, nor does it now, have a proprietary interest in this investigation (it's not the Gardner Museum Investigation brought to you by the FBI™). Anyone can grab their novelty-size magnifying glass and go find the artwork. In fact, a quick internet search will reveal that this case is simultaneously being investigated by a motley assortment of journalists, documentary filmmakers, retired Scotland Yard detectives, mobsters, self-professed art investigators, mediums and soothsayers, remote viewers, and a host of others. Not since Jimmy Durante recounted the tale of the Big W before literally kicking the bucket has there been such a disparate group of amateur sleuths searching for buried treasure.

If it's so fucking easy, you go find them.

CHAPTER 34

The Antithesis of the Perfect Crime

The self-same moment I could pray;
And from my neck so free
The Albatross fell off, and sank
Like lead into the sea.

—SAMUEL TAYLOR COLERIDGE,
The Rime of the Ancient Mariner

In December 2015, I was interviewed for an episode of CBS's *Sunday Morning*. In the segment, *48 Hours* correspondent Erin Moriarty asked me if the Gardner Museum subjects had committed the perfect crime.[1]

"No," I replied. "This was the antithesis of the perfect crime."

"It's still gone," said Moriarty, referring to the lost art.

"Nobody got any money off these paintings," I explained. "The perfect crime means you get away with it and you profit from the crime. And I don't believe that anybody has profited at all from this crime."

The Gardner Museum robbery truly was the antithesis of the perfect crime. It left a trail of murder, betrayal, and soul-crushing incarceration in a turbulent wake that spanned decades. Up until the morning after the robbery, the Gardner was an esoteric museum whose collection, while stunning, toiled in relative obscurity, overshadowed by the Museum of Fine Arts parked across the street. To the thieves, the Gardner must've seemed like an easy score. It wasn't until the following day, when a crew of bleary-eyed subjects woke to the news that they had unwittingly committed the heist of the century, that the full import of their actions finally sank in. And as time passed, the stolen artwork became a liability, not an asset. Opportunities to monetize the loot were supplanted by an existential fight for survival, a fight that many of them lost.

I've often drawn parallels between the Gardner Museum robbery and the Lufthansa heist from December 1978. Anyone who's ever seen the movie *Goodfellas* is familiar with the crime, when a crew from New York's Lucchese crime family stole $6 million from a cargo terminal at JFK Airport, making it the largest cash robbery in US history. After the subjects realized that their audacious crime had attracted way too much attention from the FBI, they made the coolly calculated decision to tie up loose ends, and over the ensuing year, at least nine members of the crew were murdered (cue "Layla").

One of the two most frequently asked questions asked of me is the dollar value of the lost artwork. "Maybe a billion," I answer, which sounds about right, especially if the reporter wants a good sound bite or a sexy headline. (Sadly, the importance of an art theft is often directly proportional to its fair-market value.) After hearing this expansive figure, the reporter's eyes will theatrically grow wide and they'll nod sympathetically. I can almost hear the cerebral gears spinning as they mentally create the headline.

But if given the opportunity to expand on my answer and discuss the true value of the artwork—that is, intrinsic value instead of fair market—I'll give a much more realistic figure: zero. The art is worthless.

Why? Because the astronomical appraisals that are bandied about for these works are based solely on their fair-market value; that is, what would the Vermeer, or *The Storm*, fetch at auction? The sobering truth is that these pieces, amongst some of the most-recognizable artwork in the world, are stolen property. They cannot be sold. If there is no market, then they have no value.

Let's assume for a moment that tomorrow all thirteen works were recovered and the museum decided to sell them off. They couldn't, since the iconic stipulation in Mrs. Gardner's will specifically forbids that from happening. To do so would be tantamount to museum suicide, since the entire collection would be liquidated and the proceeds donated to "the President and Fellows of Harvard College."

So, from a purely financial standpoint, they are worth nothing.

But they're not worthless; they're priceless.

The other frequently asked question of me is, "Will they ever be found?" Yes, I state simply, they will be found. As a student of art theft, I would've been remiss if I hadn't looked to past thefts as an indication of future success, and through years of research and firsthand experience, I've learned that stolen art is recovered in one of two ways: either shortly after its theft, or through subsequent generations. Throughout my career, I've recovered a number of pieces of art and cultural property that had been reported lost or stolen decades earlier.

In the week before my retirement, I repatriated a collection of important cultural artifacts that had been looted from Okinawa in the waning days of World War II, artifacts that had been missing for nearly eighty years.[2] In July 2023, my Art Crime Team colleague in Boston, Kristin Koch, and I repatriated a rare Hernán Cortés manuscript, dating back to 1527, which had been stolen from the National Archives of Mexico at least three decades earlier.[3] And, of course, we've already discussed Mr. Bakwin's art collection, with the last two pieces finally returned more than thirty years after the theft.

The important takeaway from these recoveries is the salient fact that to a centuries-old piece of artwork, the concept of *decades* is essentially meaningless. The FBI investigation into the Gardner Museum robbery continues, and my successor has already girded the mantle and continues the quest from the point where mine ended. And although I've officially retired, I still stay abreast of the investigation and offer advice and guidance when asked. On the day of my retirement, the case was still very active, and there were some promising leads. The intelligence is too current to discuss in this book, but perhaps they'll lead to something good. Perhaps.

The recovery of the Gardner Museum artwork will happen someday—history proves it inevitable. Someone will attempt to monetize them, and the FBI will be there, posing as a crooked art broker or a New Jersey mobster. Or perhaps the recovery will be more organic, and a distant relative cleaning out a decedent's attic will stumble across *The Storm*. Maybe *The Concert* will make its way into an auction house in Miami, or the Flinck will make a grand appearance at an antiques mall in Topeka.

Be patient. It will happen.

Afterword

Tomorrow we will run faster, stretch out our arms farther...
And then one fine morning—so we beat on,
boats against the current,
borne back ceaselessly into the past.

—F. SCOTT FITZGERALD, *The Great Gatsby*

The FBI frowns on outside employment, since its agents must be available to respond twenty-four hours a day, seven days a week. For the bulk of my employment with the Bureau, however, I also considered myself as an employee of the Gardner Museum, or at least an honorary one. The week of my retirement, I stopped by my other workplace. It would be my last visit to the museum as an FBI agent, my last visit as official caretaker of the investigation into the world's largest art heist. It was a position that I had simultaneously loathed and cherished for more than two decades. I swiped my employee ID card at the employee's entrance, waved to the guard on duty, and made my way into the galleries.

Of course, I visited the Dutch Room, and as I'd done a thousand times before, I stared at those eviscerated frames. They stared right back at me impassively, mute crime victims bearing witness to an outrage suffered so many years ago. I was humbled, and maybe even a bit haunted, to have been such a key figure in the stolen provenance of this infamous collection within a collection. It was an assessment underscored by the conversations of the handful or so visitors who milled about the gallery that morning, studying the artwork on the walls, the floor, even the ceiling. As with previous visits, I could overhear them talking quietly amongst themselves, and I picked up snippets and scraps of their discussions, which invariably centered around the heist:

> "...dressed as police officers...world's largest heist...FBI...that's why the frames are empty...never been found..."

It brought me back to the Museum of Natural History in New York, to the moment when I'd first heard about the Gardner Museum, eavesdropping on those two ladies as they discussed that audacious robbery. And there I stood in the Dutch Room, still marveling at the fact that twelve years after that chance overhear, I would be an FBI agent in Boston, embarking on the arduous journey to get back those stolen treasures.

And what a journey it's been! For more than two decades, I traveled the world, peeking in musty attics and moldy basements, peering in garbage cans and china cabinets, interviewing charlatans and priests, billionaires and murderers, sifting through the detritus of an oftentimes bizarre world where art intersects with crime. There were so many close calls, so many occasions when I truly believed a recovery was imminent, and then heartbreak. Despite setbacks and disappointments, I gathered myself up and moved on to the next lead, a boat against the current, always determined that tomorrow I would run faster, stretch out my arms farther...always hoping for that one fine morning.

As I wrapped up my final visit to the museum, I reflected on how the Dutch Room looked thirty-four years earlier, with crime scene tape draped across furniture like shed snakeskin, its bright fluorescence contrasting so starkly with the muted colors and rich woods of the hallowed room's ancestry. A sprinkle of broken glass and a stack of empty frames, deposited with reckless abandon, littered the mottled tile floor. A sheepish museum guard stood outside the entrance, twelve hours too late. I wasn't there that day; I was twelve years too late, and I wouldn't come to know about the Gardner Museum heist until I overheard those elderly ladies chatting about it in the shadow of a giant blue whale. But I had the crime scene photos, tangible memories of a terrible loss, poking out of a bulging case file and plastered above my desk, grim mementos of a day that really came to shape both my career and my life.

I also have *Christ in the Storm on the Sea of Galilee*. A few years ago, Sonia secretly ordered me a full-size replica on canvas. After it arrived, she sliced the factory edges with a razor blade, an atavistic homage to the indignity suffered by the original. After fraying the edges, she drove over the piece a few times with her car, hoping that the resultant creases and wrinkles would impart some authenticity. Finally, she hung it in the stairway to the basement, where I would later find it. Some would call it a cruel and callous prank, but they don't know my wife, a cruel and callous woman. And so *The Storm* still hangs in the basement stairwell, a tongue-in-cheek conversation piece for all our friends who've playfully theorized over the years that I probably have the original stashed away someplace safe, waiting for retirement and the promise of the multimillion-dollar reward.

"Yeah, it's just a fake," I always say. But then I add with a wink, "Or is it?"

Twenty-two years with the same case. Although I don't have hard statistics, I have to assume it must have set some kind of record within the FBI. I've never met another agent who worked the same case for more than a few years, at least anyone who was willing to admit to it.

During the course of my career, I worked a number of fugitive cases. Some evenings, in the midst of the hunt, I'd stare up at the moon—if there was one that night—and wonder if my quarry was looking up at the same moon. Almost like a kind of synergy, joining us together. I can't say the same for these fugitives. Perhaps I lack the perspicacity to personify these objects in a manner that's worthy of the metaphorical allusion that I created for this very book. They're not staring up at the moon; they are neither dreading capture nor pining for rescue. They are, after all, inanimate objects. If I were to snatch one from up in the attic, or pluck its partner out from under the bed or behind the furnace, it would make no difference to them in the least.

But it would matter to me, and so they remain my thirteen perfect fugitives.

Endnotes

Chapter 1

1 All information about Mrs. Gardner and her museum are obtained from the Isabella Stewart Gardner Museum website, isgm.org.

Chapter 3

1 Andy Dabilis and John Ellement, "$200m Gardner Museum Art Theft," *The Boston Globe*, March 19, 1990, https://www.bostonglobe.com/metro/1990/03/19/gardner-museum-art-theft/0tDN3k6ncPtdeyUVERNXWL/story.html.

2 Andy Dabilis, Kevin Cullen, and Thomas Coakley, "$1m Reward Offered for Trail to Stolen Art," *The Boston Globe*, March 21, 1990.

Chapter 5

1 FBI memorandum, dated 09/09/1991.

Chapter 8

1 Richard E. Abath, *Pandora's Laughter* (Unpublished) (2015).

2 Stephen Kurkjian, "Was Anyone Watching the Gardner Museum Watchman?," *The Boston Globe*, March 9, 2013, https://www.boston.com/news/local-news/2013/03/09/was-anyone-watching-the-gardner-museum-watchman/.

3 Personal interview of Jon-Paul Kroger, May 9, 2025.

4 Email from Emily North, August 31, 2025.

5 Personal interview of Rob Fisher, May 9, 2025.

6 Personal interview of Dick Egan, February 25, 2025.

7 Personal interview of George Gormley, February 28, 2025.

Chapter 9

1 Stephen Kurkjian, "Anne Hawley's Best Lead," Last Seen: Reporter's Notebook, November 12, 2018, https://www.wbur.org/lastseen/2018/11/12/anne-hawley-best-lead.

2 Stephen Kurkjian, *Master Thieves* (PublicAffairs, 2015).

3 Stephen Kurkjian, "The 'Master Thieves' Behind Boston's Greatest Cold Case," March 12, 2015, Radio Boston.

4 Anthony A. Amore, *The Woman Who Stole Vermeer* (Pegasus Crime, 2020).

5 "Vermeer Theft Denial," *The Guardian*, March 8, 1974.

6 Anthony A. Amore, *The Woman Who Stole Vermeer* (Pegasus Crime, 2020).

7 Ralph Blumenthal, "Five Years And $300 Million—A Special Report; The Maddening Mysteries Of the Greatest Art Theft Ever," *The New York Times*, December 15, 1994.

8 Andrea Holbrook, "'Whitey' Arrest Recalls Gloucester IRA Gun Run," *The Gloucester Times*, June 25, 2011, https://www.gloucestertimes.com/news/local_news/whitey-arrest-recalls-gloucester-ira-gun-run/article_004086f6-cde7-5092-b02e-59da8dfa6aac.html.

9 Casey Sherman, "Art Detective Eyes IRA in Gardner Museum Art Heist," *Boston Herald*, April 22, 2019, https://www.bostonherald.com/2019/04/22/art-detective-eyes-ira-in-gardner-art-heist/.

10 Ed Power, "The Billion Dollar Art Hunt: Searching for a Vermeer with Martin 'The Viper' Foley," *The Irish Times*, October 20, 2020, https://www.irishtimes.com/culture/tv-radio-web/the-billion-dollar-art-hunt-searching-for-a-vermeer-with-martin-the-viper-foley-1.4385980.

11 Personal interview of Rich Teahan, May 19, 2025.

12 Lloyd Schwartz, "Here Are The 13 Artworks Stolen the Night of the Gardner Museum Heist," August 20, 2018, https://www.wbur.org/news/2018/08/20/lastseen-gardner-heist-missing-art.

13 All information regarding *Operation Masterpiece* obtained from Robert K. Wittman and John Shiffman, *Priceless* (Crown, 2011).

14 Kim Willsher, "On Corsica, the Intrigue of Crime and Politics Claims Another Life," World News, *The Guardian*, October 20, 2012, https://www.theguardian.com/world/2012/oct/20/corsica-intrigue-crime-politics.

15 Personal interview of Michael McGowan, March 24, 2025.

16 Peter Allen, "The FBI Told Us to Do It! Seven Robbers Go on Trial Accused of £20 Million Art Heist," *The Daily Mail*, November 28, 2011, https://www.dailymail.co.uk/news/article-2067124/The-FBI-told-Seven-robbers-trial-accused-20-million-art-heist.html.

17 Tom Mashberg, "Stealing Beauty," *Vanity Fair*, accessed October 19, 2025, https://archive.vanityfair.com/article/1998/3/stealing-beauty.

18 "Conviction For Figure In Art Case," *The New York Times*, October 2, 1997; Tom Mashberg, "Isabella Stewart Gardner Heist: 25 Years of Theories," *The New York Times*, February 26, 2015; Ed Butler, "The Art of the Heist," Art and Design, *The Guardian*, November 18, 2000, https://www.theguardian.com/artanddesign/2000/nov/18/arttheft.art; and Mashberg, "Stealing Beauty."

19 Mashberg, "Stealing Beauty."

Chapter 10

1 Personal interview of Anthony Amore, March 10, 2025.

2 Bud Collins, "Monet? So What! Gardner Has Manet," *The Boston Globe*, February 11, 1990.

3 Personal interview of Myles Connor, May 29, 2025.

Chapter 11

1 Anthony Flint, "Braintree Man Eludes Prosecutors," *The Boston Globe*, January 20, 1996.

2 Lara Chicofsky and Nina Jobe, *The Planning of the Plymouth Mail Robbery*, Double Deal, aired December 20, 2021; postalmuseum.si.edu.

3 postalmuseum.si.edu; "Brink's Holdup Suspect Seized by FBI in Kentucky," *The Boston Globe*, October 2, 1970.

4 Commonwealth v. Dominico (Appeals Court of Massachusetts, Suffolk., 1974), https://law.justia.com/cases/massachusetts/court-of-appeals/1974/1-mass-app-ct-693-1.html.

5 Michael Blanding, "FBI: The Set Up," *Boston Magazine*, May 15, 2006.

6 John Dillon, "Two men sought in fatal shooting in Chinatown," *The Boston Globe*, October 14, 1981; Anthony Flint, "Braintree Man Eludes Prosecutors," *The Boston Globe*, January 20, 1996.

7 Doris Sue Wong, "Drug Suspect Said to Offer Stolen Art in Bid for Mercy," *The Boston Globe*, May 28, 1992.

8 Tom Mashberg, "Meet the Suspects: David Allen Turner," *Boston Herald*, March 22, 2008, https://www.bostonherald.com/2008/03/22/meet-the-suspects-david-allen-turner/.

9 "Revere Man Found Slain in Trunk of His Car," *The Boston Globe*, September 25, 1991.

10 Mass AG's file review.

11 Shelley Murphy, "The Last Surviving Person of Interest in the Gardner Heist, Mobster Robert Gentile, Has Died," *The Boston Globe*, September 22, 2021,

https://www.bostonglobe.com/2021/09/22/metro/robert-gentile-mobster-linked-by-officials-gardner-museum-theft-dies/.

12 Wong, "Drug Suspect Said to Offer Stolen Art."

13 Mass AG's file review.

14 Clerk of U.S. District Court, District of MA, in the case of U.S. v. Turner et al, CR-99-10098-RGS.

15 Personal interview of David Nadolski, March 10, 2025.

16 All information regarding Loomis plot obtained from publicly-available records maintained by the Clerk of U.S. District Court, District of MA, in the case of U.S. v. Turner et al, CR-99-10098-RGS.

17 United States v. Merlino et al, No. 99-10098-RGS (United States District Court, D. Massachusetts. March 7, 2002), https://law.justia.com/cases/federal/district-courts/FSupp2/204/83/2429110/.

18 United States of America v. William Merlino (United States District Court District of Massachusetts November 21, 2007), https://www.govinfo.gov/content/pkg/USCOURTS-mad-1_99-cr-10098/pdf/USCOURTS-mad-1_99-cr-10098-0.pdf.

19 Personal interview of David Donahue, March 10, 2025.

Chapter 12

1 "Dorchester Man Resentenced for Role in Plot to Rob Armored Car Depot," United States Department of Justice, November 13, 2019, https://www.justice.gov/usao-ma/pr/dorchester-man-resentenced-role-plot-rob-armored-car-depot.

2 United States v. David Turner, No. 03-2608 (United States Court of Appeals, 1st Circuit August 31, 2007), https://law.justia.com/cases/federal/appellate-courts/ca1/03-2608/03-2608-01a-2011-02-25.html.

3 US v. David Turner, 2007.

Chapter 13

1 Myles J. Connor, Jr. and Jenny Siles, *The Art of the Heist* (Harper, 2009).

2 Shelley Murphy and Stephen Kurkjian, "Six Theories behind the Stolen Gardner Museum Paintings," *The Boston Globe*, March 18, 2017, https://www.bostonglobe.com/metro/2017/03/18/six-theories-behind-stolen-gardner-museum-paintings/JmwHou86qo5MtBzX1fb9cI/story.html.

3 William F. Doherty, "A 6th Guilty Plea in Fixing," *The Boston Globe*, May 5, 1979.

4 Stephen Kurkjian, "FBI Searched Suffolk Track for Art from Gardner Heist," *The Boston Globe*, December 28, 2015.

5 "Murder Charged in Guard Death," *The Boston Globe*, December 3, 1966.

6 "Murder Charged," 1966.

7 Stephen Warmiel, "2 Killers Escape during Furlough," *The Boston Globe*, May 1, 1974.

8 Joan Vennochi and Diane Lewis, "Cleared of Murder Charge, He Wants to Forget the Past," *The Boston Globe*, August 31, 1992.

9 Vennochi and Lewis, "Cleared of Murder Charge."

10 Martie Barnes, "Co-Defendant's Statement May Free Man," *Danville Register & Bee*, August 30, 1992.

11 Personal interview of Anthony Amore, May 29, 2025.

12 Boston Herald Staff, "Museum Brushes off Tip on Theft," *Boston Herald*, February 24, 2009, https://www.bostonherald.com/2009/02/24/museum-brushes-off-tip-on-theft/.

13 Personal interview of Anthony Amore, May 29, 2025.

14 Public records, Quincy Police report, March 1991, reviewed by author. Public records can be found in person at the Quincy Police Department.

15 Boston Herald, "Museum Brushes off Tip."

16 Public records, Boston Police report, June 1991, reviewed by author. Public records can be found in person at the Boston Police Department.

17 Many news agencies reported that the FBI officially announced that Reissfelder and DiMuzio were involved in heist, including ArtNet: Sarah Cascone, "After 25 Years, FBI Knows Who Was Behind Daring Isabella Stewart Gardner Heist," Artnet, March 31, 2015, https://news.artnet.com/art-world/isabella-stewart-gardner-heist-solved-283368.

18 Shelley Murphy, "Link Suggested between Slaying, Gardner Heist," *The Boston Globe*, February 28, 2022, https://www.bostonglobe.com/2022/02/27/metro/investigators-suspect-link-between-gardner-museum-heist-an-execution-style-murder-lynn/.

19 Bob Ward, "New England Unsolved: How a Lynn Murder Is Providing a New Lead in Gardner Art Heist Investigation," Boston 25 News, February 22, 2022, https://www.boston25news.com/news/local/new-england-unsolved-how-lynn-murder-is-providing-new-lead-gardner-art-heist-investigation/NVS6SKXQMVHDLLOMAKDJVGCFAU/.

20 "Lynn Murders Match 1990 Total," *The Daily Item*, February 22, 1991.

21 Ward, "New England Unsolved."

22 Personal interview of Bob Ward, May 4, 2025.

Chapter 14

1 Personal interview of Christina Conlon, March 11, 2025.

Chapter 15

1 *The Love Boat* theme song, lyrics by Paul Williams, 1977.

Chapter 16

1 All of the historical information on Gentile is derived from the Clerk of U.S. District Court, District of CT, in the case of U.S. v. Gentile, 3:12-CR-00072-RNC-01, 05/09/2013 and U.S. v. Gentile, 04/20/2015; Edmund H. Mahony, "A Hartford Wise Guy and a $500 Million Museum Heist," *The Hartford Courant*, May 18, 2013, https://www.courant.com/news/connecticut/hc-gardner-gentile-0513-20130518-story.html.

2 Public records, USDC of CT, US v. Robert V. Gentile and Andrew Parente, Criminal No. 3:12CR34 (RNC)

3 Personal interview of Ed Mahony, May 6, 2025.

4 Public records, USDC of CT, US v. Robert V. Gentile and Andrew Parente, Criminal No. 3:12CR34 (RNC)

5 Jay Lindsay, "Four Alleged Mobsters Deny Drug Ring," Associated Press, July 9, 1999

6 Ward, "New England Unsolved."

7 Murphy, "Link Suggested between Slaying."

8 "Unsolved 1991 Murder 'Very Likely' Related to Largest Art Heist in U.S. History, Police Say," Oxygen, March 1, 2022, https://www.oxygen.com/crime-news/authorities-believe-murder-of-james-marks-related-to-gardner-museum-art-heist.

9 Ward, "New England Unsolved."

10 All information regarding the 2012 federal prosecution of Gentile is obtained from public records, USDC of CT, US v. Robert V. Gentile and Andrew Parente, Criminal No. 3:12CR34 (RNC).

11 Personal interview of Michael McGowan, March 24, 2025.

Chapter 17

1 Mahony, "Hartford Wise Guy."

2 Dave Collins, "Former Top Connecticut Prosecutor Austin McGuigan Dies at 77," AP News, March 24, 2021, https://apnews.com/general-news-d7d8639ff19075e125a118d08fa70ca3.

3 Personal interview of Ryan McGuigan, April 4, 2025.

4 Kurkjian, *Master Thieves*.

5 Personal interview of Ryan McGuigan, April 4, 2025.

6 Personal interview of Christina Conlon, March 11, 2025.

Chapter 18

1 Personal interview of Jamie Lawton, May 29, 2025.

2 Public records, USDC of CT, US v. Robert V. Gentile, Criminal Case No. 3:15-mj-00056-TPS; Mahony, "Hartford Wise Guy."

3 "Hartford's Last Powerful Mobster Dies," NBC Connecticut, December 29, 2010, https://www.nbcconnecticut.com/news/local/hartfords-last-powerful-mobster-dies/1858767/.

4 Edmund H. Mahony, "Reputed Mobster's Associate Adds New Mystery to Gardner Museum Art Heist," *Hartford Courant,* January 3, 2016, https://www.courant.com/2016/01/03/reputed-mobsters-associate-adds-new-mystery-to-gardner-museum-art-heist.

5 Personal interview of Ryan McGuigan, April 4, 2025.

6 Mahony, "Mobster's Associate Adds New Mystery."

7 Stephen Kurkjian and Shelley Murphy, "Suspect in Gardner Theft had Prison Sentence Reduced," *The Boston Globe,* January 14, 2016.

8 Luke Kenton, "Suspect in Isabella Stewart Gardner Museum Art Heist Is Released," *The Daily Mail,* November 14, 2019, https://www.dailymail.co.uk/news/article-7686201/Suspect-infamous-Isabella-Stewart-Gardner-Museum-art-heist-released-prison-21-years.html; Shelley Murphy, "Man Suspected in Gardner Museum Heist Set Free," *The Boston Globe,* November 14, 2019.

Chapter 20

1 Mahony, "Hartford Wise Guy."

Chapter 21

1 Information that the FBI interviewed Luisi reported in *The Boston Globe,* Stephen Kurkjian and Shelley Murphy, "Notorious Boston Mobster-Turned-Pastor Has Clues about Gardner Heist," *The Boston Globe,* July 27, 2016, https://www.bostonglobe.com/metro/2016/07/26/from-capo-christian-mobster-tale/5yTwaVj47owP8d4JfuDAOM/story.html.

2 "Boston Mob Boss Resurfaces in Memphis as Pastor," KGW, August 2, 2016, https://www.kgw.com/article/life/boston-mob-boss-resurfaces-in-memphis-as-pastor/283-286189385.

3 Kurkjian and Murphy, "Notorious Boston Mobster-Turned-Pastor."

4 All information regarding FBI sources obtained from public records, USDC of CT, US v. Robert V. Gentile and Andrew Parente, Criminal No. 3:12CR34 (RNC).

5 Information about Sammy, including his true name, provided through personal interview of Gentile's attorney, Ryan McGuigan, April 4, 2025.

6 Bowes v. State of Florida, No. 84-2715 (Florida District Court of Appeals December 23, 1986).

Chapter 22

1 Personal interview of Dave Schratwieser, April 30, 2025.

Chapter 23

1 Personal interview of Ed Mahony, May 6, 2025.

2 "New Hartford Woman Gets 5 Years Prison for Tax Fraud," *Country Times Insider*, January 31, 2016, https://www.ctinsider.com/news/article/New-Hartford-woman-gets-5-years-prison-for-tax-16900680.php.

3 All information regarding this tax case obtained from publicly available court records and "New Hartford Woman Sentenced to Prison for Tax Fraud and Structuring Offenses | United States Department of Justice," January 25, 2016, https://www.justice.gov/usao-ct/pr/new-hartford-woman-sentenced-prison-tax-fraud-and-structuring-offenses.

4 US DoJ, "New Hartford Woman Sentenced."

Chapter 25

1 Personal interview of Steve M., February 13, 2025.

Chapter 28

1 All information regarding the 2015 firearm sale obtained from public records, USDC of CT, US v. Robert V. Gentile, Criminal Case No. 3:15-mj-00056-TPS.

2 "Suspected Mobster Arrested on Federal Charges," NBC Connecticut, April 17, 2015, https://www.nbcconnecticut.com/news/local/suspected-mobster-arrested-on-federal-charges/50839/.

Chapter 29

1 Personal interview of Rob Fisher, May 12, 2025.

2 Press Release – "Historic Footage Connected to Gardner Museum Burglary Released – Public Assistance Sought," U.S. Attorney's Office, District of MA, August 6, 2015.

3 "Gardner Museum $500m Art Heist Video Has Led to Tips but No Arrests," *The Daily Mail*, November 23, 2015, https://www.dailymail.co.uk/news/article-3330552/Gardner-Museum-heist-video-led-FBI-leads-no-arrests-made.html.

4 Rodrigue Ngowi and William J. Kole, "2 Suspects in Boston Art Theft Worth $500 Million Are Dead, FBI Says," *The Washington Post*, August 7, 2015, www.washingtonpost.com/national/2-suspected-of-boston-art-theft-worth-500-million-are-dead-fbi-says/2015/08/07/b6cf9846-3d3a-11e5-9c2d-ed991d848c48_story.html.

Chapter 30

1 Public records, USDC of CT, US v. Robert V. Gentile and Andrew Parente, Criminal No. 3:12CR34 (RNC).

2 Stephen Kurkjian and Shelley Murphy, "Dying Mobster Gives No New Gardner Heist Info," *The Boston Globe*, October 1, 2016.

Chapter 31

1 "West Virginia Man Sentenced on Fraud Charges | United States Department of Justice," May 15, 2018, https://www.justice.gov/usao-ma/pr/west-virginia-man-sentenced-fraud-charges.

2 Kelly Horan and Jack Rodolico, "In Latest 'Last Seen' Episode, Digging Up Hope In Florida," WBUR, November 12, 2018, https://www.wbur.org/news/2018/11/12/last-seen-the-big-dig-episode-nine.

Chapter 32

1 Personal interview of Ed Mahony, May 6, 2025.

Chapter 33

1 Murphy, "Last Surviving Person of Interest."

2 Personal interview of Ryan McGuigan, April 4, 2025.

3 Personal interview of Bobbie Gentile Jr, June 6, 2025.

4 Personal interview of John Durham, March 27, 2025 and June 16, 2025.

Chapter 34

1 Olga Khvan, "FBI Agent: Gardner Museum Heist Is the 'Antithesis of the Perfect Crime,'" *Boston Magazine*, December 7, 2015, https://www.bostonmagazine.com/2015/12/07/gardner-museum-heist-cbs-sunday-morning;

2 "Twenty-Two Historic Artifacts Repatriated by the United States to the People of Okinawa," Boston FBI, April 30, 2024, https://www.fbi.gov/contact-us/field-offices/boston/news/twenty-two-historic-artifacts-repatriated-by-the-united-states-to-the-people-of-okinawa.

3 "Manuscript Signed by Conquistador Hernán Cortés in 1527 Repatriated to the People of Mexico," Boston FBI, July 20, 2023, https://www.fbi.gov/contact-us/field-offices/boston/news/manuscript-signed-by-conquistador-hernan-cortes-in-1527-repatriated-to-the-people-of-mexico.

Acknowledgments

When my good friend and colleague, Anthony Amore, first suggested that I write a book about the Gardner Museum heist, I scoffed at the idea, and with good reason. For starters, I'd never written a book before, and more to the point, there was no way the FBI was going to let me write about a pending and active criminal investigation. Anthony convinced me to start writing anyway, and if it weren't for his guidance and support, as well as his willingness to answer the thousand questions which were posed to him at all hours, this book would never have been written. Ta, Anthony.

I wish to thank my literary agent, Sharlene Martin at Martin Literary Management, for taking a flyer on a retired FBI agent with dubious writing credentials, and especially for her guidance throughout the entire process. I'm also thankful for the support I received from my editor, Debby Englander, and the entire team at Post Hill Press, whose thoughtful edits to my manuscript were always insightful, albeit painful. And thank you to Jon Ford, who, despite my affinity for one particular form of punctuation, performed a wholly merited semi-colonoscopy on the first draft. And thank you to Gretchen Koss at Tandem Literary for skillfully guiding me through a whole new industry with patience and unerring wit.

I'm indebted to my colleagues at the FBI for their support throughout this project, especially executive management at FBIHQ, who understood the importance of the Gardner Museum heist and allowed me to write a book about that aforementioned pending and active criminal investigation. Along those lines, I'm grateful to the Prepublication Review Office for their expeditious and thorough vetting of the subject matter contained in my manuscript, as well as to Colleen Childers of the Art Crime Team for her thoughtful and meticulous fact-checking.

Jamie Lawton, my co-case agent for nearly a decade, was instrumental in moving this book forward. We spent many hours together, huddled over pitchers of cold beer, recollecting the significant facts of the investigation and nailing down an accurate timeline. More than the firearms, drugs, and explosives, the investigation in Connecticut yielded a close friendship, and I'm grateful for that. I'm thankful to our good friends on the ad hoc Gardner Theft Task Force for their invaluable contributions to this investigation over the many years and for their assistance on this latest project: Brian Kelly, Rob Fisher, John Durham, and Steve M.

I'm grateful to Christina for taking the time to provide me with her critical recollections about her uncle and the stolen artwork. She didn't have to make that first call, which is what makes her assistance all the more profound.

I'd like to thank the entire staff at the Isabella Stewart Gardner Museum for their unwavering support of the FBI and our investigation, especially Steve Kidder and Director Emeritus Anne Hawley. And I'd be remiss if I didn't thank Mrs. Gardner for her eternal gift to all of us here in Boston. It truly is a jewel.

I'm grateful to my mom for supporting her son's crazy dream to become an FBI agent. I'd like to thank Jack and Will for being such good boys, and for their wonderful cards and pictures which decorated my desk over the years. And finally, I want to thank my wife, Sonia, for her love and constant support—not only through the book-writing process—but through the more than two decades of FBI service. Without complaint (well, mostly), she endured the late nights, the missed holidays, and the last-minute travel plans that are endemic to the wife of a cop. Without her, this book, and the career which underpins it, would never have been written.